Breastfeeding
...naturally

A

nursing mothers'
ASSOCIATION OF AUSTRALIA

PUBLICATION

Edited by **JANE CAFARELLA**

Published by Merrily Merrily Enterprises Ltd
3 Monomeeth Drive, Mitcham, Victoria 3132
on behalf of the Nursing Mothers' Association of Australia

First published 1996

© Nursing Mothers' Association of Australia 1996

All rights reserved. No part of this publication
may be reproduced, stored in a retrieval system,
or transmitted in any form or by any means,
electronic, mechanical, photocopying, recording
or otherwise, without the prior written permission
of the Publisher.

       Breastfeeding – naturally

       ISBN 0 949637 87 4

       1. Breastfeeding. 2. Breastfeeding – Australia
       3. Infants (Newborn) – Care. I. Cafarella, Jane.

       649.33

Edited and designed by Pagemasters Pty Ltd, Carlton, Vic.
Printed in Australia by New Litho, Surrey Hills, Vic

Oh boy! Are we in trouble!

Throughout this book, we have used the pronoun "he" to refer to the baby. We know that at least 51 per cent of new born babies are girls, but we also know that, despite the efforts of modern science, 100 per cent of mothers are still women. Using the pronoun "she" for both mother and baby can be very confusing. Therefore, we hope you will understand why, in this instance at least, we chose clarity above political correctness.

CONTENTS

Foreword viii
Introduction x
Acknowledgements xii

CHAPTER ONE
The decision to breastfeed 1

CHAPTER TWO
How breastfeeding works 21

CHAPTER THREE
Before baby is born 32

CHAPTER FOUR
Position, position, position! 48

CHAPTER FIVE
Emotional rescue 66

CHAPTER SIX
The learning period 97

CHAPTER SEVEN
Surving the early weeks 126

CHAPTER EIGHT
Common problems 142

CHAPTER NINE
Breastfeeding and paid work 172

CHAPTER TEN
An expression of love 192

CHAPTER ELEVEN
As your baby grows 207

CHAPTER TWELVE
The importance of sharing 221

NMAA services 225
Telephone counselling 225
Index 226

FOREWORD

Breastfeeding is the very best start in life – it is as simple, and as complex, as that. Simple, because there is no equal to the amazing health-giving, intellectual, emotional and environmental benefits breastfeeeding offers babies, parents, our community and our environment. Complex because, after more than 30 years of informing and nurturing breastfeeding families, Nursing Mothers' understands that it is not always as simple as it seems.

Breastfeeding is a learning process, for your baby as well as for you. We hope that *Breastfeeding ... naturally* will be a valuable part of this process.

Thanks to scientific research, we now understand a great deal more about lactation – about how breastfeeding works and about the causes of breastfeeding problems. The information in this book is soundly based on the latest scientific research, but this knowledge is not all you will need. Not every problem has a scientific solution. Sometimes patience, the will to persist and the ability to take one day at a time while you and your baby learn about each other are just as important. That is why this book is also based on the practical experience of breastfeeding women. It gives you liberal doses of realism and encouragement along with research-based information.

The many thousands of mothers who call upon NMAA each year find the consistent, quality care they need and the support and acceptance of other mothers. *Breastfeeding ... naturally* is an extension of this care. We hope it will start you on the road to breastfeeding success. Along the way, you may experience more complex situations than it has been possible to cover in this book. Remember that Nursing Mothers' is there to help you. We hope that you will choose to become a Member of the Association. In doing so you add to your experience of breastfeeding, and to the accumulated pool of wisdom which benefits mothers both now and in the future.

We hope you enjoy *Breastfeeding ... naturally* and enjoy breastfeeding your baby.

Jill Day
President, Nursing Mothers' Association of Australia

INTRODUCTION

Imagine a food that is deliciously sweet, portable, always available at just the right temperature, easily digested, nourishing, rich in antibodies, and environmentally friendly. Imagine a food that is able to change to meet the changing needs of the person consuming it, and which is so complete that it provides everything needed for the first six months of life – and which is available free to every human infant on earth. If it came in a tin, this food would no doubt be labelled 'Miracle Food' and every mother would do whatever she could to give it to her baby. If I told you that after years of research, a team of scientists had produced this miracle food, you would probably believe me.

If I told you that every mother on earth could produce it herself, with no more effort than it takes her to breathe, and at no cost other than maintaining her own food supply, would you also believe me?

This food, of course is breastmilk, the perfect natural food for babies, produced naturally by women for centuries. It is to this food that we owe our survival as a species, and it is by this food and method of feeding that we identify ourselves as mammals. But it is the very fact that this food does not come in a tin that makes it so undervalued. There is no money to be made from the marketing and promoting breastmilk, and in fact it competes directly with a substitute product which earns billions of dollars in profit for large multinational companies.

Yet the advantages of breastfeeding for both baby and mother remain undisputed.

Not only is it the best and most convenient food for your baby, it helps protect him from a wide range of illnesses and has been shown to offer health benefits which go on into later life. Studies have shown that breastmilk is also the best food for optimum brain development, so breastfeeding will literally give your baby a head start.

But how can you make an informed choice about the best food to feed your baby when there is so much promotion of one product and so little of the other. And if you want to breastfeed, how can you get the support and knowledge you need? Unless you have grown up in a family where the children were breastfed, you may not have seen many women breastfeeding their babies.

As a young woman after leaving home, you may have had little to do with babies or young children, until you considered having your own. You may also have heard a lot about the 'convenience' of bottle-feeding – but very little about the convenience of breastfeeding.

And you may not have heard about the pleasure most women get from breastfeeding their babies, the enormous health advantages for the babies, and the special relationship it encourages. Whether you are considering breastfeeding or already doing so, a good place to start is right here. This book is designed to inform you, to support you in your decision to breastfeed your baby, and to entertain you.

The Nursing Mothers' Association of Australia was formed in 1964 by a small group of mothers in Melbourne, who like you, wanted the best for their babies. For the past 30 years, the Association, which has had more than 145,000 members, has been promoting breastfeeding and helping Australian women to breastfeed successfully. This book represents that accumulated wisdom.

Throughout the book, you will find factual information, photos and illustrations, as well as the personal stories of women just like you, who have successfully breastfed, mostly without problems, but sometimes despite illness, discouragement from family, or other difficulties.

Above all, this book aims to help and encourage you and your baby to breastfeed successfully, and to enjoy that special closeness and satisfaction and the undisputed health advantages that breastfeeding brings.

ACKNOWLEDGEMENTS

Nursing Mothers' gratefully acknowledges the assistance of the following people, without whom this book would not have been possible:

Joy Anderson
Sue Byrne
Jill Day
Debra Digby
Jan Kirkup
Lesley McBurney
Anne McDonald
Yvette O'Dowd
Kerry Paine
Robyn Wainwright

Special thanks to:
Carol Fallows
Dr Stephen Juan
Fiona Kautrill
Maureen Minchin
Rosemary Stanton

Our grateful appreciation to Associate Professor Peter Hartmann, of the University of Western Australia, for his invaluable advice.

CHAPTER ONE

The decision to breastfeed

- Making the decision to breastfeed
- Advantages for baby, mothers, the community, the environment
- Factors affecting the decision – family, peers, society
- Exploding the myths surrounding breast vs bottle

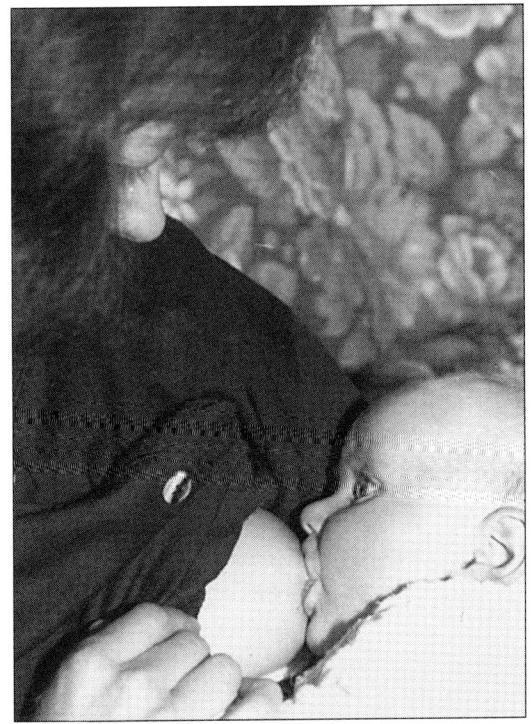

Photograph by Yvette O'Dowd.

The 1989-90 National Health Survey showed that 77 per cent of women who had a child aged five years or less had breastfed or were breastfeeding
— Australian Bureau of Statistics publication 'Women's Health' 1994, Catalogue Number 4365.0

Photograph by Dianne Griffiths

LEARNING ABOUT BREASTFEEDING

Breastfeeding is a natural function – not a science – and millions of women all over the world do it without ever referring to a book. In fact, millions do it without ever having learned to read. However, in our culture, doing what comes naturally is not always easy. While a vast amount of knowledge is gained in some areas, such as science and technology, other knowledge, more ancient and basic, is sometimes lost. The loss of this knowledge – knowledge that for millions of years has been vital to human survival – has meant a loss of confidence for mothers in caring for their babies, the loss of a vital source of nourishment and a loss of power for women.

Man may have walked on the moon, but in many parts of the world, the simple, womanly function of breastfeeding a baby may seem more difficult and fanciful than the moon walk. Yet successful breastfeeding does not require any special equipment and costs nothing but time and patience, knowledge and support. It is this knowledge and support which is so vital in ensuring successful breastfeeding. While you may have read avidly about labour before your baby was born, remember that labour may last from anything from one to 36 hours (if you're really unlucky), but a successful breastfeeding relationship can last from six months to up to four years, or longer if you wish. A healthy baby is the obvious aim of labour, but it is breastfeeding that will ensure that your baby remains healthy and has the healthiest start in life.

If your baby has not yet arrived, now is the best time to talk to your midwife or doctor, family and the hospital (if you are planning a hospital birth) about breastfeeding and the support that they can offer.

Talk to other women who have breastfed or who are breastfeeding. Just as when you were first pregnant, you may have suddenly noticed other pregnant women; once you start breastfeeding, or consider it, you will notice breastfeeding women everywhere. They are great examples of how breastfeeding works – and may be your greatest allies.

> *One chubby fist is playing with my hair; one knowing-brown eye is gazing up at my face; one small warm body is curled around my own. Breastfeeding time. Time for lunch, time for cuddles, time for love. Precious time ...*

EXPLODING THE MYTHS BETWEEN BREAST AND BOTTLE

> *'Bottle-feeding is so expensive. I calculated it cost $1500 a year (for infant formula alone). It's $30 a week for two tins of formula. Of course it's not rebatable. Pharmaceuticals are, but it's not – which I think is wrong. If you use disposable nappies too, that's half your allowance (of the Supporting Parents Pension).'*
> *– Sue, aged 42, mother of James, 10 months.*

Breastmilk is indisputably the best food for your baby. Most women know this, yet some elect to feed their babies artificially. While some do so by choice, there are many who feel that breastfeeding was so difficult for them that there really was no choice. It is this that makes them so defensive and angry in discussions about breastfeeding. They feel they have been told what they should do, but that they did not get the right support or information to enable them to do it successfully.

Sadly, this is why breastfeeding is such a touchy subject among many mothers. This is why a book like this is so important.

Breastfeeding may be the natural way to feed a baby but it is not culturally promoted and women are often uninformed about how to do it, or misinformed about how it works and what to do if problems arise.

Breastfeeding may be done anywhere or anytime, but in our culture there are restrictions, both stated and unstated, on when and where it is done, which sadly only serve to undermine the confidence of mothers and sabotage their attempts to breastfeed.

Unless women see other family members breastfeed, or unless they happen to visit the changing and feeding rooms in a large shopping centre, they may not have even seen a baby at the breast. Yet, the image of a baby or toddler sucking a bottle is everywhere.

Whether a woman chooses to breastfeed or not, her choice should be an informed one and she should be supported and aided in that choice so that her nurturing role is a happy one.

So how do breastfeeding and bottle-feeding compare and why, despite the many advantages of breastfeeding, and the many risks associated with bottle-feeding, even with modern day hygiene, do some women choose to bottle-feed?

BREASTMILK – WHAT'S IN IT FOR BABY?

There is a common misconception, even today, that the only difference between bottle-feeding and breastfeeding is the vessel – one comes in a breast and one comes in a bottle, and while the breast may be conveniently attached, the bottle is even more conveniently detached so that others can feed the baby too.

Even if this were true, there is no doubt that babies would prefer the nice warm soft breast to a hard plastic or glass bottle. But the truth is that in comparing infant formula with breastmilk, you are not comparing equals.

While science has improved infant formulas considerably and modern hygiene makes their delivery less risky, there is no formula that comes close to the life-giving and life-saving properties of breastmilk, a fact that the infant formula companies do not dispute.

Just as nature has provided goat's milk for baby goats and dog's milk for puppies, it has provided the human infant with a food perfectly tuned to its needs.

Colostrum, the first fluid produced by the breasts at the onset of lactation, provides special protection for the new infant. The small, soft curds of the mature milk are more easily digested. Breastfed babies are subject to fewer allergies, with a risk of one-seventh that of children fed on cow's milk.

The calcium in breastmilk is more easily absorbed and the iron absorbed through the milk is sufficient to maintain normal reserves for at least six months. The anti-infective properties in breastmilk are maintained for as long as breastfeeding continues.

Breastfeeding provides protection against bowel and respiratory illnesses and there are now indications that it may also protect against middle ear infection and urinary tract infections, well after weaning.

There is no contamination because breastmilk is delivered straight from breast to baby , and there are no storage problems.

A mother does not have to be literate to breastfeed, and human error cannot affect the composition of breastmilk. It is low in salt and aluminium. Tooth decay is rare in breastfed infants and breastfeeding guards against obesity in later life. Fully breastfed infants are rarely constipated, and also have less risk of gastroenteritis.

Cuddling is a natural by-product of breastfeeding and the release of relaxing hormones in the mother while feeding helps her to bond with her child.

Breastfeeding is also less work as there are no bottles to wash and sterilise and no formula to make up.

It costs nothing apart from a small increase in the mother's food intake. It aids the contraction of the uterus, helping it return to its non-pregnant state sooner, and the baby smells sweeter as its breath and bowel motions are pleasant-smelling.

Bottle-feeding by comparison is expensive, not only for the purchase of the infant formula , but for the resources needed to produce it and to provide and boil the water for its preparation. Another cost factor rarely taken into account is the medical backup required if the baby becomes ill due to contamination of the milk or through lower resistance to infection.

A bottle-fed baby is also more vulnerable if money is short and the mother cannot afford more formula (something that aid agencies in Australia report is quite common, particularly if mothers are depending on the subsistence pensions or benefits).

The bottle-fed baby is also more vulnerable during power blackouts or during natural disasters.

A bottle-fed baby may sleeper longer between feeds as he has to digest the larger tougher curds of cow's milk, but when woken may take longer to settle, as bottles have to be prepared and warmed, and bottle-feeding does not provide the same comfort.

Breastfeeding your baby is an investment in his future health, an investment which will not only benefit him as an individual and you as a family, but the community in general.

In short, from your baby's point of view, breast is best.

WHY BREAST IS BEST FOR BABY
- Provides all babies nutrients for first six months
- Provides antibodies which help fight infection
- Contains fatty acids important for brain development
- Enhances eyesight, speech and jaw development
- Increases resistance to infection, meaning fewer doctor's and hospital visits
- Lowers risk of Sudden Infant Death Syndrome (**SIDS**)
- Lowers risk of developing juvenile diabetes in the future; may also lower risk of heart disease
- More convenient
- More pleasurable

WHAT'S IN IT FOR YOU?

If you are considering whether to breastfeed or bottle-feed, consider this: it's 2am and your new baby is crying for a feed. The rhythmic, almost primitive, cry has wrenched you from a deep sleep, full of confused dreams from the emotional and physical exhaustion of adjusting to your new role.

You can nudge your husband or partner to bring your baby to you, roll on your side, putting your baby to your breast while cradling him with your arm and drift gently back to sleep, aided by the release of relaxing hormones triggered by the baby's sucking.

Or you can put on your dressing gown and slippers, turn on the kitchen light, remove the bottle of infant formula – which you made up earlier that evening after disinfecting the bottle, teat and other equipment – and boil some water to heat it up. (You can't use the microwave as it may heat unevenly and burn your baby's mouth.) You can then return to your now screaming baby and sit up in a chair or your bed while feeding.

When the baby has finished and perhaps drifted off to sleep, you can then put him back in his bed and return to your own.

In these circumstances, which in the early months, may occur several times a night, which would you prefer – breastfeeding or bottle-feeding? Which do you think your partner would prefer and, more importantly, which would your baby prefer?

If you are bottle-feeding, the need to carry infant formula, disinfected bottles, teats and water for mixing, everywhere you go can be wearing and worrying.

Artificial feeding also means your baby is vulnerable during power blackouts or any other circumstances where access to clean water, methods of boiling water, and heating and refrigeration of milk is limited.

If you have your breastfed baby with you, getting stuck in a traffic jam, being held up while waiting at the doctor's, sitting in at a meeting which has run overtime, or even being faced with a screaming hungry infant while you are in a department store are all circumstances that are easily dealt with.

The bottle-feeding mother can return to paid work whenever she is ready – but so can the breastfeeding mother if she is given regular breaks to express milk or breastfeed baby. Continuing to breastfeed may also help alleviate the guilt that, regrettably but inevitably, seems to haunt mothers in paid work, as you can be reassured that you are still providing the best food for your baby.

Breastfeeding also helps you return to your pre-pregnant figure more quickly. As your baby gains weight, you may even find that you lose any excess weight gained during pregnancy.

Research has shown that mothers who breastfeed lower their risk of breast and ovarian cancer, heart disease and osteoporosis. Menstruation is also usually delayed if you breastfeed your baby exclusively. This is more convenient for you, saves money, and lessens the impact of tampons and napkins on the environment.

Breastfeeding can also delay the return of fertility in many women, acting as a natural contraceptive.

In short, for the independent woman, breastfeeding gives her the most independence and makes mothering more pleasurable.

WHY BREAST IS BEST FOR YOU
- **Hastens the return of your pre-pregnant figure**
- **Lowers your risk of breast and ovarian cancer, heart disease and osteoporosis**
- **Delays the return of menstruation**
- **Acts as a natural contraceptive**
- **More convenient**
- **Cheaper**
- **More pleasurable**
- **Provides a sense of fulfilment**

POLITICAL REASONS

Having your own child suddenly changes your perspective, domestically and globally. Images in the media of suffering mothers and children which you may have taken for granted before, may suddenly be extremely disturbing to you, as you identify more strongly with them.

If this is so, then you may like to consider your decision to breastfeed as a political statement, as well as something that benefits you and your baby.

Advances in science and stricter controls on the composition and advertising of infant formula, as well as better hygiene, have made bottle-feeding less of a risk in the Western World. But in many developing countries, where resources such as water and energy are limited, and many women are illiterate, the difference between bottle-feeding and breastfeeding can mean the difference between life and death.

Despite the World Health Organisation International Code on the Marketing of Breast-milk Substitutes relating to baby foods, approved by 188 countries in 1981, babies in developing countries are still dying at an alarming rate due to the promotion of these products in an environment where it is impossible to use them safely.

Your commitment to breastfeed your own child shows solidarity with mothers who are struggling to do so all over the world against great odds. And by not purchasing infant formula yourself you are not endorsing their promotion here or in the developing world.

HOW GREEN IS MY BABY?

Breastmilk is possibly the greenest food your child will ever have. No, you will never produce green milk, but what you do produce will be at little cost to the physical environment (provided you do not eat takeaway food served in polystyrene plates as your staple diet while lactating!) and the health-inducing effects for your baby will save limited resources that are needed to create medicines and other items that might otherwise be needed to maintain health.

Yet the same person who may be applauded for paying special attention to her own diet or that of other family members by purchasing organic foods, or by avoiding artificial foods, may be encouraged to give a second-rate, artificial food to the most vulnerable person in her family – her baby.

The difference is that many people have been educated about the benefits of an organic whole food diet compared to a diet of processed foods, yet few have been educated about the real benefits of breastfeeding.

This means that those who choose to breastfeed sometimes find it difficult to get the right knowledge and support to help them in their choice.

Thankfully, this is changing. As more people are realising what's good for them, more are also realising what's good for baby and the environment.

Gabrielle Palmer in her book 'The Politics of Breastfeeding' (*See Further Reading*) talks about the economic value of human milk – something that is rarely, if ever, stated.

'Human milk is a commodity which is ignored in national inventories and disregarded in food consumption surveys, yet it does actually save a country millions of dollars in imports and health costs.'

It also saves energy and resources. No forests are depleted to provide fuel to boil water for breastfed babies, no tin is mined and discarded, no physical and intellectual resources are used to manufacture formula, no large tracts of land are needed to breed animals to provide the milk, no fertiliser is used to maintain the land and which pollutes water, and no plastic or glass is needed.

Breastfeeding not only saves lives, it saves energy, natural resources and money not just for the breastfeeding mother but for the whole nation.

SWEET AS A ROSE

Your breastfed baby will have another advantage over those who are formula fed: he will smell better. Let's face it: babies can be messy creatures: what goes in eventually comes out, sometimes at both ends, hopefully not simultaneously. A breastfed baby's bowel motions are sweet-smelling and are softer than that of artificially fed infants. In the first few days after birth, your baby's bowel motions will be a sticky black and greenish substance, known as meconium. Gradually, this will change to a more loose, unformed motion, ranging in colour from yellow through to greenish gold. The occasional green bowel motion is nothing to worry about in a healthy baby as the stools sometimes turn green when they are exposed to the air.

The bowel motions of a breastfed baby are looser than those of a bottle-fed baby. However, this does not mean that your baby has diarrhoea. Another advantage of breastfeeding is that breastfed babies rarely suffer from diarrhoea. However, frequently watery stool that are unusually foul-smelling are a sign that your baby is not well, particularly if they are accompanied by other signs of illness.

Breastfed babies are seldom constipated either, so don't be too concerned if your baby sometimes appears to strain and go red in the face. Unless the motion is formed or hard, this is not a sign that he is constipated.

In the early weeks, your baby may have a bowel motion at every feed, or twice a day. As he gets older this can even occur as infrequently as one every eight to 10 days or so. Some babies are regular, others change from day to day or from week to week.

When you begin to wean your baby from your breast and introduce solids, you will find that his bowel motions become more solid and like those of adults.

Photograph by Dianne Griffiths.

EROTICA VERSUS NURTURE, AND THE POWER OF ADVERTISING

So why, when the advantages of breastfeeding are so obvious to mothers, babies and society, is it still sometimes seen as more 'natural' and preferable to bottle-feed?

The symbol of the feeding bottle to represent a baby is as pervasive in our culture as the McDonald's arches, the Coca-Cola symbol and the light bulb is to the cartoonist who wants to represent an idea.

The symbol of the breast is also pervasive. Despite campaigns to wipe out sexist advertising, the breast is still used both overtly and covertly to advertise everything from jeans to luxury holidays.

In short, in Western culture the breast is an erotic symbol rather than a symbol of nurture.

This can create quite a mental hurdle for some women who are considering breastfeeding, or trying to breastfeed.

To feed your baby in a crowded cafe, for example, you must overcome your own embarrassment and that of other people around you who may have been constantly confronted with breasts in their erotic function but seldom in the nurturing function.

Fortunately, with more and more women breastfeeding their babies and more people recognising breastfeeding as a natural womanly function, attitudes are changing.

Unless it is for your own comfort, there is no need to isolate yourself while feeding. In fact, breastfeeding exposes less of the breast than normal beachwear; and while baby has his lunch, it is a good opportunity to have yours.

Breasts can be beautiful and sexy, but they are also functional and a woman who chooses to breastfeed confidently in public is making a positive statement about her own power as a woman.

On 14 April 1994, the Equal Opportunity Board (Victorian) ruled that Lynch's restaurant had discriminated against Juliette Borenstein and her husband Greg Chambers when it refused to allow them to bring their five-week-old daughter, who was asleep in a capsule, into the restaurant. The Board ruled that in February 1992, Mr Lynch had been unreasonable, when he turned them away. However, the Board warned that its decision was not meant as a general policy statement, but that restaurants should exercise their judgement about what was reasonable under the circumstances.

- Source, 'The Age', Melbourne, 14 April 1994, 15 April 1994 and 17 May 1994.

WILL MY PARTNER/HUSBAND FEEL EXCLUDED?

Sometimes, women are discouraged by their husbands or partners from breastfeeding because they fear that they may be excluded from bonding with their baby or because they are jealous of the physical and emotional closeness between mother and child.

The birth of a new baby is an emotional time for everyone, especially if this is your first baby, as you adjust from being a couple to a family.

In the past, stereotypical notions of how men and women should behave meant that fathers were excluded from most aspects of child care, not just feeding. These days, however, most fathers are enthusiastic partners in the preparation for birth, the birth itself and the care of the child.

Fathers need to be reassured that while feeding is vital for your baby's survival, so too is cuddling, bathing, playing and loving. These are all things that fathers can do very well and which will help them get to know their babies. Talk to your partner about why you want to breastfeed, and discuss your feelings together. Encourage him to read this book and any other relevant material and to talk to other fathers whose partners have breastfed.

All fathers, as well as mothers, want the best for their babies, and breastfeeding is indisputably the best food a baby can have. Reassure your partner that the best thing he can do for his baby, apart from cuddle and care for him, is to support your decision to breastfeed. He may also be surprised at the rewards he receives, too. Fathers often report that seeing their baby breastfeeding is an intensely emotional and rewarding experience.

FEELINGS OF DISCOMFORT AND DISTASTE

Negative attitudes towards our body's natural functions sometimes lead to misunderstandings. This has led some people to view breastmilk as waste matter that is eliminated from the breast, rather than as a food.

Breastmilk is not an excretion, but a secretion. As Virginia Phillips says in her book *Feeding Baby and Child*, it is not related to waste products such as urine or sweat but is 'a living fluid', different from, but more closely related to blood. Just as blood contains living substances which it brings to the body to give it energy, breastmilk carries nutrients from mother to baby.

Cow's milk is also a secretion. However, the same people who are revolted by the idea of breastmilk, find the idea of quaffing huge quantities of cow's milk udderly delightful!

Perhaps if breastmilk was packaged differently, in cardboard cartons with pictures of sports people on them, or if cow's milk was drunk straight from the udder, the correlation would be more obvious.

If it is not the milk, but the very notion of somebody sucking on your breast that is distasteful to you, then it may help to talk to other women about what breastfeeding actually feels like, particularly those who may have felt uncomfortable about it at first. Some women who may have been 'turned off' at the idea but who tried it anyway, have been surprised to find it not unpleasant at all. In fact most women are surprised to find it very pleasurable indeed.

The experience of pregnancy and birth bring many physical and emotional changes. In a society that reveres the body shape of the immature woman, slim and taunt, it is very confronting for a woman to find her body ripening and expanding.

A woman may feel very vulnerable, but she may also feel very powerful. It is a tremendous and amazing thing to be able to produce another human being from your own body and then to be able to nurture that being solely from your own body for the first six months. It is a great achievement, and many women, including those with brilliant careers, see it as their greatest achievement. Viewed like this, breastfeeding can help you feel more positive about your body and about being a woman.

MUM BOTTLE-FED ME, AND I'M HEALTHY

When you become a mother, you often begin to understand your own mother more, and to want to be close to her, both geographically and emotionally.

You may find that she enjoys helping you care for your baby and this may also mean encouraging you to do as she did.

Photograph by Dianne Griffiths.

If your mother breastfed, this will be an invaluable support; but if she did not, you may find that your choice to breastfeed your baby conflicts with her notions of how a baby should be fed. She may be unable to support you simply because she is not fully informed about how breastfeeding works.

Having raised her own children successfully on infant formula she may be unable to see any obvious differences between bottle-fed babies and breastfed babies. She is probably unaware that studies have shown that breastfed babies grow into healthier adults, with less risk of developing juvenile diabetes and heart disease, and that breastfeeding will also reduce your risk of developing cancer of the ovaries or breasts.

Although you may not want to undermine your own mother's mothering techniques or to jeopardise your relationship, your decision to breastfeed your baby should not be based on whether your mother breastfeed her children 20 or more years ago, but on what is best for your baby today. Like you, your mother probably based her care and feeding of you on the best knowledge and support that was available to her and on her own ability and circumstances.

By choosing to feed your baby naturally, you are not going against family tradition or undermining your mother. You are making a decision about what is best for your baby based on current knowledge and your own preferences and abilities. Some fathers, grandparents or other relatives may think that your baby's dependence on you for food may mean they will be excluded from the care of the baby or involvement in it's life. Fortunately, this is not so.

There are many things that fathers and grandparents can do to bond with the baby, apart from feed it. By supporting you in your decision to breastfeed they are ensuring the best for the baby, too.

The best way to ensure the support of other family members is to involve them in your decision to breastfeed. Let them know that, like them, you want the best for your baby and that breastmilk alone is the best food you can offer in the first six months.

Reassure them that as long as your baby looks healthy, is producing six to eight wet cloth nappies each day, and is gaining some weight, he is getting enough milk. If you use disposable nappies, your baby will produce fewer wet nappies as disposable nappies hold more moisture. A healthy baby may produce three or four wet disposable nappies a day, depending on the quality of the nappy used. A good test is the weight of the nappy. If it is heavy and obviously holding a lot of moisture your baby is getting plenty of fluids.

Your family may also be unfamiliar with the bowel motions of a breastfed baby. A breastfed baby's bowel motions are more frequent and looser than those of a bottle-fed baby, and may range in colour from mustard yellow to orange or even green. This does not mean that your baby has diarrhoea or is ill.

Encourage your family to read relevant parts of this book and discuss ways they can help, such as freeing you of other household chores while you concentrate on establishing your milk supply. They may not be able to prepare a feed for the baby in the early days, but feeding the rest of the family will no doubt be a welcome offer.

WILL IT HURT?

Breastfeeding your baby should not hurt if the baby is attached properly and sucking well. In fact, for most mothers it is a pleasurable experience. While some problems can occur in the early stages, with the right information, support and treatment, they can be easily and quickly solved.

Breastfeeding is not about a mother having to suffer for the good of her child. If a mother is experiencing pain, there is something wrong and it should be attended to immediately.

It is impossible to nurture your child if you are doing it through gritted teeth and indeed, persevering through pain defeats one of the benefits of breastfeeding, which is to build a positive nurturing relationship with your baby.

DO I HAVE TO GO ON A SPECIAL DIET TO BREASTFEED?

You do not have to eat or drink anything in particular in order to breastfeed successfully, although you may find you are thirstier and hungrier than usual in the early days.

Breastfeeding is designed so that your baby gets top priority, when the nutrients are handed out, no matter what you eat. Your body will still produces nourishing milk for your baby even if the you are undernourished. You can live on cola and French fries without diminishing the quality of your milk.

However, you are obviously going to feel better (and look better) if you are eating a normal healthy diet.

FIGURING OUT WHAT'S BEST FOR YOU

'You'll have boobs down to your waist!' is a common retort when a mother breastfeeds, and especially if she continues to feed past infancy. Not only is this a fallacy, the facts point as firmly as a Marilyn Monroe bra in the other direction.

Breastfeeding, especially immediately after birth, encourages the uterus to contract and the placenta to be expelled more easily, and this continues when feeding in the early days and weeks after birth.

These contractions allow the uterus to return to its former size more quickly so that the breastfeeding mother returns to her former shape sooner.

However, the contractions only work on the inside muscle. Any outside flab that has accumulated during pregnancy needs a bit more help from you, such as walking or swimming. (*See chapter 7 on How To Look After Yourself.*) These uterine contractions also minimise bloodloss after birth, thus reducing the risk of postnatal haemorrhage.

Breastfeeding is often unfairly blamed for figure changes that occur during pregnancy; but studies have shown little difference between the bodies of mothers who have breastfed and those who have bottle-fed. The reality is that motherhood brings a maturing of the female body that is not only discouraged in our culture, but which is openly despised. Unless you have the discipline and money (especially for child-care) to train your body back to its taunt youthful state, you may have to accept the new you.

This is not an excuse to let yourself go. Moderate exercise will help you look and feel better; but, in the final analysis, you will probably look and feel different after giving birth – and this is natural. Your new role may mean a loss of your youthful shape, but it will also bring many more gains as you mature and grow as a mother.

NURTURING RATHER THAN FEEDING

Breastfeeding is not just a feeding relationship, but a nurturing relationship. Eating for us involves much more than just satisfying our hunger. We eat for enjoyment, comfort (even if we try not to) and as a social act.

Similarly, a baby who has had plenty to drink may want to continue sucking because he enjoys the warmth and comfort. A baby who has just fed, but who is tired and grisly may want to feed some more to help him go to sleep. A baby who is sick may want to breastfeed to ease the distress.

All of this means that much more of your time will be taken up feeding and nurturing your baby than you may have imagined.

It will not be just a matter of giving a bottle for 10 minutes and leaving the baby to sleep for four hours. In societies where this is understood, the other work undertaken by mothers, whether paid or not, is put on the back burner. It is recognised that the mother also needs to be nurtured at this time.

It is important that you and your family realise this so that you will be supported in your decision to breastfeed.

> 'While awaiting the birth of my first baby, I tried to envisage what life might be like after he/or she was born, and considered doing a course of study as I thought the baby would sleep for a minimum of four hours between feeds. How else would I fill in all that time, I worried? Little did I know!' – Lynne

Mothering is not a temporary state but a life-long relationship. Your child's need for you at first will be vital for his survival and breastfeeding will not merely help him survive, but thrive.

Sometimes, breastfeeding is made easier if you understand that it is natural and essential for his survival for your baby to want to be with you and to want to breastfeed when he is hungry, tired, sick and scared. If you understand this, the demands of your new baby may still be a shock, but you will probably find them easier to accept.

Ideas about mothering are also coloured by the values our society places on that role and what other roles are expected of us.

The fact that, until recently, only paid work was seen as real work, hid the real work of parenting from many young people.

Parenting, particularly mothering, where much more physical intimacy is demanded, is extremely hard work.

Real babies may be cute and cuddly, with skin as soft as an angel's wings, and tiny ears, tiny noses and tiny toes. But their needs are far from tiny. Babies are also human beings with human needs – none of which they are capable of fulfilling themselves yet. Like you, they get

> When the NMAA first started in 1964 only 23 per cent of mothers were breastfeeding on discharge from hospital, compared with a standardised (ie adjusted for ethnic group and age) breastfeeding rate of 85% in 1993.

hungry between meals, they get uncomfortable, they get sick, tired, itchy, grumpy and bored. The difference is that they can only cry about it, while you can talk about it. There will be times when you will want to cry about it, too: when the demands of this little person seem unreasonable and impossible to meet, when it seems that nobody is meeting your needs and yet your are expected to meet everybody's.

If you are feeling tired and overwhelmed, let something else go while you and your baby rest. The vital nutrients your baby gets from your milk are far more valuable to him than a tidy house, in both the short and long term.

When your baby is newborn, being held close to your skin while feeding, and hearing the familiar sound of your heartbeat, will help him learn that the world is a safe and good place. As your baby grows, he will use this time to get to know you, gazing into your eyes, patting your breast fondly, playing with your hair and jewellery. It is these moments of joy that make the hard work of mothering worthwhile.

CHAPTER TWO

How breastfeeding works

■ How milk is produced and delivered by the body (anatomy and physiology of lactation).

PRIDE AND PREJUDICE

Over the years, on the road from girlhood to womanhood, you have probably thought and worried a lot about your breasts: their size, their shape, whether they are high or low, long or pert, and so on. In a culture obsessed with appearances and sex, the type of breasts a woman has can influence her feelings of femininity, self-esteem and even her posture. Throughout all of this, though, it is highly unlikely that anybody told you that no matter what their size or shape, your breasts are nothing short of miraculous in how they are made and what they can do.

No matter how you felt about your breasts before pregnancy, the changes that occur during pregnancy and birth, the realisation that they can make milk to nourish your baby and the experience of breastfeeding can give you a new perspective on your body and its amazing abilities. In fact, breastfeeding can help you take new pride in your body and your power as a woman.

THE ANATOMY OF YOUR BREAST

Your breast is made up of glandular tissue, supporting connective tissue and protective fatty tissue. The amount of fatty tissue determines the size of the breast, which is in turn largely determined by genetics. So your mother and grandmother will influence

Structure of the Breast

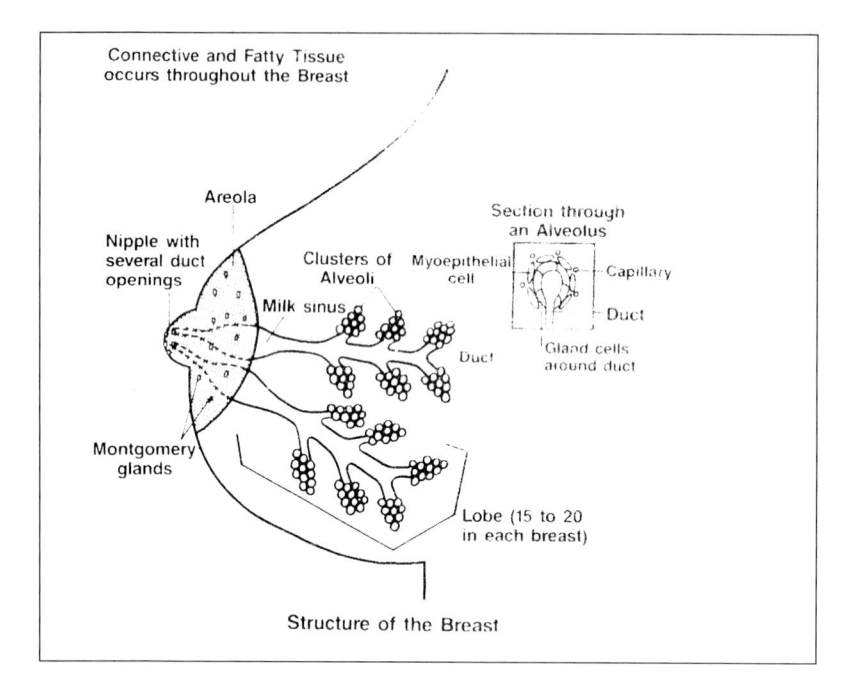

(Diagram labels: Connective and Fatty Tissue occurs throughout the Breast; Areola; Nipple with several duct openings; Clusters of Alveoli; Myoepithelial cell; Milk sinus; Duct; Montgomery glands; Lobe (15 to 20 in each breast); Section through an Alveolus; Capillary; Duct; Gland cells around duct)

the size of your breasts – but not your ability to breastfeed. The milk-producing part of your breast is the glandular tissue. The shape and size of your breast has nothing to do with how much glandular tissue you have. A big-breasted woman may have a small amount of glandular tissue and a large amount of protective fatty tissue, while a small-breasted woman may have little fat and a lot of glandular tissue.

You do not need a particular amount of glandular tissue to breastfeed. Women with a small amount of glandular tissue are still able to breastfeed successfully. It is extremely rare for a woman not to be able to breastfeed. Even women who have had breast surgery often find that are able to breastfeed with the right advice and support.

In fact, there is no such thing has having the 'wrong' type of breasts, or the 'wrong' nipples. Women who have been told this simply have the wrong advice.

While breast size can vary enormously, all breasts have the same basic structure.

Each breast has 15 to 20 lobes of milk-making glandular tissue composed of clusters of alveoli, which are the cells where breastmilk is produced. From these lobes run special channels called ducts, which expand to form sinuses directly beneath the areola (the coloured area which surrounds the nipple). These sinuses are reservoirs for the collection of milk, and it is from there that the milk flows out through tiny openings in the nipple.

The areola, or darker area around the nipple, contains special glands called Montgomery's tubercles, which provide natural lubrication. This lubrication also helps prevent bacteria growing on the nipples.

YOUR NIPPLES

Your nipples play an important role in helping you to breastfeed successfully. In fact, the role of the nipple is analogous to the role of the penis in intercourse. It's not the size or shape that matters, but the ability to become erect!

The nipple has smooth muscle which enables it to become erect in response to stimulation – touch, heat or cold, or sexual activity. This muscle also plays a part in controlling the release of milk from the milk sinuses.

However, your baby needs to have more than just your nipple in his mouth to allow him to milk your breast. The baby needs to be able to take a good mouthful of breast, enclosing much of the areola so that the milk sinuses are between his jaws. Just chewing on your nipple will hurt you and frustrate him, as he will not get any milk.

When it is not erect, the nipple looks slightly flat, but when you are aroused, either by cold or sexual excitement or contact with your baby, it stands out. When the baby sucks, the nipple extends to form a teat, which is up to three times its original length.

Your nipple contains anything from six to 25 openings, or nipple pores, that come from the milk sinuses.

Some women's nipples become erect easily. Others have to be coaxed out, and some seem to be flat or even around the wrong way, going in, instead of out. Nipples which go in rather than out are known as inverted nipples. If you have nipples like this you may need a little extra help to encourage your nipples to stand out, but there is no reason why you cannot breastfeed. Your breasts and nipples can change dramatically throughout pregnancy so you may be surprised to find that nature has done her job and that your 'introverted' nipples have gradually become more 'extroverted' as your breasts have grown. (*See Chapter 3*)

UNDERSTANDING HOW YOUR BREASTS MAKE MILK

It is much easier to breastfeed if you understand how your breasts make milk. Understanding this will help you to avoid or overcome some of the problems that have been associated with breastfeeding in the Western world.

Firstly, you do not need abundant breasts to breastfeed, but you do need a baby with an abundant appetite.

Frequent sucking by your baby at the breast is the best way to establish a good milk supply and to increase your supply if your baby seems particularly hungry.

Fortunately, almost all babies are born with this strong instinct to suck, known as the sucking reflex. However, the type of sucking action a baby uses to 'milk' the breast is very different from the type we would use to suck milk from a straw or a baby would use on a bottle teat.

When properly attached (*See Chapter 4*) the baby encloses not only the nipple but a large part of the areola in his mouth, and using its jaws and tongue, draws the milk out of the breast.

Whenever the baby sucks at the breast, nerve impulses are carried to the brain, causing the release of hormones. One (prolactin), is responsible for the manufacture of milk by the milk-producing glands in the breast, while another (oxytocin), causes the 'let-down', or ejection of milk.

When the baby attaches to the breast, the nipple is drawn into the back of his mouth and is held there by suction so that the sinuses are between his upper and lower jaw.

The action of the tongue and jaw compress the sinuses and rhythmical, undulating tongue movements express milk into the back of the baby's mouth.

A baby cannot bite while he is breastfeeding correctly because the tongue lies over the bottom gum and teeth.

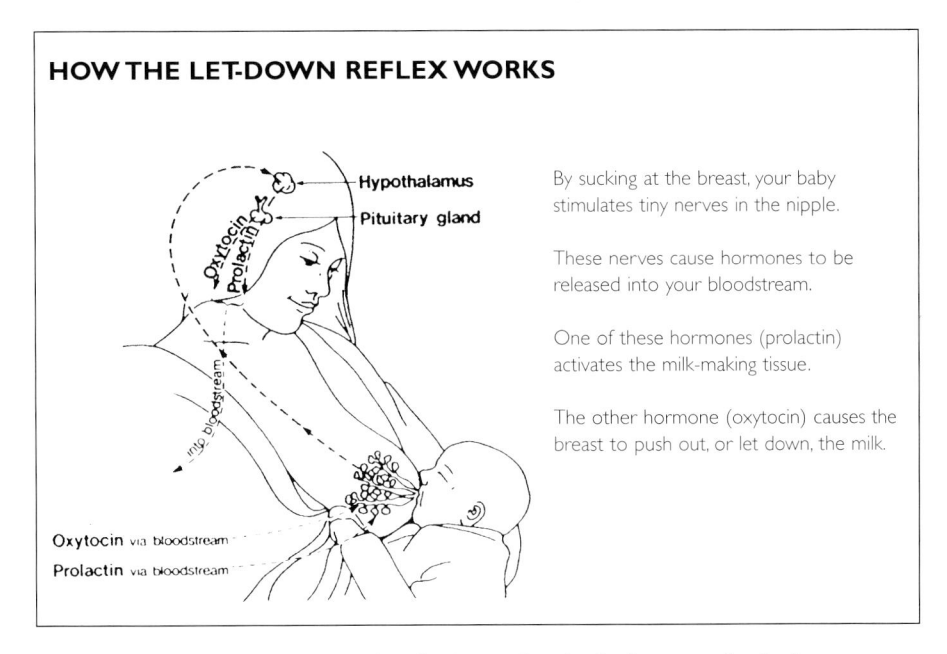

HOW THE LET-DOWN REFLEX WORKS

By sucking at the breast, your baby stimulates tiny nerves in the nipple.

These nerves cause hormones to be released into your bloodstream.

One of these hormones (prolactin) activates the milk-making tissue.

The other hormone (oxytocin) causes the breast to push out, or let down, the milk.

If the nipple is not fully drawn back into the baby's mouth, it is liable to move in his mouth, causing friction and then pain.

The effect can be felt by sucking your own thumb. The deeper the thumb is in the mouth, the less rubbing there is on the end of it.

The skin covering the nipple contains many nerve endings which are stimulated by the baby's sucking. This stimulation causes the milk to be released.

This release is commonly called the let down reflex (also called the milk-ejection reflex). It is the removal of the milk by the baby which causes more milk to be produced.

The let-down reflex works something like a valve, or tap. It is this reflex that makes most of the milk your breasts have made available to your baby.

The cells surrounding the alveoli contract and squeeze out the milk, forcing it down the ducts towards the nipple. This may feel like a tingling sensation, or a sudden fullness.

Sometimes you may notice milk dripping from the other breast. Some women do not experience these signs, but all can see a change in the baby's sucking rhythm as the milk starts to flow. In the early days, you may feel your uterus contracting when you let down, especially if this is not your first baby.

These are known as 'after-pains' and may be as strong as the early contractions you experienced during labour.

The let-down reflex is a conditioned response, caused by your baby's sucking. Just as your mouth may begin to water, when you are hungry and smell something delicious cooking, the let-down reflex can be encouraged by simply the sight or sound of your baby, or even just by thinking about him.

It can also be triggered by stimulation of the breast and nipple area by your fingers; but this can also work the other way. If you are anxious, extremely tired, upset or in pain, the let-down may be slow or inhibited.

The let-down reflex occurs more than once during a feed, but most mothers will only notice the first. Oxytocin is released in a pulsing manner throughout the feed.

How much milk your breasts make depends on your baby's sucking – causing the release of prolactin and oxytocin and a local control mechanism (that is, how often your baby sucks and how much milk he takes).

A special protein found in breastmilk regulates how much is made. As the breasts fill up with milk, the concentration of the protein builds up in your glandular tissue, your breasts receive the message that enough milk has been made and to slow down production. The more milk that is removed, either by your baby's sucking or by expressing, the lower the level of the protein and so your breasts get the message to increase milk production.

This explains why one breast may appear to produce more milk than the other. In this case, the fuller breast may have been emptied more effectively, perhaps because the baby was offered it first and was hungrier and therefore sucking more strongly.

This also explains why some mother's milk supply seems slow to build up, despite frequent feeding. A baby who is weak or sick may not be sucking effectively, which in turn will not drain the breast. Protein levels in the milk will then remain high, sending the message that no more milk is needed.

While the removal of milk from the breast is vital to the production of more milk for subsequent feeds, babies rarely empty a breast – they stop feeding when they have had enough.

Many mothers don't need to use both breasts at each feed. Occasionally, a mother may only be able to feed from one breast, for example if she has had surgery. In this case, the 'good' breast will get twice the stimulation and so will be capable of supplying enough milk for the baby.

Similarly, mothers breastfeeding twins are able to make enough milk in each breast for one baby.

If all this sounds very complicated, try to imagine a technical description of what happens when you eat – how the food is masticated, the part your teeth play, how it is swallowed, the role of the oesophagus, and how the food travels to the stomach and is digested. Sounds complicated – except that we do it without thinking, and enjoy it, too.

The same goes for breastfeeding. Just as it is helpful to know about the digestive system when you need to treat problems associated with it, it will help you to resolve any breastfeeding problems you may encounter if you understand how breastfeeding works.

In most cases, neither you nor your baby need to understand how breastfeeding works in order to do it successfully.

WHAT'S IN A BREASTFEED?

A breastfeed is like a good long warm drink and a hot meal, all in the one package. The first milk your baby receives at the beginning of the feed, known as the foremilk, looks a little like skim milk, pearly and fine and may sometimes appear bluish. This is designed to quench your baby's thirst. As the feed continues and the let-down occurs, the fat content of the milk increases as it gradually changes to the fat-rich hindmilk. This looks creamier and satisfies your baby's hunger.

This is why it is so important to allow your baby to set the pace of feeds, rather than timing them by the clock. A baby who is removed from the breast after only a few minutes, particularly in the early days when he may not be as efficient at milking the breast, will only receive the warm drink, not the hot meal. Your baby will be hungry and your breasts will receive the message that less milk is required and so will produce less.

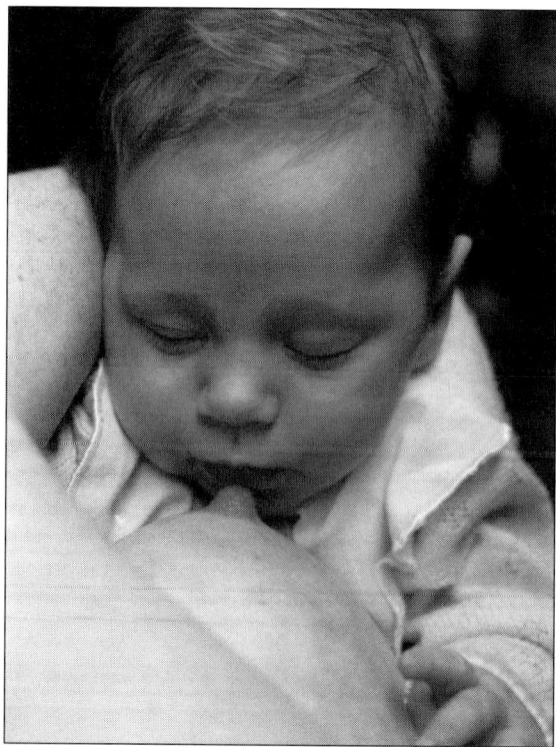

Photograph by Dianne Griffiths.

If this pattern continues, the hungry baby, when put to the breast again, will receive less, and will not be satisfied. The baby's distress, combined with well-meaning but misinformed advice about your milk not being 'good enough', can cause you to lose confidence, and ultimately, cease breastfeeding.

By comparison, a baby who feeds on the first breast until he comes off by himself, receives the right balance of both foremilk and hindmilk. Research has also shown that efficient removal of the milk is extremely important to ensure that more milk is produced.

Sometimes your baby may be satisfied with just one breast. That is fine. Just make sure you alternate the breast you feed from first to ensure that each breast is drained well at alternate feeds. A safety pin or other marker attached to your bra on the side you fed last may help you remember.

COLOSTRUM – IT'S COLOSSAL!

As your pregnancy advances, you may notice a thick, yellowish fluid may leak or be expressed from the breasts. This is colostrum, the first milk produced by the breasts and which is present from around the fifth or sixth month of pregnancy.

Although you don't need to express it, most women could produce up to two to three millilitres of pre-colostrum before their baby arrives. Up to 38 millilitres has been recorded, but many women don't see it at all.

Colostrum is high in protein, immunoglobulins (factors which boost your baby's immune system), lactoferrin, chloride and sodium (salt) and low in lactose (milk sugar), and fat and is the first milk that you will produce for your baby. It has a low volume, which causes minimum work for your baby's immature kidneys.

Colostrum provides protection for your baby when he is at his most vulnerable and provides conditions for the right bacteria for his gastro-intestinal tract to get his system working well. It also helps him to pass meconium, the black, sticky faeces that are first bowel motions. Passing meconium effectively in the first few days also helps prevent jaundice. Colostrum will protect your baby from infection and nourish him for the first one or two days after birth depending on when your milk 'comes in'. The small volume is perfectly suited to his needs at this time.

Frequent sucking by the baby will ensure that your milk comes in quickly, but do not worry if there is a delay. As long as you continue to put your baby to your breast whenever he seems hungry, he will be well nourished by your colostrum. Almost all babies lose some weight in the first few days after birth, whether they are breast or bottle-fed, as the baby's physiology adjusts to his new environment outside the womb. This weight loss does not mean that your baby needs complementary feeds. In fact, filling him up with formula or water will simply reduce his desire to suck at your breast and will impair the establishment of breastfeeding.

WHAT YOUR MILK LOOKS LIKE

We are so accustomed to seeing homogenised and pasteurised cow's milk, which is consistently white, that the appearance of breastmilk can come as quite a surprise. Cow's milk looks white because of the casein (protein) in it. For about two weeks after the birth, your breasts will produce both colostrum and milk, making your milk look creamier than 'mature' breastmilk which is translucent, sometimes bluish. This cocktail of colostrum and mature milk is sometimes known as transitional milk.

This does not mean that your breastmilk is losing its goodness. That is how mature breastmilk looks at the beginning of a feed. The water content in the foremilk is essential for quenching your baby's thirst. The hindmilk, produced later in the feed, is creamier and satisfies your baby's hunger. Together, it makes a perfectly balanced meal.

Mature milk has more lactose and fat than colostrum, but breastmilk does not lose its nutritional value with time. In fact, continuing to breastfeed past your baby's first year can be an important complement to his diet and still provide important protection from infection as he begins to make contact with other adults and children outside the home. During weaning, your milk will begin to resemble colostrum again, with more sodium, protein and immunoglobulins, and less lactose.

AM I MAKING ENOUGH MILK?

When your milk 'comes in' your breasts may feel very full and large. The veins, which stood out as your pregnancy advances, may look like a map of a complex system of waterways leading down to your nipple. Squeezing the areola may result in jet streams or sprays of milk, and the free breast may leak while baby is feeding from the other. It is easy to feel then, that your breasts are full of milk. However, only part of the initial fullness is breastmilk. The rest is blood and tissue fluid in the breast, which subsides after a few days.

As your breasts settle down and begin to adjust the amount of milk they are making to the amount of milk your baby is taking, you will find that they no longer look as 'full'. This does not mean that you are losing your milk, or that your breasts are not making enough milk. It means that your body has fine-tuned the delicate balance between demand and supply.

The best indication of whether you have enough milk is your baby. Is he reasonably content? Does he have six to eight wet (cloth) nappies a day and regular, soft bowel motions? Is he gaining some weight? If you are using disposable nappies, three or four very heavy nappies a day will show that your baby is getting enough to eat, if he is only getting your milk. As you continue to breastfeed, your breasts may not be much bigger than they were before your pregnancy and may not look full at all, unless you miss a feed.

You will then notice that they begin to feel full and unless you express or feed your baby soon, your breasts may become engorged. This makes the breasts painful and lumpy and may lead to blocked milk ducts and inflammation. Feeding your baby often is the best way to avoid this.

Despite slang references to breasts being 'jugs', your breasts are not at all like jugs of milk which can only hold a limited amount of fluid and which are obviously lighter and empty when the milk is poured from them. As one NMAA Counsellor put it, the human breast is more like the Magic Pudding, from the tale by Norman Lindsay. Whatever is eaten is replenished, producing a constant supply perfectly matched to the demand.

CHAPTER THREE

Before baby is born

- **Preparing for breastfeeding by reading appropriate literature**
- **Preparation for breastfeeding classes**
- **Finding out about support groups importance of support from partner, family**
- **Changes to body (breast size and colour)**
- **Reassurance about small breasts and flat/inverted nipples**
- **Helpful products – breast pads, Meh Tai, nursing nighties**

PREPARING FOR BREASTFEEDING

From the earliest days after you announce your pregnancy, you will notice that apart from constant queries about 'What are you hoping for?' and 'Is this your first?' the focus will be on preparation for labour.

While preparing for labour is important, it is equally important, if not more so, to prepare for breastfeeding. Labour may last anything from one hour to 36 depending on how lucky you are, but a successful breastfeeding relationship can last for years.

It is important that your baby's entry into the world is as peaceful and loving as possible, but arriving safely is only the first step on the road to surviving and thriving. His journey throughout life will be a lot healthier and easier if he receives the best nurturing and nourishment that you can give him, and breastfeeding indisputably provides this.

So how can you prepare for breastfeeding? Perhaps the best preparation you can make, apart from reading about breastfeeding and watching and talking to breastfeeding mothers, is by choosing a birth environment that supports your decision to breastfeed your baby.

If you decide to give birth at home, you will have more control over your environment and who you choose to help you during and after the birth. However, most Australian women – even some of those who planned to give birth at home – give birth in hospital. The hospital you choose therefore will play a big part in helping you to establish breastfeeding.

Most hospitals which cater for maternity patients conduct classes to help new parents prepare for the birth of their child and relaxation exercises learned at antenatal classes can be helpful for some breastfeeding mothers. Some of these also now conduct separate classes on breastfeeding.

Luckily, there are no special exercises you need to do to learn about breastfeeding, and the only panting and blowing you will ever do is when you run to your local NMAA meeting carrying your baby and his nappy bag. However, breastfeeding classes can help you understand how breastfeeding works and give you the confidence in your body's ability to nourish your baby. Breastfeeding classes will explain why breast is best, how your breasts make milk, the importance of positioning and attachment and how to get and ask for help if problems occur. You may also see a demonstration by a breastfeeding couple.

Your labour, whether it is long or short, and your delivery, whether vaginal or by caesarean, may also affect your plan to breastfeed. That is why it is important to choose a birth environment and support people which will support your decision to breastfeed and who can be flexible and helpful under a variety of circumstances.

BABY-FRIENDLY HOSPITALS

In my grandmother's day, the difference between giving birth at home and giving birth in hospital was chloroform. 'They put the mask on and I knew nothing about it,' she said proudly, discussing the births of her three children in country hospitals. In such hospitals, the mother was a 'patient' rather than a participant in the birth, and the baby was delivered and packaged, stamped, labelled and sorted as efficiently as a parcel at a post office; blue for boys, pink for girls, all 'protected' from the germs of their parents and visitors behind a glass wall in the nursery. It was no wonder that breastfeeding was often difficult under these circumstances. By separating the mother and baby, the mother's breasts missed that vital stimulation of her baby's suckling and her milk would have been slower to 'come-in'. The rigid feeding schedules of the day would also have inhibited the mother's milk supply as the amount of milk made depends on the stimulation of sucking.

These days, Australian hospitals would class themselves as 'baby-friendly' in that they try to create the best possible environment for the baby's safe arrival and to ensure that the mother and baby are together as soon as possible after birth, so that bonding and breastfeeding can begin.

However, at the time of writing, there are only two Australian hospitals which have been accorded the 'Baby-Friendly' status according to the criteria set out by the United Nations Children's Fund (UNICEF) and the World Health Organisation to promote breastfeeding and thus infant health.

These are Mitcham Private Hospital and the Royal Women's Hospital, both in Melbourne, Victoria.

This does not mean that there are no other hospitals in Australia which are suitable for mothers who wish to breastfeed. On the contrary, hospitals these days support breastfeeding, and many are also working towards the special Baby-Friendly accreditation.

However, hospitals that are Baby-Friendly recognise that active support of breastfeeding requires much more than just putting the baby to the breast. An accredited hospital must follow certain steps. *(See box)* For example, mothers are actively informed about the benefits of breastfeeding and are encouraged to breastfeed. Infant formula is not offered unless the mother clearly chooses to use it, or there is no breastmilk available, or without the formula, the child's life would be threatened.

All nursing and midwifery staff at Baby-Friendly Hospitals are expected to be knowledgeable about breastfeeding, and are expected to attend professional educational programs several times a year.

A Baby-Friendly Hospital is also likely to have breastfeeding classes separate from antenatal classes, which usually focus on the birth.

A Baby-Friendly Hospital may also have a breastfeeding clinic where a lactation consultant can help both inpatients and outpatients with any breastfeeding problems.

If complementary feeds are necessary, where possible breastmilk will be given by cup or spoon rather than bottle, so that the baby does not become confused between the two different types of sucking.

Infant formula is not banned, but nor is it supplied. Mothers who wish to use infant formula must purchase and prepare their own. This includes the disinfection of bottles and mixing of the formula. This makes good sense as proper hygiene and correct measuring is vital to ensure the safety of artificial feeding and it is best that parents who wish to feed this way learn to do it under supervision and as soon as possible.

The lactation consultant may also do follow-visits after the mother has returned home to make sure that breastfeeding is progressing well.

The policy in Baby-Friendly Hospitals is that a mother should decide how she will feed her baby, but her decision should be an informed one.

Some Baby-Friendly Hospitals also recognise the importance of human contact in the progress of premature and sick babies and encourage both staff and parents to carry these babies around in specially designed slings.

Some hospitals, like birth centres, also have double beds to allow the mother to breastfeed in bed more easily and her partner to join her for an important family cuddle whenever they wish. Despite some claims that such hospitals are not 'mother-friendly', a baby-friendly policy does not mean that a mother would be forced to breastfeed against her wishes.

Change is always difficult, especially if it challenges what was previously thought to be correct. Making formula feeding a second best rather than a choice between equals is not fanatical or unfair. It merely acknowledges the undisputed scientific facts about the superiority of breastmilk as the ideal food for babies.

A hospital which actively supports breastfeeding is particularly important in states which have a policy of early discharge for mothers, or if you choose to return home early.

In some Australian states, mothers who have normal deliveries are sent home within three days after the birth, while mothers who have had caesareans are sent home on day five. Pregnancy and childbirth are not illnesses and there are many mothers who feel more comfortable at home and are well enough to cope.

However, as breastfeeding is not usually fully established until anytime between 36 and 72 hours after birth, early discharge means that many mothers return home before breastfeeding is established.

Positioning and attaching the baby on the now very full breast when your milk comes in may be very different and more difficult than before, when your baby was receiving the first milk, or colostrum, and your breasts were smaller and softer.

If possible, it is good to be able to choose to stay longer if you are having difficulties breastfeeding or feel that you just need an extra day or two to recover and be fully confident when you return home. If this is not possible, you may be able to have a community midwife, a lactation consultant or your child health nurse visit you at home to help you position your baby correctly and avoid any problems such as sore nipples.

The Ten Steps to Successful Breastfeeding, developed by WHO and UNICEF are

1. Have a written breastfeeding policy
2. Train all health staff to implement this policy
3. Inform all pregnant women about the benefits of breastfeeding
4. Help mothers initiate breastfeeding within half an hour of birth
5. Show mothers the best way to breastfeed
6. Give new born infants no food or drink other than breastmilk, unless medically indicated
7. Practise 'rooming-in' by allowing mothers and babies to remain together 24 hours a day
8. Encourage breastfeeding on demand
9. Give no artificial teats, pacifiers, dummies or soothers
10. Help start breastfeeding support groups and refer mothers to them. Ask too, if they have a lactation consultant to help with any problems you may have.

BIRTH CENTRES

Many hospitals these days have birth centres where you can give birth with the security of medical intervention nearby should you need it, yet in the privacy of a home-like environment.

A birth centre may be set up like a large bedroom with an ensuite or kitchen where you, your partner, midwife and support people are in control. The advantage of a birth centre to the breastfeeding mother is that, if all goes well, it is a relaxing environment where it is easier to give your baby his first feed lying on your side in bed or propped with pillows.

However, the policy in most birth centres is for very early discharge, so it is important that you arrange to receive breastfeeding support, either from a visiting lactation consultant, your midwife or your child health nurse or a NMAA Counsellor once you are discharged. Alternatively, you may like to inquire about the possibility of moving into the postnatal ward after you leave the birth centre if you are not confident about breastfeeding or wish to sort out any problems before you return home. Make sure that you ask the hospital staff about their policy on this before you go into labour, as it is best to make such arrangements when you are at your least vulnerable and most assertive.

YOUR DOCTOR

Your choice of doctor or obstetrician may also affect your breastfeeding relationship with your baby. Discuss your decision to breastfeed early in your visits and enlist your doctor's help in preparation and referral to breastfeeding classes and helpful organisations. Make sure that your doctor understands and accepts that you wish to breastfeed as soon as possible after birth. Even if you are well during your pregnancy, and do not foresee any emergencies such as a caesarean delivery, it is wise to talk to your doctor about what can be done to ensure a good start to breastfeeding if things do not go as planned.

THE LABOUR WARD

Despite their best intentions, some women find that they end up in the labour ward rather than the birth centre, with much more medical intervention than they had hoped for. If this happens to you, you

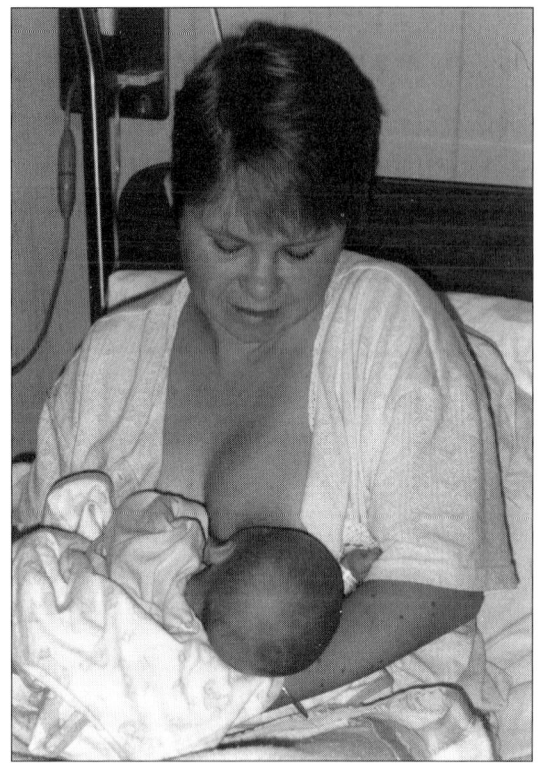

Photograph by Yvette O'Dowd.

may be too exhausted to be assertive about wanting to breastfeed your baby as soon as possible after birth, or you may be under anaesthesia after an emergency caesarean. This is where you partner and support people can step in if you and your baby are well enough. Make sure you have a birth plan which includes breastfeeding as soon as possible after birth, and that your support people can lobby on your behalf if necessary. However, don't be too concerned if things don't go according to plan. You can successfully establish breastfeeding, even if you don't get off to an ideal start.

YOUR PARTNER

While the right birth environment and doctor are important, and other mothers will be invaluable for friendship and support, a most important source of support should be your partner.

This is why it is important for him to be well-informed about breastfeeding too.

Encourage him to read this book and any other material you would like to share with him, and talk to him about your discoveries and feelings about breastfeeding.

Your partner may also have some strong and confusing feelings about your desire to breastfeed your child. He may feel proud, fascinated, and passionate about it, or even jealous. Or he may feel concerned about whether you will be able to produce enough milk and whether breastfeeding will be tiring for you. He may have heard about other women who had difficulties breastfeeding or fathers who felt excluded by the closeness between the breastfeeding mother and child.

Encourage him to talk about his feelings with you. It is also important for him to talk to other men about how they felt when their partners were breastfeeding and about what they did to support the breastfeeding relationship. This may include emotional support, or practical things such as preparing meals, fetching drinks and pillows.

Some men fear that the intimacy of the breastfeeding relationship may impinge on the intimacy between you both. While the breastfeeding relationship is often intense, and there is no question that the bond between mother and child is great, there is no reason why a father need feel excluded. Love is not a limited resource and the love a mother feels for her child, although different from the love she may feel for others, does not detract from the love she feels for her partner. The difference is in the way she is expressing it, (pardon the pun!).

Bearing a child, nurturing it from within her body while she is pregnant, and then again while breastfeeding, is a profound expression of love not only for the child, but for its father.

If you and your partner have shared in the experience of birth and caring for your new baby together, you will find that your love for your baby does not come between you, but is an extension of the love you feel for each other. Caring for your baby together and watching him grow is a new and different, but richly rewarding way of expressing your love for each other.

A father cannot breastfeed, but he can develop his own unique relationship with his child simply be cuddling and talking to him lovingly and sharing his care. He can also give his baby the best nutritional start in life, by supporting you in your choice to give your baby the optimum nutrition.

YOUR CHANGING BODY

When you are pregnant, the focus is often on your growing belly. However, the changes to your breasts may be less obvious to others, but just as dramatic. In fact, for many women, enlarged, sensitive or tingling breasts is the first exciting sign that they are pregnant.

Your breasts will undergo several changes during pregnancy and after birth, not only in size but in appearance.

Initially, the veins on your breasts will appear to stand out like rivers on a map. This is because of the increased blood supply to the breast necessary to produce milk. This will also settle down in time.

Sometime after the fifth or sixth month of pregnancy, you may have noticed purplish streaks across your breasts, thighs or tummy. These, unfortunately are stretch marks.

Some women are more prone to stretch marks than others, but contrary to popular views, it is not breastfeeding but pregnancy that causes these. Put simply, it means that your body has expanded faster than your skin would allow, stretching the skin.

A big increase in breast size or weight gain during pregnancy and your skin type may all be factors influencing whether or not you get stretch marks.

You may have tried to avoid stretch marks by using a special cream throughout pregnancy. However these creams, while they increase the moisture and suppleness of the skin, are no guarantee against stretch marks, despite the manufacturers' claims.

Eventually, these marks will lose their purplish or bluish appearance and fade to silvery streaks which may appear crepe-like when you are cold.

Women who have stretch marks on their breasts or dislike the changes caused by pregnancy often blame breastfeeding. You may be warned not to breastfeed if you want to keep your breasts (and your man!). Fortunately for the survival of our children and our relationships, this is not so.

The breasts of any woman who has borne a child are different from those of a woman who has not, whether she breastfed or not. Glandular tissue proliferates and fat mobilises in the breast during pregnancy causing the breasts to increase in size.

It is this increase that causes the changes to the shape of the breast, not breastfeeding.

Some women choose to wear a supportive bra to try to minimise the effect of these changes. This may make you feel more comfortable, but it is no guarantee against droopy boobs.

The fact is that the immature breast is higher and firmer; the mature breast is lower and curved.

Chances are your breasts will not return to their original *shape* after pregnancy and breastfeeding. But if you wean gradually studies have found that fat (which affects the size of the breast) are more likely to be redeposited in the breasts and help them to return to approximately the same *size*. Very flat chests are usually the result of lactation suppression or sudden weaning.

The reverence in our culture for the high firm breast can perhaps be linked to the reverence for youth, as high firm breasts are a sign of youth. This may also have something to do with the power of advertising and the mass media. The popular image of the breast projected in the media is of the young breast, so this has come to be accepted as the norm.

The longer, mature, curved breast is seldom seen except in news bulletins or documentaries about starving women in developing countries who are often depicted with a tiny wizened baby at a long or withered breast.

Is it any wonder then that some mothers see their own mature breasts as disfigured? Perhaps if more women breastfeed and both men and women become more accustomed to seeing the breast perform its nurturing function rather than its sexual function, this distorted view may change. The darker nipple of the mother, which may range from a dark pink in fair mothers to virtually black in dark-skinned mothers, and which is caused by hormone changes during pregnancy, can be just as beautiful as the rosy pink nipple of the young girl.

The soft, lower, curved breasts of the mother, (whether breastfeeding or not) can be just as beautiful as the high pert firm breasts of the teenager.

Motherhood is a time of great change, both physically and emotionally. Rather than be disappointed at the changes in your breasts, you may like to view them as a mark of your passage from womanhood to motherhood.

SMALL BREASTS, BIG BREASTS, WHAT'S THE DIFFERENCE?
You do not need abundant breasts to breastfeed, nor do they need to be any particular shape. The ability to make milk depends on the number of lobes of milk-making glandular tissue, which are composed of clusters of alveoli.

Special channels, called ducts, run from these lobes. These expand to form sinuses directly beneath the areola. These sinuses are reservoirs for the collection of milk and it is from here that the milk flows out through the tiny openings in the nipple. Much of the breast is fatty and connective tissue rather than milk-producing glands.

However, the size of your breasts (and don't forget that this can change dramatically throughout pregnancy and lactation), may affect the feeding position that is best for you and your baby. The aim is to position your baby so that your nipple points to the back of the roof of his mouth.

If you have large breasts, you may need to support them from underneath while feeding. If the breasts are very heavy, the weight can pull them down and may pull the nipple out of position in the baby's mouth. This can cause nipple damage.

To avoid this, you can cup the breast in your hand, or make a sling which goes under your breast and over your shoulder or around your neck. (You may need to ask for help in this case, as the sling and cupping may distort the nipple position in your baby's mouth.)

Alternatively, you may like to tuck your baby under your arm with his legs pointing behind you and cup his head in your hand. You will also need to make sure that your baby opens his mouth very wide to latch on properly.

If you have small breasts you may need to lift your baby to the breast, by lying the baby on a pillow or cushion. The size of your nipple is also unimportant as the baby needs to suck at the breast, not just the nipple.

The size of the areola, also varies greatly between women, and does not affect the ability to breastfeed.

INVERTED NIPPLES

If your nipples do not become erect, you may have what is known as flat or inverted nipples. This does not mean you cannot breastfeed. You may just need a bit of extra help preparing your nipples before baby is born and when feeding to help baby latch on.

An inverted nipple retracts or inverts into the breast instead of protruding when a baby tries to suckle.

Deeply inverted nipples are rare, but many women have nipples which will not easily draw out from the breast.

How do you know if your nipples are inverted? The best way of telling is to try this simple test: squeeze or gently pinch the areola between your forefinger and thumb, just behind the base of the nipple.

If the nipple reacts by coming out, even a little, it is not truly inverted. However, if the nipple shrinks back into the breast when the pinching test is done, it is inverted and requires attention.

The appearance of the nipple alone will not tell you whether it is inverted. An apparently well-formed nipple may shrink back when pinched, while an apparently flat nipple may pop out.

You may also try an ice pack or manual stimulation to see how your nipples react. Truly inverted nipples will retract: flat or pseudo-inverted nipples will become firmer and more erect, although this may only be slight.

The breast undergoes some dramatic changes during pregnancy and in the early days of lactation, and inverted nipples may improve as your pregnancy progresses. Research has shown that specific antenatal preparation is probably of no benefit.

The normal changes during pregnancy and the immediate postnatal period cause most nipples to become larger, more prominent and supple. If your nipples remain flat or inverted, you will require some extra help to attach your baby for the first feeds.

WHAT TO WEAR

Imagine how difficult breastfeeding would have been for women in the 16th Century, when the fashion was for corsets of leather, bone or even metal which completely flattened the breast and the nipple.

Not only did such fashions damage the health of the mother, they probably would have damaged the developing breast tissue and made breastfeeding almost impossible. No wonder it was the custom for fashionable women to hire a wet-nurse to breastfeed for them.

The current flexibility of fashions makes it easier for women to breastfeed anywhere and everywhere than ever before. These days, a T-shirt or windcheater and jeans or skirt are considered appropriate for women to wear almost anywhere, and this loose, comfortable clothing is ideal for breastfeeding. Patterned clothing tends to camouflage any damp patches that might appear.

A T-shirt or jumper may be lifted just enough to allow the baby access to the nipple without exposing the whole breast.

The only special item you might need for successful breastfeeding is a good maternity bra. This will provide proper support and, as it has a special opening, will also be more convenient.

The changes to your breasts throughout pregnancy and lactation may mean that you start as AAA cup and end up a AA after the baby is weaned, but in between you may increase to a DD.

Whether you choose to buy a maternity bra or not will depend on your personal preference and the size of your breasts. Some women prefer to wear no bra while pregnant or breastfeeding. Others find that as their breasts grow throughout pregnancy and lactation, they like the extra support a maternity bra offers.

Not so long ago, maternity bras looked about as feminine as surgical boots. These days, however, there are several designs on the market which are discreet and pretty and which provide excellent breast support. Maternity bras are relatively expensive, especially as you will need two or three, but some women find them a good investment in comfort and convenience.

If you do buy a maternity bra, to ensure that you are confident about breastfeeding in public, practise opening and closing your bra without looking. After a little practice most designs can be easily undone with one hand without looking.

BREASTFEEDING ... NATURALLY

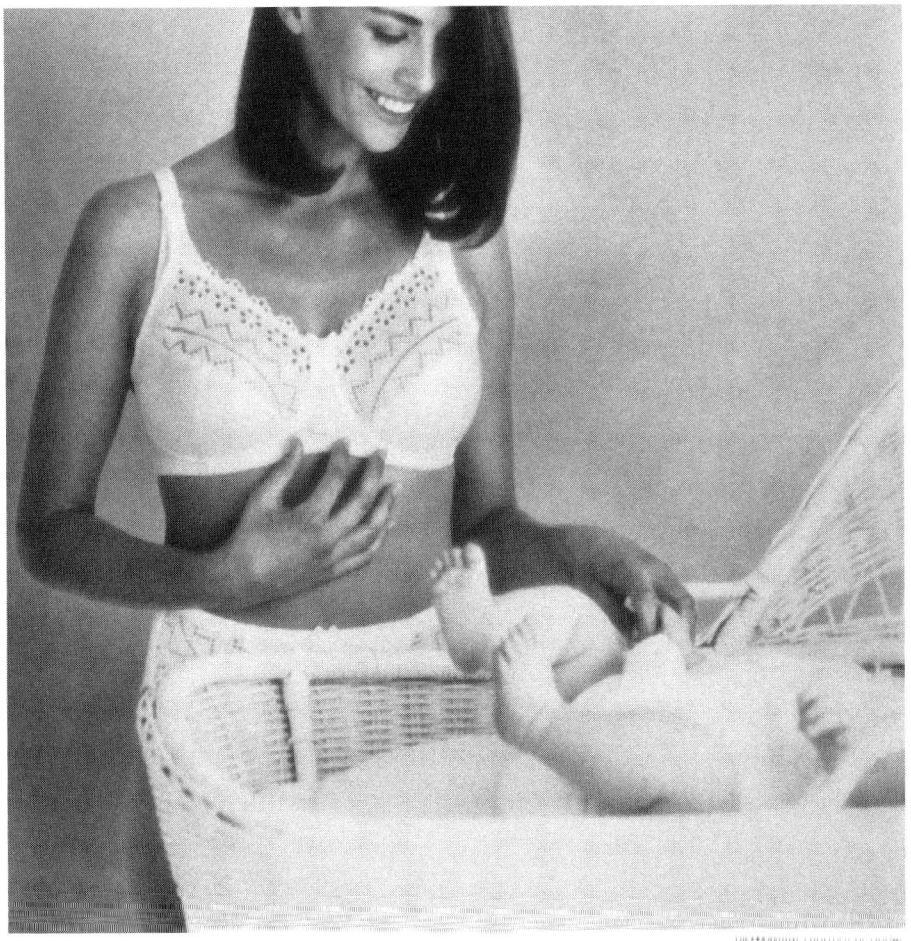

Photograph courtesy of Berlei.

Once your bra is undone, put your baby in the feeding position and lift up as much as necessary of your top. Allow the shirt or jumper to fall down just as baby pulls away, then do up your bra.

You may also like to invest in a few skirts or pants with elasticised waists. Even if you were careful with your diet during pregnancy, most women find that they are a little rounder and thicker in the waist soon after giving birth and their usual clothes may feel a little tight for a while. By choosing the right wardrobe, you need not feel that you are on show while breastfeeding in public. Choosing comfortable clothes which allow you to feed discreetly will give your more confidence to go out with your baby.

Although there are an increasing number of special breastfeeding clothes on the market that may offer a little more convenience, some are little more than gimmicks that are just an unnecessary expense at a time when most women have to forgo their earning abilities and money is short. Apart from a maternity bra, the only other specially-designed product which may be of use while breastfeeding in front of visitors if you are in hospital, or for convenience at home, is a maternity nightie. NMAA has several designs available, and there are others available in speciality and department stores.

HELPFUL PRODUCTS

When you become a mother you may suddenly find that the world is no longer geared to your needs, nor those of your baby. There are steps leading to your local bank that make it inaccessible with a pram; doors open outward making pushers hard to manoeuvre; there are few places, other than the ladies toilet, to change a nappy; bench tops have sharp corners at just the right height for banging little heads, and so it goes on.

However, there is one area in which you and your baby are welcome, and that is as consumers. In the past few decades the number of products aimed at parents and children have escalated as manufacturers have realised the potential market.

Some of these have been helpful and even lifesaving, such as baby car restraints: others are just gimmicks. Talking to other parents is a good way of finding which is which.

Breastfeeding mothers are not good consumers as breastfeeding requires no special equipment. However, there are a few products which may be helpful. These are:

Breast pads: These can be disposable or cotton round light pads which may be placed inside the bra to absorb leakage both during pregnancy and lactation. Breast pads must be changed regularly to prevent the nipples becoming moist and so predisposed to cracking and infections. The washable pads are more economical. Some mothers whose breasts leak copiously find these invaluable. Others who do not leak may never use them. You may be asked to include breast pads in your list of things to bring to hospital.

Breast pumps: There is a range of hand-operated and electric breast pumps available for mothers who need to express their milk. (*See Chapter 10, Expressing and Storing Breastmilk.*)

Meh Tai baby sling: This medically approved baby sling is one of the simplest, yet most effective on the market. It is a simple cotton sling which can be tied in a variety of ways and which allows baby to be carried in a variety of positions and supported, leaving your hands free. It allows you to comfortably carry, and even breastfeed your baby while walking, shopping or attending to household chores.

Photograph by Prue Carr.

CHAPTER FOUR

Position, position, position!

- **Positioning and attachment, explained and illustrated**
- **Getting started – colostrum, milk coming in, engorgement (how to avoid it), night feeds, rooming in, complementary feeds and the problems they present, jaundice, weight loss, nipple soreness, dummies**
- **What's normal?**
- **How often to feed and how long feeds last**

GETTING STARTED

You've seen the real estate advertisements? When it comes to buying a home, position is everything. A house in the right position will guarantee a return on your investment later. The same goes for a breastfeeding baby. Correct positioning in the first days will help ensure that your baby is properly attached and sucking well, which in turn will help avoid sore or cracked nipples, and will get your breastfeeding relationship off to a good start. So it is worth investing some time into reading up about 'positioning and attachment,' the words commonly used to describe the process of putting your baby to your breast so that he can drain it effectively without damaging your nipples.

Some nipple tenderness is common in the early days of breastfeeding. The nipples are more sensitive in the first few days after birth, and it does take a little time to become accustomed to the strong sucking of a healthy baby.

Sometimes mothers are advised to limit feeds in the early days to try to lessen any early discomfort. However this has been shown to merely delay the soreness. Restricting your baby's time at the breast may also lead to a build-up of milk and increased engorgement, resulting in further soreness.

Many mothers find that sore nipples improve quickly once they learn how to attach their babies correctly to the breast.

When your baby is properly attached to the breast, the nipple is drawn into the back of his mouth and is held there by suction so that your milk sinuses are between his upper and lower jaw.

The action of the tongue and jaw compress the sinuses and his rhythmical, undulating tongue movements express milk into the back of his mouth.

Your baby cannot bite you if he is attached correctly as his tongue lies over the bottom gum (and later teeth).

When the nipple is drawn back to the baby's soft palate, friction from his tongue cannot cause pain on the end of the nipple. Try sucking your own thumb. The deeper the thumb is in the mouth, the less friction there is on the end of it.

Your skin covering your nipple contains the many nerves which are stimulated by your baby's sucking. This stimulation causes your milk to be released. This release, which you may feel as a tingling feeling, is commonly called the let-down reflex. The removal of the milk by the baby is the signal for more milk to be produced.

You and your baby will probably need help getting positioned in the early days. Breastfeeding is a learned art and it is normal to feel awkward at first.

Your baby is also trying to learn how to breastfeed and may take time to learn how to milk the breast effectively. Don't hesitate to ask the midwifery staff at the hospital for help, or other nursing mothers.

POSITION CHECKLIST

A detailed description of how to position your baby follows in this chapter under the heading 'The First Feed' but here is a quick check list to help you recognise if your baby is well-attached:

- **Baby's mouth covers your nipple and a large amount of the areola**
- **His chin is touching your breast**
- **His nose is clear of, or just touching your breast**
- **His upper and lower lip is opened out or 'flanged' over the breast**
- **You are not in pain**

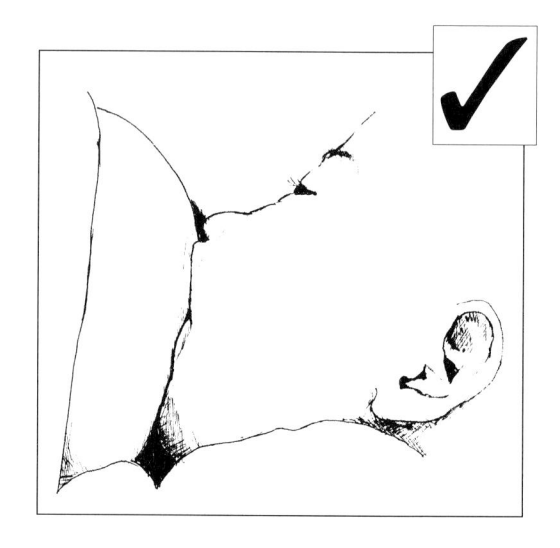

COLOSTRUM

The sticky, clear or yellowish fluid that may have leaked from your breasts will now be your baby's most valuable aid. This is colostrum and is the first food your baby receives from your breast in the first few days after birth, until your milk production increases.

Colostrum is perfectly designed for all your baby's nutritional needs and he will not need any complementary feeds of water or formula. In fact, giving your baby any other fluids will reduce his desire to suck at your breast, deprive him of important colostrum and delay your milk coming in. In a few days, with the stimulation of his sucking and the change in your hormones, this rich first meal will gradually change to mature breastmilk.

YOUR MILK COMES IN

Anytime between 24 and 96 hours after you give birth, you will notice that your breasts are fuller and heavier and that the milk is finer and more plentiful. This means that your milk has come in and your body's task of matching your supply with your baby's needs has begun.

At this stage, correct positioning is even more important as your breasts will be fuller and may be more difficult for your baby to grasp. Incorrect positioning will cause nipple soreness and other problems, and may also mean that your baby is not able to milk the breast effectively.

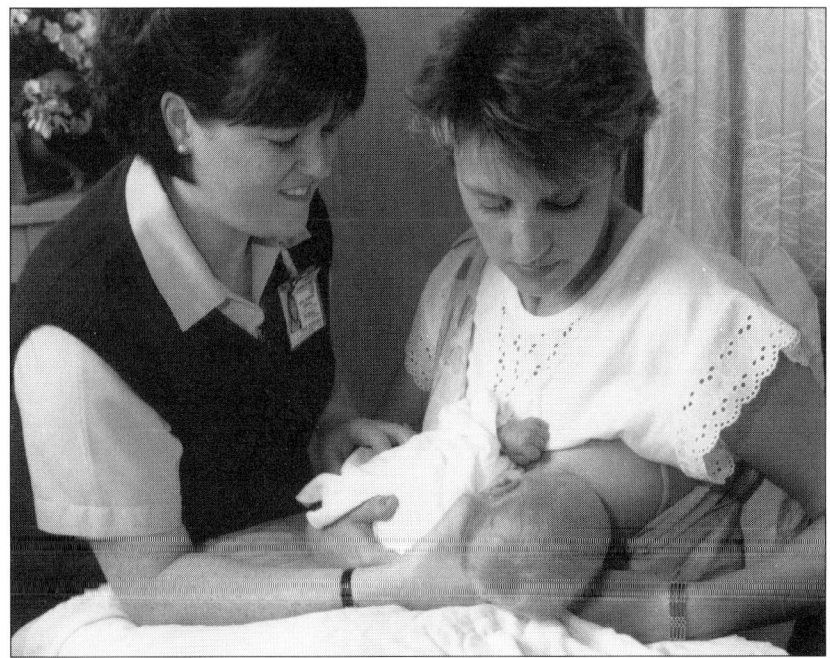

Photograph by Robert Madden.

THE FIRST FEED

Ideally, your baby's first feed will be as soon as possible after birth. Studies have shown that the newborn is at his most alert and responsive at this time. Many babies are not ready to feed until half to one hour after birth. If possible, and enough time is available, wait for cues from your baby, such as hand to mouth movements.

Make sure your doctor and midwives have already been informed about your desire to feed your baby as soon as possible. Your baby will prefer the warmth of your body and the familiar sound of your heartbeat to any heated crib, and he will certainly feel a lot better about having his first bath if he has had the reassurance of your breast and your arms first.

If you gave birth on a delivery table, you may like to feed your baby lying down, using a couple of extra pillows to tuck under your shoulder or behind your back. Lie on your side, with your body slightly curved so that your baby can snuggle in next to you.

Put the baby on his side, his mouth in line with your nipple. Place your arm on the bed, above his head. Or you could try placing him in the crook of your elbow, bringing his head closer to your breast. Pull your baby in close to you, aligning his body at a slight angle to you with his chin closer to your breast than his nose. Make sure that his mouth is directly opposite your nipple. Cup your breast with your other hand, four fingers underneath and the thumb on top to tilt the nipple towards your baby's nose and offer the breast by tickling his lips with your breast. Wait for him to search or nuzzle and open his mouth wide. Centre his mouth over your nipple, guiding it over his tongue, and pull his body close against yours so that he takes a good mouthful of nipple and areola.

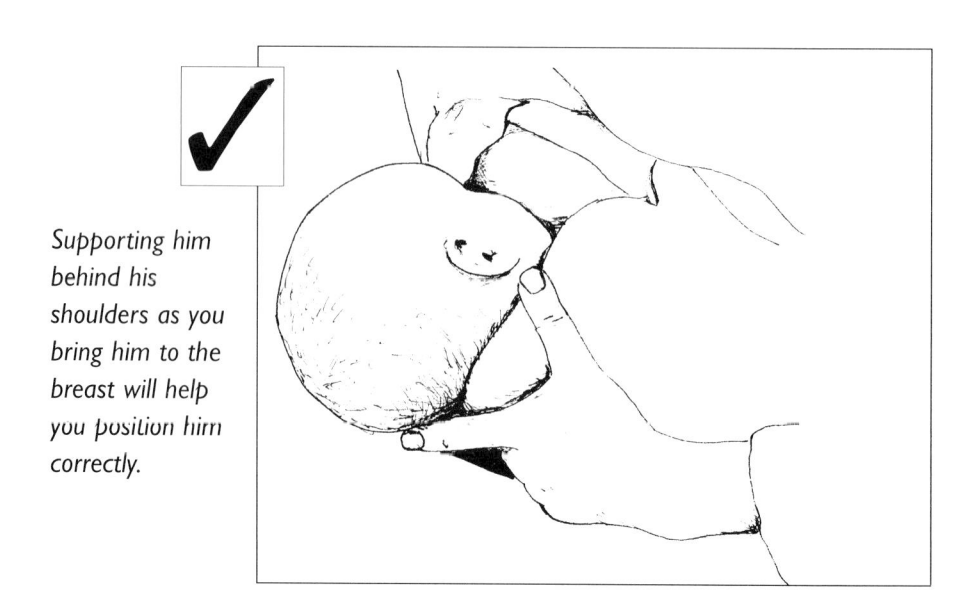

Supporting him behind his shoulders as you bring him to the breast will help you position him correctly.

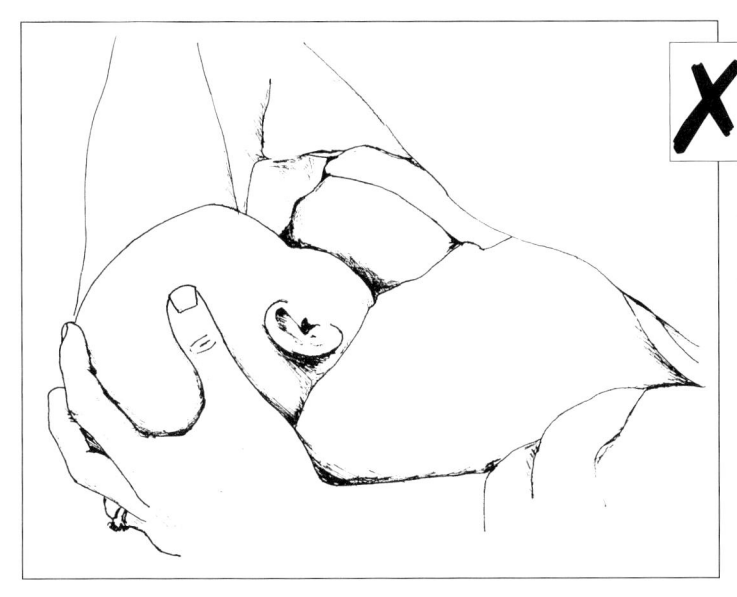

Pushing your baby's head onto the breast may mean his nose makes contact before his chin.

Make sure he is close enough to you so that he does not have to strain to hold on to the nipple. It is important that the baby takes in as much of the nipple and areola as possible.

Avoid pushing the back of your baby's head forward as this can press his nose into the breast causing him to struggle to breathe and hurt your nipple in the process. This can also change the position of your nipple in his mouth, so that it hurts you when he sucks.

If your baby is properly attached, his tongue will have come forward to take a good bit of the underside of the areola as well as the nipple in his mouth, his head will be tipped back a little so that his chin is touching your breast and his bottom lip will be turned out rather than sucked in.

If your baby lets go of the breast, make sure that he attaches correctly again. A baby who is properly attached at the breast should not hurt you as he feeds. If it does hurt, place a clean finger in your baby's mouth at the corner to break the suction, remove your nipple from his mouth and start again.

If you prefer to sit up, a pillow on your lap will help support your baby's weight and keep him up level with your breast. Once again it is important that his mouth is directly opposite your nipple. Remember, chest to chest, chin to breast, is the optimum position for feeding your baby.

A normal healthy baby will be born with a strong sucking instinct, but sometimes a newborn may be affected by drugs administered during labour, or may be tired, or will not seem interested.

Sometimes your newborn baby may also seem to fight the breast, moving his head from side to side and perhaps crying. If that is the case, don't worry. He may just need a little encouragement.

Express a little colostrum by squeezing the areola firmly (your midwife may be able to help you with this while you cradle your baby) and let a few drops fall into your baby's mouth. Sometimes, this first taste is enough to awaken interest or to help a frustrated baby persist and try to latch on.

Above all, do not force your baby's head or get frustrated yourself. These things take a little time and patience. And while patience may have to be learned by both of you, you have plenty of time.

Don't be concerned if your baby only feeds for a few minutes. He may be too tired to suck any more or may have had enough. You are both off to an excellent start. Your baby will have received valuable nutrients and antibodies from the colostrum in your breasts, and the reassurance that life outside your womb is likely to be just as warm and secure as it was inside.

LATER FEEDS

Your baby will be well nourished by the colostrum in your breasts for the first few days after birth and if given the opportunity to feed frequently will not need any other fluids. In fact, if you are in hospital, it is important to let staff know that you are fully breastfeeding and that your baby does not need extra fluid. Any extra fluid will reduce his appetite and his desire to suck and therefore inhibit your supply. Depending on the hospital's policy, a friendly note pinned to the crib may help as a gentle reminder.

Anywhere between 24 and 96 hours after the birth you will notice that your breasts seem fuller and that your baby is obviously swallowing, or perhaps even gulping, at feeds.

This means your milk has 'come in', which can sometimes be a gentle euphemism for discovering that over night your lentils have turned into pumpkins. This will settle down once your baby starts feeding regularly and your supply begins to match your baby's appetite.

At this time, you may feel a tingling sensation in the breast a few minutes after the baby begins to suck as the 'let-down' reflex occurs and the milk is released.

The breast that he is not feeding from may also drip or even stream milk and you may experience painful contractions, similar to those you experienced in early labour, especially if this is not your first baby.

The contractions will not continue at every breastfeeding session, but may persist for a few days. These contractions are a hormonal reaction and will help your uterus to return to its normal pre-pregnancy shape more quickly. The let-down reflex will continue to occur at each feed, sometimes more than once, although perhaps not with the same intensity. Some mothers do not feel it strongly at all, while others notice the first let-down but not later ones that occur during the feed. Later, especially if you express your milk for your baby, you can learn to trigger it yourself.

Babies have three different types of sucking. The first is the ravenous, hungry suck which occurs before the let-down. When the milk is let down from the back of the breast, babies change to a deep, nutritive suck-and-swallow action. As the feed progresses your baby may swallow less frequently and pause from time to time. Comfort sucking occurs toward the end of a feed and is faster and more gentle than the earlier sucking actions, with babies swallowing only occasionally.

The need to comfort suck is strong in most babies and helps to remove the very nourishing hindmilk from the breast. If your nipples are sore, you can shorten this comfort-sucking time by offering a clean finger.

In the first few days after birth, you may be feeling sore or tired, or unsure of yourself and may need some help in getting your baby properly attached to your breast. Do not be afraid to ask for help. Most hospitals today support breastfeeding and their midwives have knowledge of breastfeeding which should be constantly updated, or they may have a lactation consultant who can offer support and advice.

Do not feel embarrassed if you find that you need their support and advice often. That is what they are there for. They understand how important it is to help you to feel confident and to get your breastfeeding relationship off to a good start.

You will probably need to experiment a little with how you sit or lie to feed before you find a position that suits you. If you are sitting in a chair, it may help to put your baby on a pillow to raise him to the correct height and to put your feet on a low stool. If pain from stitches is making it difficult to relax, speak to your medical adviser.

In the first few days, you will probably prefer some privacy as you learn to breastfeed. Make sure that other staff or visitors are alerted to this by hanging a sign on your door and keeping it firmly closed. If someone still persists by knocking or opening the door, don't feel shy about politely asking them to wait outside or to return at a more convenient time.

Getting your baby feeding well and building your confidence about breastfeeding is the most important thing at this stage. You will have plenty of time to catch up with friends later. Most people understand that this is a special learning time for you and your baby.

Make sure your nightie and bra are open well enough to allow your baby close contact with the breast. NMAA's 'Melissa' nighties unbutton to the waist, allowing easy access to the breast. You may like to remove t-shirts or other tops as you learn to breastfeed, rather than tuck them under your chin. Some mothers use a clothes peg to secure the bottom part of a shirt to the shoulder, or tuck it under a bra strap to keep it out of the way.

Unwrap your baby and hold him close. You can do this by supporting his head and shoulders on your forearm, or hold him with your opposite arm, with your outstretched hand supporting his shoulders and forearm holding the baby close.

You can tuck his lower arm around your waist. Make sure he is at the same level as your breast, with his mouth level with your nipple.

Gently touch your baby's mouth with your nipple. Your baby will instinctively open his mouth and you can bring him to the breast. If you need to support your breast as your baby attaches, make sure your fingers are behind the areola so they do not get in the way of his mouth.

Encourage your baby to open his mouth wide. As you brush your

BREASTFEEDING ... NATURALLY

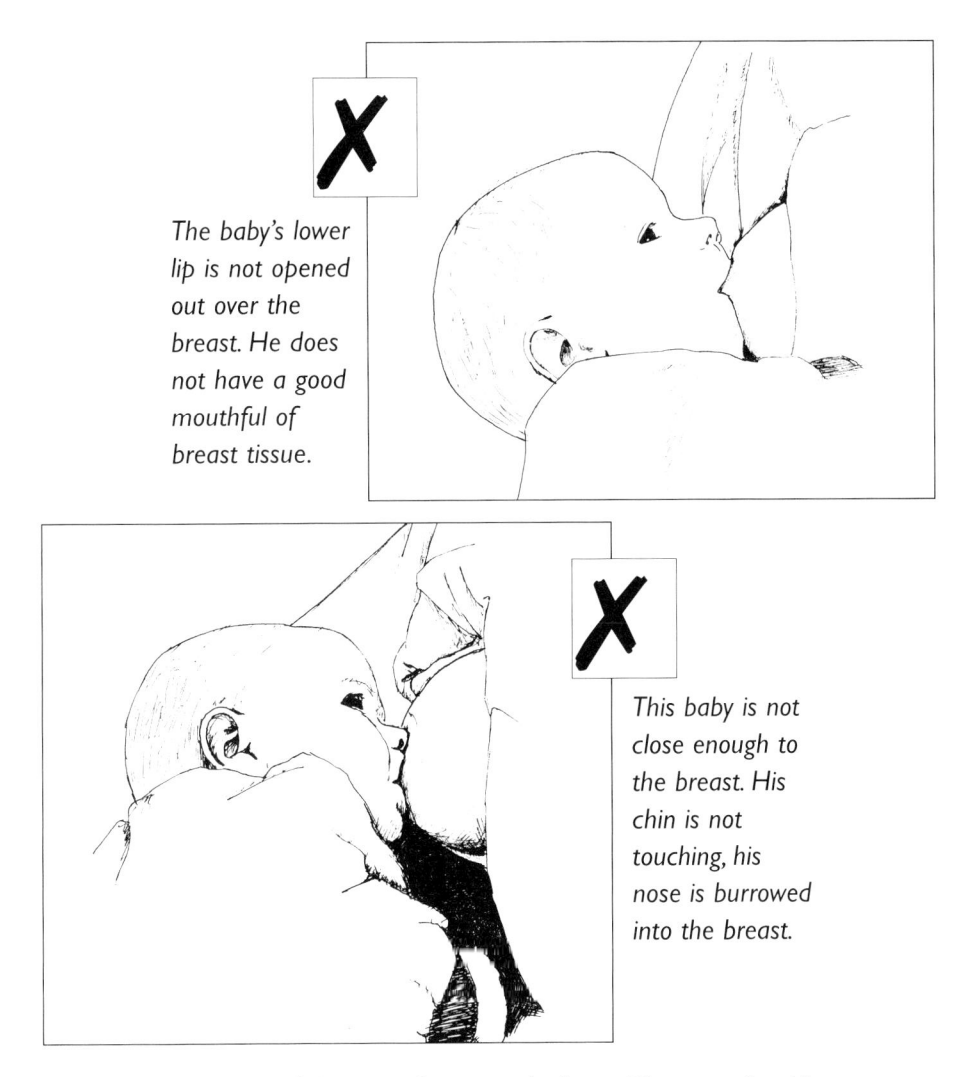

The baby's lower lip is not opened out over the breast. He does not have a good mouthful of breast tissue.

This baby is not close enough to the breast. His chin is not touching, his nose is burrowed into the breast.

nipple and breast against this mouth, your baby will gape for the breast. Do not move your breast or chase his mouth with your nipple. His natural rooting reflex will help him find it. When he opens his mouth, his tongue will come forward and you can quickly bring him to the breast.

Bring your baby to the breast, not your breast to the baby. Move his body gently but quickly towards yours. This will place his mouth over the nipple and breast before he has the chance to close it.

Don't push his head on to the breast or his nose will make contact before his chin. He will not like this and will probably pull away and cry.

When your baby is well-attached to the breast his mouth will have a good mouthful of nipple and breast. More of the areola should be visible above the top lip than below the bottom lip. His top and bottom lip will open out over the breast, with his chin touching and his nose clear.

A correctly-attached baby will be able to breathe while feeding. Most mothers find they do not need to hold the breast away from the baby's nose. Doing so may pull the nipple from his mouth or even block the milk ducts below. You may be surprised by the force of your baby's jaw as he latches on. We tend to think of gums as soft and pink, but your new baby's gums may feel surprisingly hard. If your baby is particularly hungry and keen to attach, it may feel more like an iron clamp on your breast. Don't worry, as breastfeeding progresses he will learn that his hunger will soon be eased and he will relax.

However, if you experience pain beyond the initial attachment, your baby may be positioned wrongly. Break the suction by inserting a clean finger in the corner of his mouth between his gums and try again. If you are having any trouble attaching your baby to the breast, it is best to ask for help to get it right.

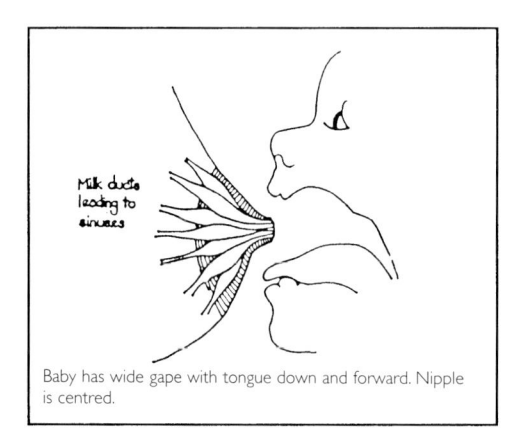

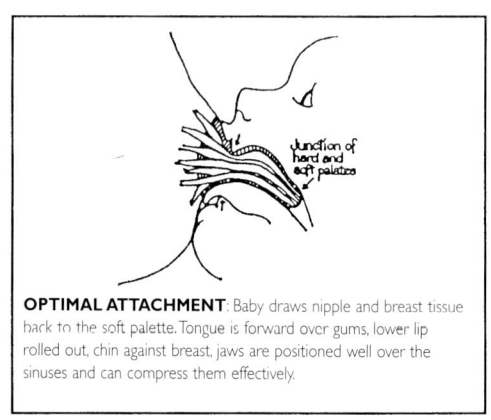

Baby has wide gape with tongue down and forward. Nipple is centred.

OPTIMAL ATTACHMENT: Baby draws nipple and breast tissue back to the soft palette. Tongue is forward over gums, lower lip rolled out, chin against breast, jaws are positioned well over the sinuses and can compress them effectively.

From *Breastfeeding Review* (May 1989) article Ros Escott, pages 34-37.

SORE NIPPLES

Early nipple soreness can sometimes take the enjoyment out of breastfeeding, but this is usually short-lived. For most mothers, taking care in getting the baby on and off the breast, and some simple first aid treatment, time and patience are all that is needed to solve the problem.

If pain persists after the first week or so, or your nipples become very sore, red, blistered or bruised, it is time to consult your medical adviser, child health nurse, or perhaps chat with a NMAA Counsellor, (all Counsellors are experienced breastfeeders).

Your skin is more easily damaged when it is either too dry or too moist, so keeping the nipples healthy and supple is important in preventing soreness.

If your breasts are leaking milk make sure that your bras and clothing do not become soggy. Breast pads (either disposable or washable) worn inside your bra can help absorb moisture and keep your nipples dry, provided they are changed regularly. Plastic-backed pads may be worn for special occasions, but they are best avoided because of the moisture they hold against the breast. Going braless or leaving your bra open for a while after a feed, also helps the nipples to dry naturally.

Do not use any drying agents such as methylated spirits or tinct. benz to dry your nipples. Nor should you scrub them with anything harsh to toughen them. Even soap can dry out the skin so that it is more prone to cracking. Nature provides the best lubricant during pregnancy and lactation as special glands in the areola produce natural oils that clean and lubricate the nipples. Rinsing with water during your daily bath or shower is all that is needed.

WEIGHT LOSS

Babies may lose up to 10 per cent of their birth weight in the first few days and may take five days or longer to regain it. This is normal and does not mean your baby is starving. As long as he is given free access to your breast he will be receiving valuable colostrum and stimulating your breasts to supply the mature milk that he needs after the first few days. Some weight loss is no cause for concern in a baby who is allowed to suck freely, and if is doing so happily, does not need any other fluids.

However, if your baby is obviously having trouble milking the breast or is not thriving, he may be incorrectly positioned and may not be milking the breast effectively to gain adequate nourishment. If repositioning or advice from a lactation consultant does not resolve this, your baby may have a medical problem and should be checked by your doctor.

ENGORGEMENT

The breast size that you (or your husband!) may have sometimes fantasised about may not be too ideal in practice if it means that your breasts are suddenly very full and tight.

Pregnancy usually causes several changes in breast size as your breasts prepare to make milk, but you may be surprised at how quickly even mole hills can become mountains when your milk comes in properly. Your breasts may suddenly feel enormous and quite uncomfortable, so you may be relieved to know that this is temporary.

The engorgement is caused not only by the increased volume of milk but also by the increased blood supply to the breasts, needed to begin their milk-producing function.

The best treatment and prevention of engorgement is to feed your baby often, with some of those feeds being at night, and to ensure he is correctly attached.

However, it may also help to use cold compresses. Cold packs, or thoroughly washed and dried, crisp, cold cabbage leaves, applied over the affected breast can provide relief. Remove any large veins from the leaves which could press on milk ducts. Cut a hole for your nipple as the cabbage may irritate some delicate skins.

Change the cabbage leaves approximately two hourly or when they become limp. At each change, inspect the breasts to check whether the engorgement has eased. Stop using the compress as soon as your breasts feel comfortable. If treatment continues for too long, your milk supply could be inhibited. Gently massaging the breasts before and during feeds may also improve milk flow.

Engorgement may make it difficult for the nipple to protrude. If this occurs express a little milk before offering your baby your breast. This will soften the breast around the nipple and areola, allowing your baby to draw the nipple well into his mouth and preventing him from chewing on it.

If engorgement is causing extreme pain, it may be best to express your breasts completely, once, either by hand or with a pump. (See

Expressing and Storing). To ensure breasts are drained evenly, start each feed on the opposite side from which you started your last feed.

AM I LOSING MY MILK?

When engorgement subsides and breastfeeding becomes more established, your breasts will return to a more manageable size and will not feel as full. This does not mean you are losing your supply. On the contrary, it means that your baby's needs are being better met as your body matches how much milk it makes to how much he takes.

DECLINING COMPLEMENTS

A healthy, newborn baby, who has unlimited access to the breast, needs no other fluids. Your colostrum or breastmilk will not only provide him with fluids and nutrients, but will protect him from infection. Colostrum is of great value to your baby as it is particularly rich in antibodies and will increase his resistance to many infections. Most babies lose weight in the first few days and this is not an indication that they need a complementary feed.

Infant formula, or even bottles of water, can interfere with the establishment of breastfeeding as they fill the baby up and reduce the time he spends at the breast.

Research has shown that babies may lose more weight when they are given fluids other than breastmilk in the early days. Your body is making more milk all the time and your breasts are never completely empty. In fact your breasts have another full feed available half an hour after you started the last feed.

If your baby does not settle after a feed, try putting him back on the breast for a 'top-up' after 20 minutes or so. The extra milk he gets may be just what he needs to settle down. The extra sucking will stimulate and increase your supply too.

If, for any other reason, your baby must have extra fluid, ask that he be given expressed breastmilk or plain, boiled water, rather than infant formula.

This is especially important if your family has a history of allergy or asthma, eczema or hay fever as your newborn baby can become sensitised to the foreign protein.

Extra fluids should be given by cup or spoon, not bottle, as the baby may become confused by the different sucking actions required to milk the breast and the bottle.

JAUNDICE

If, by day three or four, your baby seems to developing a deep olive or ochre complexion while the rest of the family are pink, white or freckly, do not fear a recessive gene, or worse still, that you have the wrong baby. It is likely that your baby has physiological jaundice.

Jaundice occurs when your baby's body is having trouble breaking down or getting rid of bilirubin, which is usually expelled through the liver or bound to albumin in the bloodstream. Bilirubin (a compound produced when foetal red blood cells are replaced by normal red blood cells) is yellow, which is why babies who are jaundiced look yellow.

Jaundice is a common and easily treated problem in the newborn baby. It is estimated that between 30 and 75 per cent of babies develop jaundice, which is generally a benign, temporary and easily treated condition, not a disease.

Physiological 'normal' jaundice appears on the third or fourth day and is gone by the seventh day and usually requires no treatment.

It was once thought that breastfeeding and jaundice were linked, that breastfed babies had a greater risk of jaundice, and even that breastfeeding caused jaundice.

This is now known to be false. In fact breastfeeding in the early days is an important part of the treatment for jaundice as the first food produced by your breasts, colostrum, has a natural laxative effect that helps your baby to pass meconium.

Inaccurate feeding advice, such as limiting the amount of colostrum and breastmilk you give your baby in the first few days, is likely to be one cause of jaundice. Babies affected by jaundice are usually very sleepy and need to be encouraged to feed more often.

Do not give your baby water as this will not reduce his bilirubin levels and will decrease his desire for the breast, exacerbating the problem and affecting your supply.

TREATMENT

Treatment of jaundice can be as simple as feeding more often while sitting with baby near a sunny window, exposing your baby to the natural ultraviolet rays (Although you will have to be very careful not to damage your baby's sensitive skin).

If this does not lower the levels of bilirubin, your medical adviser may recommend phototherapy.

Your baby will be placed in a special humidicrib using phototherapy for anything from a few hours to a few days.

In short, your baby is off to a tropical island for some extended sunbathing. His clothes and his nappy will be removed and a towel will be placed under his bottom, and he will be fitted with a special mask to protect his eyes. Sometimes this is a tiny felt eye patch, held in place by a hair net. A special arm hole in the crib will allow you to stroke and touch your baby while he receives treatment.

There is no reason why you cannot continue to breastfeed under these conditions. Phototherapy has been shown to be more effective if it is intermittent rather than continuous, and your baby should be taken out for feeds as often as he needs.

Having a break from the lights will also reduce his risk of dehydration, skin rashes, diarrhoea and any other possible effects of prolonged treatment. He will also need the comfort and reassurance of your presence.

Although you may understand that this treatment is for his own good, it may frighten you or distress you that you cannot hold and comfort your baby.

Remember too, that jaundice usually occurs on the third or fourth day after birth, when your hormone levels may also be readjusting. Your baby's yellow period may therefore coincide with your 'blue' period, making this a distressing time for both of you. Some hospitals allow babies who are still under going phototherapy to room-in with their mothers.

BREASTMILK JAUNDICE

Breastmilk jaundice only occurs in one in 200 breastfed newborn babies. In otherwise healthy babies, bilirubin levels rise on the fourth to seventh day and peak at two weeks then slowly drop to normal at between four and 16 weeks.

No treatment is usually required, but phototherapy may be recommended if bilirubin levels rise above 340 um/l. This may not be evident until after you and your baby are discharged from hospital, so it is important to keep a close watch on your baby's yellowness.

Your baby may need to be readmitted to hospital for treatment, or to be reassessed to rule out other possible causes. You may also be advised to stop breastfeeding temporarily, expressing milk and feeding your baby an alternative milk till the bilirubin levels return to normal.

THRUSH

The most common cause of pain in the nipples and breast is faulty positioning and attachment. If this has been rectified and pain persists, thrush should be suspected.

If breastfeeding your baby causes sharp excruciating pain, you may have thrush, a yeast-like organism which occurs naturally in the digestive tract, but which can cause infection in the breast. This can cause breast and nipple pain in breastfeeding mothers.

Thrush in the nipples can come as a surprise to some women who may be (unfortunately) familiar with vaginal thrush, but may not be aware that it can also be present on the nipples and in the mouth. The pain caused by thrush may be severe and may be present both throughout and between feeds, sometimes radiating throughout the breast.

Signs of nipple thrush may include redness, shiny areas, flaking or white spots, or there may be no outward signs. Symptoms include itching, knife-like pain, burning, deep pain or throbbing in the breast, sometimes extending to the arm or back. As well as being sore, nipples are often very sensitive to the touch and you may not be able to bear having your clothes rub on them.

If you suspect thrush, see your doctor who may prescribe an anti-fungal cream. Your doctor will also check your baby's mouth for white curd-like spots or coating which does not come off when scraped with a finger. You will also be checked and treated for vaginal thrush if it is present.

Scrupulous attention to hygiene is vital in getting rid of thrush. Wash your hands before and after feeds, nappy changes and wash towels, face washers and bras frequently. Boil any toy or dummy that your baby sucks, and change dummies regularly.

There is no reason to stop breastfeeding if thrush is diagnosed. Treatment will not affect baby's desire or ability to suck. In fact, treating the thrush may help him regain his appetite and enthusiasm for sucking as thrush in a baby's mouth can cause some babies to not want to feed because of the pain.

Thrush organisms (candida albicans, sometimes called monilia) are normally present in everyone's bowel and usually only cause problems if the body's resistance is lowered. Some women are more susceptible to vaginal thrush during pregnancy or if they have been taking antibiotics.

Nipple thrush is most likely to occur if you have a cracked nipple which allows the infection to penetrate, or it may enter through the natural crevices present in the nipple face.

Thrush can be transferred from your vagina to your baby's mouth if you have an infection during childbirth, and from your baby's mouth to your nipple and vice versa.

That is why it is important for all possible sources of infection to be treated at the same time. Your partner may also have to be treated if it is suspected he also has thrush.

Even if you have not resumed intercourse, any sexual contact may cause the infection to pass from penis to hand to mouth and to nipple and back again.

Consult your doctor immediately if you suspect you have thrush. He or she will probably prescribe an antifungal treatment.

There are various forms (creams, gels, pessaries) for different parts of the body. Some women also find a low-yeast or low-carbohydrate diet helps, or eating yoghurt, which has natural acidophilus. However, consult your doctor or a nutritionist before you make any changes to your diet.

CHAPTER FIVE

Emotional rescue

- **What's normal?**
- **How often and how long feeds last**
- **Settling baby**
- **Mother's emotions**
- **Dealing with any disappointments or unrealised expectations**
- **Caesareans**
- **Premature babies**
- **Twins**
- **How to ask for (and receive) assistance from staff and deal with conflicting information**

FEEDING AGAIN? WHAT'S NORMAL?

'Feeding again! He'll be sick!' Comments like this are not uncommon from people who are not accustomed to breastfed babies. You may be warned that by feeding every two to three hours, or topping up after 20 minutes, or an hour, will make your baby sick, fat, spoiled or worse still it will be a sign that your milk is not 'good enough'. Fortunately none of this is true. By feeding your baby frequently you will ensure that your supply is maintained and that he is properly nourished as well as given the vital comfort and security that he needs.

Your milk is extremely well absorbed by your baby and unlike cow's milk will not take long to digest. His stomach, unlike yours, is also very tiny, and does not take much to fill. As the milk is so well absorbed, he may also have a bowel movement after every feed, so will feel emptier more quickly. Your breast is also a source of warmth and comfort to him and he may want the reassurance of it to help him feel safe in this new and frightening world.

Young babies feed often. It is not unusual for a young baby to want eight to 12 feeds in a 24 hour period, and some of these will be at night. Few babies younger than about eight weeks sleep for long periods between feeds and if they do, this may be balanced by a period of more frequent feeding.

Ideally, you should feed your baby whenever he seems hungry or fussy. He may only need to suck for a few minutes.

Every baby is different. Some like to linger over dinner, while others like to eat and run, so to speak. Some are robust and ravenous, while others are quieter or fussier. The frequency of your baby's feeds is best regulated by him, not by other people's expectations.

Imagine how you would feel if you were told by others when you could eat: probably hungry and frustrated.

Some call this baby-led feeding routine, 'feeding on demand' but experienced mothers know that it is really feeding according to need.

There may be times when you seem to spend the whole day breastfeeding, but these usually last for only a few days at most. If you can meet your baby's needs on these fussy days, you will soon be rewarded by a more contented and settled baby.

If you have young children or other responsibilities which cannot be shelved while your baby is very young, you may need to strike a balance between feeding according to need and some sort of routine. It will be easier if you can be flexible and perhaps set aside a time each day when you and your baby can enjoy a long leisurely cuddle when he may have unrestricted access to the breast.

If your baby is sleepy and doesn't wake as often as he may need for a feed, it may be wise to wake him, at least every three hours during the day to help maintain your supply and his need for food as well. Unwrapping him or changing his nappy can help wake him. Never shake him as this can cause serious physical damage. Try waking him when he is in the light phase of sleep – when he is twitching or his eyelids are moving. He will be difficult to arouse if he is in a deep sleep.

Let your baby feed until he stops on one breast and then offer him the other, again for as along as he wants. There is no need to wake him if he falls asleep after one breast. Just make sure you start the next feed on the opposite breast to maintain your supply and to prevent engorgement. Some babies are content to feed from only one side in the early weeks. Later, some babies even develop a preference for one side. This is fine, as long as you don't mind lop-sided breasts while you are breastfeeding.

SETTLING YOUR BABY

Giving birth and breastfeeding are natural womanly functions, but the art of mothering does not always come as naturally. If your baby seemed to be the picture of contentment in hospital, only waking for feeds and then going back to sleep, but seems to be crying and upset at home, do not despair. This is normal and does not mean that he is a bad baby or that you are a bad mother.

After birth, many babies are sleepy and do not show their true colours till they return home. Some babies adapt to their new worlds very easily, while others are jumpy and easily woken.

Settling and comforting your baby may require quite a few

Photograph by Dianne Griffiths.

different tricks and techniques. Some mothers find this seems to come naturally to them, as dimly remembered lullabies now pour forth as clearly and naturally as the milk from their breasts. If this is you, perhaps you are remembering things that your mother or father did for you, such as rocking, singing, cuddling and talking. If not, then it may help to try to consciously recall some of those old lullabies, or tricks that have been used in your family for generations.

Most babies love the sound of the human voice and do not care whether it is in tune or not. Simple songs that have definite lulling rhythms are best. You may also find that your baby responds to certain recorded music.

Experiment with different sounds. Humming noises, similar to the hums and gurgles that baby heard in the womb, are also comforting. The hum of the clothes drier or the washing machine or vacuum cleaner have all been enlisted in settling babies.

Most babies are comforted by the warmth and closeness of another human being and the sound of the heartbeat or voice, so carrying your baby around with you is the best way of meeting this need.

NMAA sells a special simple sling called a Meh Tai which is excellent for this purpose. There are also many other products on the market that will enable you to carry your baby on your front or back while you shop or go for a walk or do housework.

If your baby falls asleep on the breast but refuses to be settled by any other means, you may find yourself grounded involuntarily. While this may be enjoyable for both baby and you in the initial weeks or months, it can be difficult if you need to resume other responsibilities.

The decision to use a dummy is an individual one. Some babies find them comforting while many breastfed babies spit them out because they do not reach far enough back in the mouth (they were designed for bottle-fed babies).

If you are trying to establish your supply, especially in the early weeks or during a period when your baby seems hungrier than usual, sucking a dummy may reduce your baby's desire to suck at the breast and may inhibit your supply.

For this reason, dummies should be used with caution and are probably best avoided for very young babies. All dummies should be disinfected before use.

NIGHT FEEDS

Before your baby was born, he received a continuous supply of food from you via the placenta and never knew what it was to be hungry. Now, not only he has been wrenched from the warmth and support of your womb, but he has a strange gnawing feeling inside which is caused by new and distressing feelings of hunger. Unlike that of an adult, his stomach is extremely tiny (only six centimetres wide, on average – about the size of his clenched fist) and does not hold much. Your milk is also extremely well absorbed by him, so it is easy to understand why he cannot go more than a few hours without being fed.

That is why you will need to feed him at night, as well as during the day. Most newborn babies need feeding several times throughout the night and this may continue for weeks or months, depending on your baby's needs. Night feeds are also important in establishing and maintaining your milk supply.

While you are in hospital, however, you may be offered the opportunity to rest for the first night or two, and leave the staff to feed your baby while you sleep. This may be tempting but if you do so you will also be tempting fate as giving baby complementary feeds instead of your milk will reduce your supply and hinder your success at breastfeeding.

Unless you are so exhausted that you cannot manage the night feeds, or a doctor has advised against it, it is usually better to give your baby a night-time breastfeed and catch up on sleep during the day, when your baby sleeps.

Throughout your pregnancy you may have heard horror stories about how exhausted you will feel after getting up many times throughout the night. While some tiredness is unavoidable as you adjust to meeting your baby's needs, there are ways to minimise this.

One of these is to do what you did in hospital (if you gave birth in hospital) and 'room-in'. This practice of having the baby's crib beside the mother so that she may attend to his needs more easily is well-established in Australian hospitals, but not very well established in Australian homes.

All the work that you and your partner put into creating the ideal nursery will just mean more work for you in particular in the early months as you get up and down throughout the night to attend to your baby's needs.

Even if your baby's room is next door to yours, in the early weeks at least it is easier to have baby and all his requirements such as nappies and change table close at hand. Make sure you have a night light and a comfortable chair set up to feed in, or alternately you may like to feed your baby in bed with you, either lying down on your side or sitting up, well supported.

Ideally, your partner can change the baby's nappy and bring him to you in bed and you can feed him literally without batting an eyelid.

If you establish this routine, be warned that many people, particularly those not getting up several times a night to a hungry baby, will disapprove. (*See Chapter 6 on Sleeping Habits.*) However, one of the first and most difficult things to learn about parenthood is to do what suits you and your baby, not others.

SLEEPING THROUGH

Much of the information new mothers receive about how their babies will behave is based on the experience of mothers with bottle-fed babies. Cow's milk is ideal for baby cows, but a lot harder for baby humans to digest, as the curds from cow's milk tend to stay in the stomach longer and cause a feeling of fullness. This meant that babies fed on high-casein cow's-milk based formulas needed feeding less frequently, which some mothers viewed as a bonus, especially at night.

This, and ideas from 'experts' during the 1940s and 1950s, who believed that from an early age babies should be trained to fit into adult schedules, led to much emphasis on training babies to 'sleep through' the night.

Babies were sometimes given solid food before their digestive systems were really able to cope with it, in the hope that this would also create a fuller feeling and encourage fewer interruptions to sleep.

Some babies do sleep through at a young age. But most do not. Most babies, like adults, wake often during the night, even when they are not hungry. The difference is that adults have learned to maintain that half-conscious sleep state and simply roll over to a more comfortable position and settle themselves back to sleep. Most babies take a while to learn this, some take longer than others. The other big difference is that adults don't need food as frequently. Waking in babies is a survival strategy to ensure that they don't starve.

That is why complementary feeds of formula, or early feeding of solids, seldom make a difference to babies' sleeping patterns.

If your baby is unsettled at night, and there appears to be no physical problem, perhaps he is uncomfortable or lonely? You can help him learn to settle back to sleep by comforting him by cuddling, patting, singing or rocking, or all of these.

The emphasis in our culture on evenings being for adults, rather than children, can make parents feel particularly put out by unsettled babies and children whose constant interruptions eat into the longed-for adult time. This is especially so if one parent has been out of the house doing paid work, while the other has been at home doing the unpaid work, and both parents are looking forward to some time together at the end of the day.

Not getting this time to sleep or relax together, can cause parents to feel frustrated and angry, not to mention exhausted, especially if they are told by well-meaning family, friends or even strangers that someone else's child has been sleeping through since three months. Either way you will probably feel that you and your baby are not up to scratch.

However, there are two things that you, as a parent, will never be able to do. You cannot force your child to sleep or eat. All you can do is stick to a routine that suits you both and provide whatever comfort your baby seems to require. As long as your baby is well fed and healthy, you can be reassured that he will eventually learn how to sleep for longer.

Meanwhile, try to catch up on sleep yourself if your baby naps during the day. Your sanity is more important than the dishes or the meals. Enlist the help of friends and family where possible.

If you become distressed, exhausted or depressed through lack of sleep you may need to speak to your medical adviser or child health nurse.

Treatment for sleep disorders is seldom recommended for very young babies, whose genuine need for food and comfort is essential for

Photograph by Yvette O'Dowd

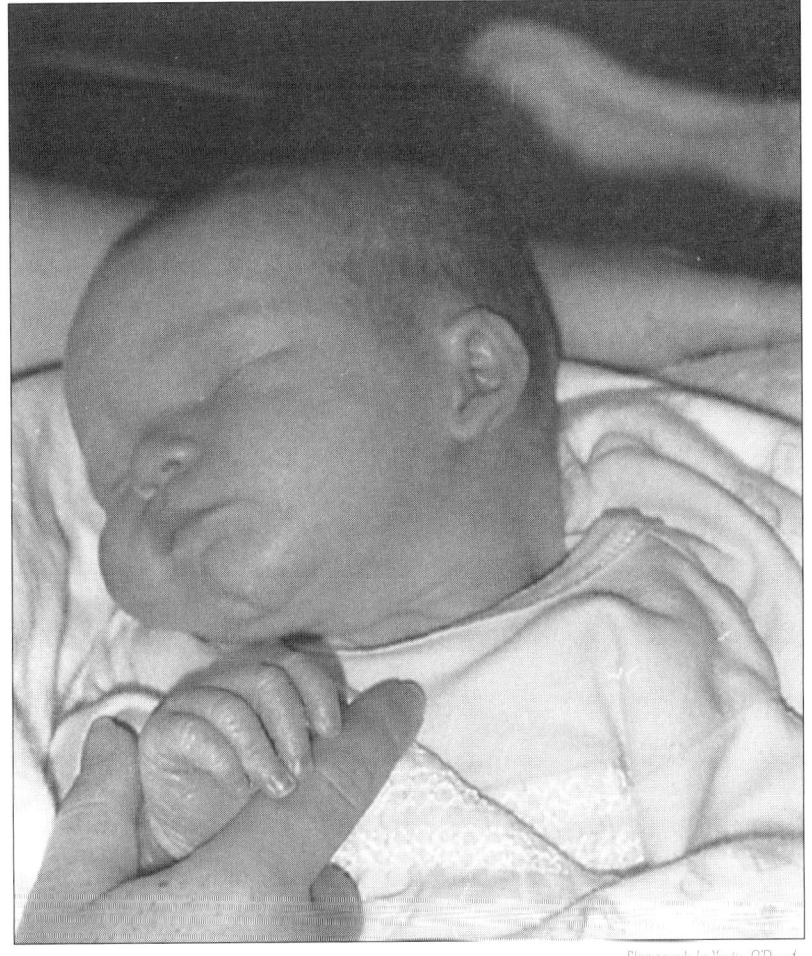

their physical and emotional survival. Opinions differ but some experts say it is best not to start before six months, others say not before 12 or 18 months, while others say such treatment does more damage than good.

Perhaps instead of trying to change your baby, you can change your own expectations and lifestyle to suit this temporary phase in your baby's life.

If you accept that this is a temporary stage (and believe me it is), and get some support for yourself, you will weather it. While it may seem endless, your baby's need for night-time comfort will not be endless. Meanwhile, perhaps you and your partner could take turns to attend to him, or you could enlist the help of a relative to attend to him once a week by giving him your expressed milk if he is still feeding at night, while you and your partner catch up on some sleep or time together.

One solution may be bringing baby to bed with you, as (discussed further in Chapter Six). This will save you from getting up frequently and may help him learn to settle back to sleep more easily. However sleeping with their babies does not suit all mothers; nor does it suit all babies. There are some babies who sleep better in their cots, and some mothers who feel that a few hours of deep but broken sleep is better than a whole night of feeling semi-wakeful.

If you and your baby prefer to sleep separately, make sure that you can meet his night needs with a minimum of fuss. New babies do not distinguish between night and day, but you can help your baby learn the difference by attending to him quietly. A night light in his room, nappies and other equipment for changing on hand close by, a comfortable chair, and perhaps a blanket, a drink for you (although nothing hot that could scald baby) and a warm room will help you both to feed and then return to sleep more easily.

Some mothers like to watch television or listen to the radio while feeding in a comfortable lounge chair or on the couch. This is great if you are a Thunderbirds fan, or want to catch up on an old movie or some Open Learning, but the stimulation may make it more difficult for both of you to return to sleep.

DEPRESSED AND DISAPPOINTED?

You had it all planned: you and your partner had toured the birth centre, your best friend had planned to be there to help your partner support you, you were hoping to have a 'natural' birth – without drugs – and of course, you were planning to have a beautiful, healthy normal, baby and to breastfeed immediately after birth.

But something went wrong. Perhaps your doctor diagnosed placenta praevia (the placenta growing in front of the birth canal making a natural vaginal birth impossible) and you had to have a caesarean.

Or perhaps you laboured valiantly in the birth centre for what seemed like centuries, only to find that your were not dilating and the baby was in distress, resulting in an emergency caesarean.

Or perhaps, despite your best intentions and all those breathing exercises, you found labour exhausting and excruciating and you welcomed the pethidine that you had vowed to refuse. Perhaps by the time it came to push, you felt like pushing your husband, your friend and your obstetrician over a cliff and then jumping yourself?

You are not alone. Many parents find that the birth of their child falls short of their expectations and disappointment and depression can lead to feelings of hopelessness, anxiety or anger, and breastfeeding troubles.

In the past, women giving birth were grateful to survive themselves and for the survival of their infants. These days, as women have fewer babies than their foremothers with better medical support, the emphasis has shifted from the survival of the mother and child to making the whole process an optimum experience for the baby and the mother.

There is nothing wrong with wanting your birth experience and the arrival of your new baby to be as natural and rewarding as possible. Nobody wants to return to the days when labouring women were drugged automatically, or laboured with no support from their loved ones, and whose babies were whisked to a nursery immediately after birth and left to cry to encourage 'moral fibre'.

Over the years, the emphasis on family-friendly hospitals which encourage the mother to remain in control during the birth, and which recognise the important role of the father has been a welcome change. But sometimes, amid all this, things can get out of perspective.

While it is possible to plan the nursery, it is not always possible to plan a birth. Your age, health, size, genetic disposition, size and health of your baby, and the support and medical help your receive have a lot to do with it.

Giving birth is an amazing and often unpredictable experience. If your baby's birth did not go as planned, it is natural to feel upset. Throughout the process, the aim is to deliver a healthy baby: it is not an endurance test for you.

How you performed throughout your pregnancy, by eating sensibly, resting, reading and preparing yourself for successful breastfeeding, is far more important and will have a more far reaching affect on your child than whether you 'gave in' and asked for pain killers, or screamed lustily during labour.

It is no doubt better for your baby if you can resist pain killers as he will be more alert at birth and better able to begin breastfeeding, but the pain of labour should not be dismissed. Many women find they need strong pain killers for period pain, let alone labour, which is far more intense and prolonged. Pain thresholds vary from person to person, as do labours.

While it may be affirming to compare birth stories with other women, try to ensure that this does not become a competition between those who succeeded at 'natural birth' and those who 'failed'. You cannot fail – unless of course you are still pregnant!

The most important thing is not how your baby arrived, but that he arrived safely. Those 10 or 20 hours or whatever of labour are only a drop in the proverbial ocean when you consider the years ahead that you and your partner will share with your child. If you found the birth traumatic or disappointing, developing a successful breastfeeding relationship with your new baby will be an excellent way to heal your feelings about a bad start.

NOT FEELING MOTHERLY?

Throughout pregnancy many women (and their partners) daydream about how their baby will look. You may have said you did not mind whether it was a boy or a girl, but in your heart of hearts or your mind's eye you may have envisaged a beautiful little boy, or a dimpled girl with bows in her hair. When a crumpled, bloody, tiny creature was placed on your tummy looking more like a cross between Frankenstein's monster and the star of the movie 'Coneheads', your vision probably burst like a bubble.

You expected a little stranger, but nothing as strange as this, and your feelings of shock and ambivalence make it seem all the stranger when you begin to breastfeed.

Many mothers feel exhausted, shocked and sore after birth, and emotionally vulnerable. Rather than feeling motherly, they feel they need mothering themselves. This is natural. As you care for your baby and get to know each other you will find these feelings pass and are replaced by ones of love and protectiveness. Breastfeeding is one of the best ways of overcoming these feelings as the special hormones that are released when the baby sucks help relax you and will help you feel more motherly. And while you are feeling ambivalent, you can be reassured that your baby will still be getting the best nourishment in the most comforting and loving way from you by being held close and feeding from your breast. If these feelings are worrying you, it may help to talk to other mothers, or to a NMAA Counsellor. However, if such feelings persist, it may be wise to consult your doctor for a referral to a specialist organisation or medical practitioner.

These negative feelings, combined with isolation and lack of support, can sometimes combine to produce postnatal depression, an illness that can not only make you feel miserable but can affect your relationship with your baby.

Depression can take many forms. Sometimes it causes a type of numbness in your heart that makes it seem impossible to find the energy to cope with caring for yourself, let alone another helpless person. At other times it can cause you to be angry and to feel that your baby is being unreasonably demanding and that it is you, not him, that deserves the loving care. Sometimes it can cause you to be overly anxious about your baby. This is a serious problem for both you and your baby if not treated. However, by talking about your feelings early on and getting help when you feel you need it, and proper treatment, postnatal depression can be overcome.

If you are affected by postnatal depression it may help to know that it is caused by a number of factors, some of them known, others unknown, and that it affects all types of women. Suffering from this condition does not mean you are a bad mother or will not be able to raise your child successfully.

If you seek treatment at a clinic where you are required to stay overnight or for longer, and you feel able to cope with your baby with some support, you can continue to breastfeed by taking your baby with you. That way you will still be providing the best care for him while you are getting vital care for yourself.

THE SICK OR DISABLED CHILD

The shock and distress of discovering that your baby is sick or disabled can throw all your plans and thoughts of how things would be after the birth of your child out the window as you try to cope.

If your baby's illness or disability means he must be separated from you soon after birth, or for lengthy periods in a humidicrib or to undergo surgery, you and your partner will naturally feel upset and worried. You may feel anxious and helpless as you watch 'experts' take over and instead of holding and feeding your baby at your breast as you planned, you may be sitting alone with a breast pump feeling miserable.

Every pregnant woman's paramount concern is for a healthy baby, and when something goes wrong, she can be consumed with feelings of anxiety and guilt.

Smoking and drinking alcohol or using other non-prescribed drugs can all adversely affect the health of your newborn baby. However, most of the things that can be wrong with a new baby are caused by factors out of the parents' control, such as genetics and the position of your baby in your uterus, or by unknown factors.

Finding out as much as possible about your baby's illness or disability by talking to your medical adviser or other parents or support groups may help ease your distress. However, by breastfeeding him, you will be making a major contribution to his well-being and giving him the comfort and love that he especially needs.

The nutritive and disease-preventing properties of breastmilk are even more vital for premature and sick babies and those with health-threatening disabilities. In fact the milk of mothers of premature infants is especially high in some components that allow for optimum growth and development.

However, breastfeeding a sick baby is not always easy, especially if your baby continues to stay in hospital after you are sent home. You will need to learn to express and store your milk to establish and maintain your supply. (*See Chapter 10 on Expressing and Storing.*)

Your anxiety, travelling to and from the hospital, lack of sleep, and the fact that your nipples are not getting the natural stimulation of your baby's suckling can make this difficult, but not impossible. As often as you need to, talk to your NMAA Counsellor and others who can support you. Remember that by keeping up your supply, you are doing the best for your baby. As he grows stronger, you will be able to put him to the breast (unless he has a physical condition that makes this difficult) and enjoy breastfeeding under more normal and relaxing circumstances.

YOUR PREMATURE BABY

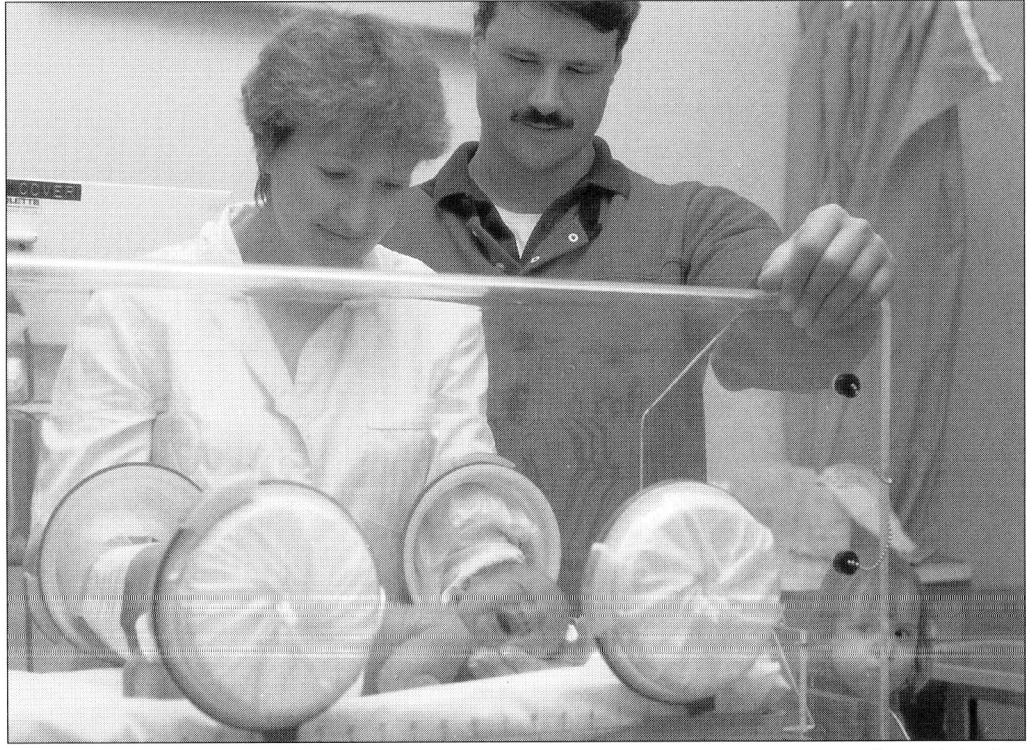

Photograph by Prue Carr.

Pregnancy is an important time for you to become accustomed to the idea of being a mother. As your baby grows, so you grow used to the idea of motherhood. That's why giving birth prematurely can be quite a shock. Even women who have a full-term pregnancy but deliver their babies very quickly, such as within an hour of going in to labour, report that it takes time to recover from the shock.

A premature baby is one who is born three or more weeks earlier than the expected 40 weeks of gestation. You may also hear the term 'low birth-weight baby'. This means a baby who weighs less than 2500g. These babies are mostly, but not always, premature, and need the same care as premature babies.

If you fully expected to carry your baby to term, giving birth prematurely will mean a change of plans. You may have planned to stay in paid work up to a few weeks before your baby was due, relaxing at home in the last weeks or making last minute arrangements for your baby's arrival.

When he arrives early, you will naturally be thrown. You may not be prepared physically or emotionally. The time you imagined as a period of contentment and slow integration may now be a period of high stress, especially if your baby's prematurity means that he is unwell or needing special care.

These days, prematurity, while still a cause for concern, is no longer the worry it once was. Thanks to the special care and medical knowledge now available, babies as young as 22 weeks gestation have a chance of surviving. Most premature babies, however, not only survive but thrive.

Breastfeeding is a vital aid in your premature baby's survival. Even if your baby is in a humidicrib or special care nursery, there is no reason why you cannot breastfeed.

In fact, now more than ever your baby needs the special protective qualities of your breastmilk to boost his immune system and give him the right nutrients for healthy growth.

However, as the suck/swallow reflex is not always fully developed until between 34 and 36 weeks gestation, it may take a while for your premature baby to learn to breastfeed effectively.

At first your baby may be getting all his nutrition through an intravenous drip and he may be fed no breastmilk at this stage. When they do start breastfeeding, many premature babies receive their mother's expressed breastmilk through a feeding tube inserted into the stomach through either the nose or mouth until they are able to suck and swallow properly. Sometimes parents can assist with tube feeds.

Your baby may also require oxygen via a ventilator, which will also prevent you from feeding him directly from your breast.

Start expressing from your breasts as soon as possible after the birth, as this will help you build up your milk supply. This milk can be frozen for later use. (*See Chapter 10 on Expressing and Storing Breastmilk.*)

Sometimes premature babies need their breastfeeds stopped for a while for medical reasons. If this happens, keep expressing so that you will have a good supply when your baby is ready for it again.

Sometimes very tiny babies may need extra vitamins and iron. This does not mean your milk is inadequate. Your baby just needs a little booster as he is so very tiny. This is to make up for what he would have received in your uterus if he had not been born so early.

The fact that you cannot feed or handle your baby directly may make you feel less motherly. You may even feel as if the baby is not yours as so many other 'experts' seems to be in charge of him. You may feel tearful, quite distant or composed, or very upset and depressed. All these feelings are normal. Make sure you talk to your partner or anyone else you trust, the hospital staff or a NMAA Counsellor about your feelings.

It can be very upsetting if you need to go home without your baby, perhaps visiting him in the special care nursery, each day. You may still feel upset at the fact that your baby came into the world under such distressing circumstances, and going home without him may exacerbate your feelings of loss and sorrow.

It may help to focus on the more positive aspects of going home, such as having more time to sleep, to express, and to talk with your partner about your feelings. This may also give you time to prepare for your baby if he arrived very early.

The special care nursery may also seem a very strange place, with lots of buzzing and beeping machines, doctors, nurses and humidi-cribs or incubators. Every time you see your baby you may have to wash and put a gown on. Try not to be intimidated. Hospital staff welcome parents' involvement. You may like to bring a lambskin for your baby to lie on and something special to hang on his crib to make it seem more personal. Stroke or touch your baby as much as you can, talk and sing to him. Your support, and your milk, will be a vital part of your baby's recovery.

Breastmilk is easy to digest, which is less taxing on your baby's immature digestive system. There is little waste, so eliminating waste will not overtax his immature kidneys. It will increase your baby's resistance to infections and in fact, the milk from mothers of pre-term babies has special qualities which allow for optimum growth and development. Even if you only manage to express a tiny amount each time, pre-term breastmilk has very concentrated nutrients, and your baby will still benefit.

It may take a while for your baby to shift to exclusive breastfeeding. Don't be too upset if he sometimes seems sleepy or uninterested. He just needs a little time and patience.

As your baby's condition stabilises you may be offered kangaroo care, a new method of caring for premature babies in hospitals which allows them to be carried around in a special pouch, or just placed inside your shirt against your skin, while wearing only a nappy and a woolly hat. (The baby, not you!)

This close contact with your body will help him maintain his own body temperature, and the contact with your breasts will encourage him to feed and will improve his sucking ability and your supply. This method of interaction with premature babies has been found to increase the mother's expressed breastmilk supply by an average of one and half times. Sometimes you can even use kangaroo care while your baby is still attached to the ventilator. Fathers may also take part in this special care. Indeed, all parents who have taken part in this have found it very rewarding.

Premature babies usually have to be sucking all their feeds (rather than tube feeding) before they go home. Some babies may become confused about how to suck at the breast if they are given bottles or dummies. If you don't want your baby to become confused ask that any expressed milk be given by syringe or a small cup or that feeds still be given by tube if you are not there.

Sometimes, some bottle-feeding of premature infants is unavoidable, and most babies are still successfully breastfed despite this.

Some babies come home being partially breastfed and formula-fed. If you want to fully breastfeed, try building your supply by breastfeeding as often as the baby seems hungry, day and night, as well as offering the breast for comfort.

If he seems hungry after a feed, wait 20 minutes or so, and top him up with another breastfeed. Aim at gradually reducing the amount of infant formula he needs. (*See Page 108, How to Make More Milk.*)

BRINGING YOUR 'PREMMIE' HOME

When your baby comes home it may feel a bit like an anticlimax. The normal visitors and congratulations may be missing or people's reactions may be inhibited by their fear that inquiring about the baby's condition may be upsetting for you.

Let them know that this is still a special occasion to you. If you want their company and help let them know. Some parents feel that nobody really understands what they went through in hospital. If you feel like this it may help to joint a support group for the parents of premature babies, or to keep in touch with other mothers from the special care nursery. Your local NMAA Group can also offer a wealth of support and information.

TWINS

Sometimes it takes a good nine months to get used to the idea of having one baby. The mother expecting twins therefore may be twice as excited – and twice as daunted. If twins are prevalent in your family (often the case), you may be able talk to other parents in the family about how they felt and managed.

If your twins were diagnosed early, you will have had time to get used to the idea. If they were undiagnosed, you will probably be both horrified and elated. You may also wonder whether you will be able to breastfeed both babies.

Breastfeeding twins is both practicable and possible, although you will need extra support yourself as you will be twice as busy, especially in the first few months.

If your twins are premature, weak or small, as some may be, the advantages of breastfeeding are doubly important. It is important to remember that breastfeeding works on a demand and supply basis – the more milk that is taken, the more is made – so if you feed whenever your babies seem hungry you should not have any trouble providing plenty of milk for them.

If your babies are in the special care nursery, you may need to express your milk to establish your supply, preferably 6-8 times a day, including at least once at night. (*See Chapter 10 on Expressing and Storing.*)

BREASTFEEDING ... NATURALLY

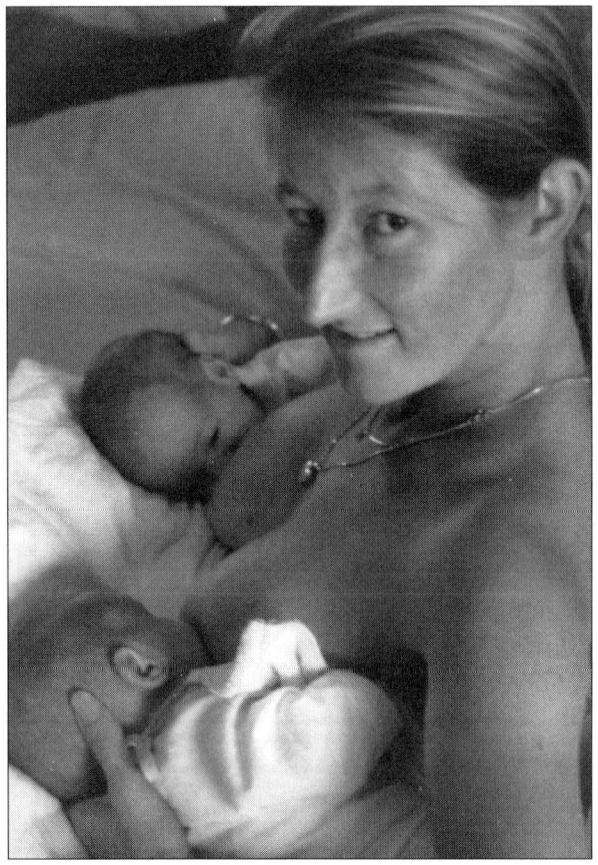

Photograph courtesy of Renee Adams.

If only one baby is in care, you may need to express from one breast while you feed from the other, alternating breasts at each feed. The baby who is feeding from the one breast will start the let-down reflex making it easier to express from the other breast.

You can either feed your babies separately or together, keep each to his own breast or alternate sides. It is up to you. Most mothers interchange, depending on the ages and stages of the babies.

If you are giving each baby his own breast, keep in mind that one breast may produce more than the other, or one baby may not be sucking as effectively as the other, which means one breast may not be emptied as well and therefore, may not make as much milk. Of course, one baby might not need as much milk as the other baby.

If you wish to continue feeding this way, it may help to express a little from the less productive breast after feeding to build up supply or to keep the baby who does not suck as well at the breast for longer to ensure that it is drained well.

If you decide to feed each separately, be prepared for the fact that you will spend twice as much time feeding, and it may be difficult to relax and feed one baby while the other is crying from hunger. You could try to give one just enough to satisfy him and keep him nearby in a pram or rocker while you feed the other. Feeding simultaneously satisfies and calms both babies and is very relaxing once you get the hang of it. The disadvantage though is that you will be stuck there unable to move for a while, so make sure that you have everything you need within reach, the telephone unplugged and a 'Do Not Disturb' sign on the door.

In the first few weeks you will probably need someone to help you to position both babies. You may also find that your babies needs and temperaments are very different and that their feeds do not coincide. It may also be difficult to feed simultaneously in public.

FEEDING POSITIONS

Breastfeeding twins requires a little extra planning. If you feed simultaneously you may need four to six pillows or a few larger cushions, on a couch or bed permanently set up for feeding. Lie a pillow on either side of where you sit, parallel to your body and have extra pillows within your reach for your lap, back and under your knees if necessary. Large, especially shaped pillows may be useful.

Lie your babies safely on the bed where you can reach them while sitting. If you use a couch or lounge, lie the babies at each end of it, safely wedged between a pillow and armrest.

Sit down, place a pillow across your lap and either raise your feet on a stool or put a pillow under your knees to save having to lean forward over the babies. Alternatively, you may prefer to sit on the floor with your back supported. Some mothers find a beanbag useful.

HOLD EVERYTHING – I'M FEEDING!
There are several different ways you can position your twins for feeding, including the football hold or clutch hold, the parallel hold, the criss-cross hold and the front v hold. If you are beginning to feel like

a ruck rover in training, take heart. Each position is really quite simple. It's just that telling you about it rather than showing you, makes it seem more complicated. If you study the pictures of each hold you will will see that it is really a matter of common sense. The one that suits you best will depend on the ages and stages of your babies.

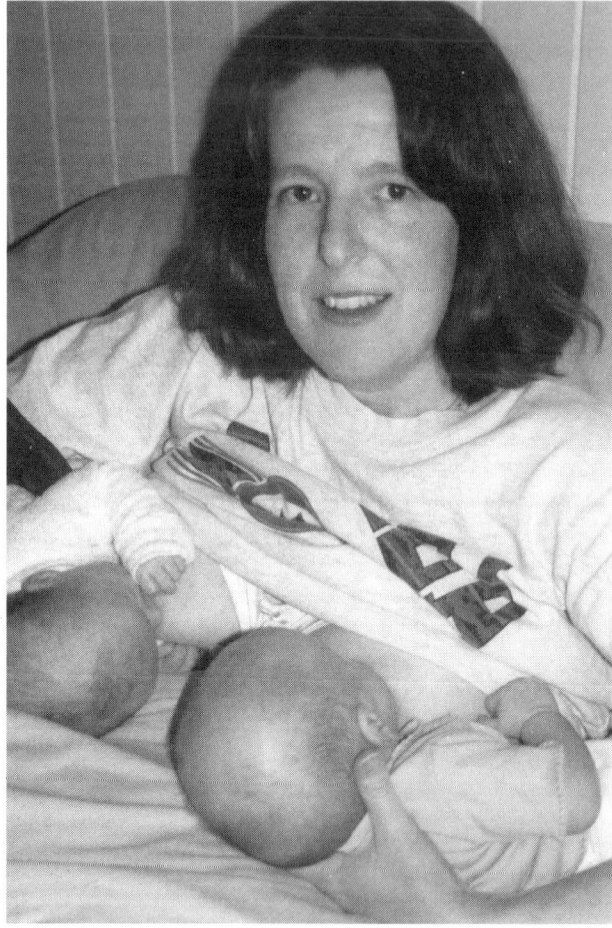

Photograph by Lesley McBurney.

FOOTBALL HOLD – OR UNDERARM HOLD

This is one of the most popular positions as it is the easiest to use when you don't have anyone around to help you. It is probably the most practical position for small babies, leaving two hands free, and puts no pressure on your abdomen if you have had a Caesarean delivery. Lie your babies with their feet facing backwards and tucked under your arms and their faces towards yours. Cup their heads in your hands and lift them to your breasts (one baby at a time while they need help attaching). Use your elbows to hug your babies to you.

Raise your knees high enough to ensure that a pillow on your lap will support the babies' heads at your breasts without you having to lean over uncomfortably. This will leave your hands free.

Photograph by Lesley McBurney.

PARALLEL HOLD

This is less conspicuous but more difficult when your babies are young. When your babies are older, you can feed like this without pillows as one baby's body will support the head of the the other. This makes it more convenient when you are feeding away from home.

Hold the first baby in the normal nursing position (across your lap).

Lie the second baby gently on the body of, and parallel to, the first baby, so that his head is at your other breast and cupped in your hand. Both babies will be lying in the same direction. Raise your knees to support your arms as you hold your babies.

FRONT 'V' HOLD
This is a good method for feeding at night and helpful if you cannot sit comfortably after delivery. It may be difficult with tiny babies as you will have limited control over their heads.

Support your back so that you can sit comfortably semi reclined. Place a baby at each breast so they are facing each other and their knees are bent and touching. Support their backs with your arms while your hands cup their bottoms.

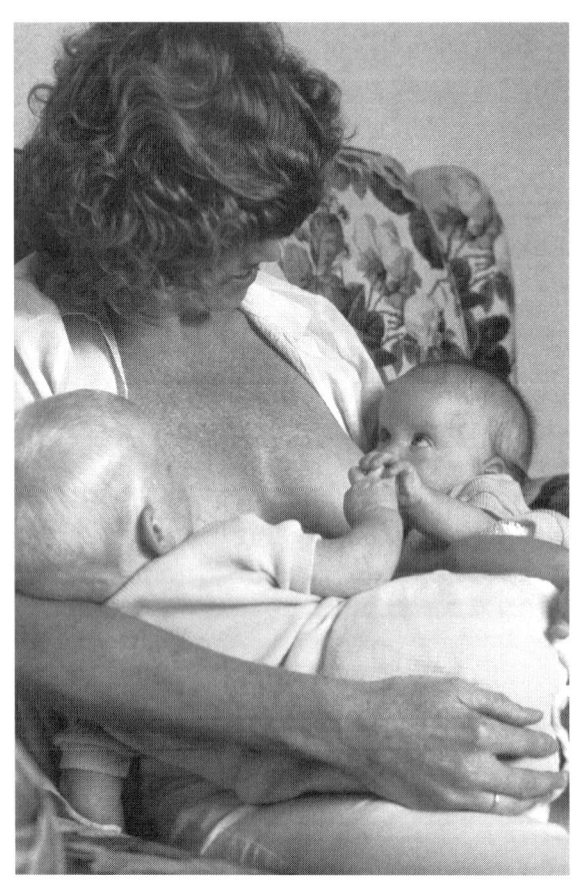

Photograph by Prue Carr.

CRISS-CROSS HOLD

This is easier after about six weeks when your babies are bigger, sucking more strongly, and can attach more easily and securely.

Make sure your elbows and back are well supported with pillows. Place the heaviest baby in the normal nursing position. Gently lie the second baby across the first so they are criss-crossed, facing each other, each at one breast. Support their backs with your arms and clasp your hands under their bottoms when you need to bring them close to you.

WHEN IT'S ALL TWO MUCH

Having twins can be twice as tiring as well as twice as exciting, and the extra demands can place a lot of stress on your family. Trying to find time for yourselves as a couple, as well as for any other children you may have, let alone time for yourselves as individuals, may seem impossible. That is why it is important to be realistic about what you can and cannot do. Stick to the bare essentials when it comes to housework and cooking and enlist the help of anyone who offers, such as friends, relatives, your local NMAA Group. You may like to join the Australian Multiple Birth Association, which can offer practical as well as moral support, including the hiring of equipment.

Try to make time for yourselves as a couple, as well as individuals. Don't be surprised if you feel completely overwhelmed and as if nobody really understands the demands being made on you. Only those who are the parents of twins themselves will probably ever understand. That's why it will be helpful to share your feelings with other mothers of twins.

Finally, breastfeeding is only one part of the art of skilled and loving mothering, so do not feel guilty or a failure if breastfeeding does not progress as you had hoped. Most problems can be overcome with encouragement and support.

However, there will no doubt be times when you think that it is all just too difficult and that your problems are related to breastfeeding. It is more likely that your problems are related to the demands of two babies rather than one, and the exhaustion that follows. Mixing formula and disinfecting bottles is hard work too, and twice as time-consuming for twins. Rather than resort immediately to bottle-feeding, you may find it more practical and helpful to get the extra support that you need (either moral or practical or both) so that you can continue to breastfeed, which will be far more convenient for you and the family in the long run.

CAESAREANS

Many women give birth by caesarean section, which means that the baby is removed from the womb via the abdomen after the surgeon makes an incision.

These days, especially if the need for your caesarean is caused by a pre-existing medical condition and is planned, you can choose to have an epidural anaesthetic which will allow your top half (from the chest up) to remain awake while the operation takes place.

You and your partner can then share the birth experience together as you planned, despite the surgical procedure. A curtain is usually placed across your abdomen between you and the surgeon, shielding your face from the actual operation.

A caesarean birth can sometimes only take 10 minutes (although stitching you up will take much longer), and if all is well, you can then cuddle and breastfeed your baby immediately. However, some women report that their arms were wrapped in a sterile sheet to keep them free from the operation site, making this impossible. If this happens to you, or you just find it too awkward to hold and feed your baby while the operation is being completed, you may find it easier to breastfeed in the recovery room later.

The recovery room is a special room where immediately after an operation a patient can be observed and her progress monitored to make sure all is well before she is returned to the hospital ward or her own room. However, whether you breastfeed straight after the birth or in the recovery room or later in your room, you will need support to position your baby.

If you received a general anaesthetic, you may have to delay your baby's first feed, but it is still important that you breastfeed as soon as possible after the birth.

If your baby is sleepy due to receiving some anaesthetic via the placenta, feed more frequently and for shorter periods. You may require medication for pain for up to 72 hours after the operation. This may be given immediately before a feed to help you position yourself with the least pain.

You will probably need help with breastfeeding for the first few days after the birth. You may find it easier to lie on your side with a pillow under your head and behind your back and your baby lying beside you.

Alternatively, you may prefer to sit up in bed with pillows around your back and under your arms and your pillow across your thighs for your baby to lie on.

You could also try sitting up in bed with your baby on a pillow beside you, turning slightly to feed.

Another option is you may like to sit up in a bed or a chair with a pillow over the incision and your baby on the pillow. A midwife will need to help you to pick up the baby and position it until you are able.

When you go home, you may need a little extra help. Contact your local NMAA group, a Caesarean support group or parenting group or your local council.

In the past there were many myths associated with breastfeeding after a Caesarean birth. It was thought that the milk took longer to 'come in'. However, studies have shown that this is not so. Lactation is initiated by the removal of the placenta, not the type of birth you have, so there is no link.

It may have been that mothers who gave birth this way took longer to establish their milk supplies because in the past they were separated from their babies for longer. The earlier you attempt to breastfeed, the earlier your milk will come in and the more smoothly your breastfeeding relationship will develop.

Your ability to breastfeed may be affected by your feelings about the birth. Some women feel very disappointed that they were not able to experience a vaginal birth. Others may feel inadequate, guilty or depressed. These feelings are normal. If your Caesarean was planned, you will have had a chance to get used to the idea. If your Caesarean was performed after a long and difficult labour you may feel upset and angry at the way your labour was managed. All these feelings may affect your let-down reflex and the quantity of milk being produced.

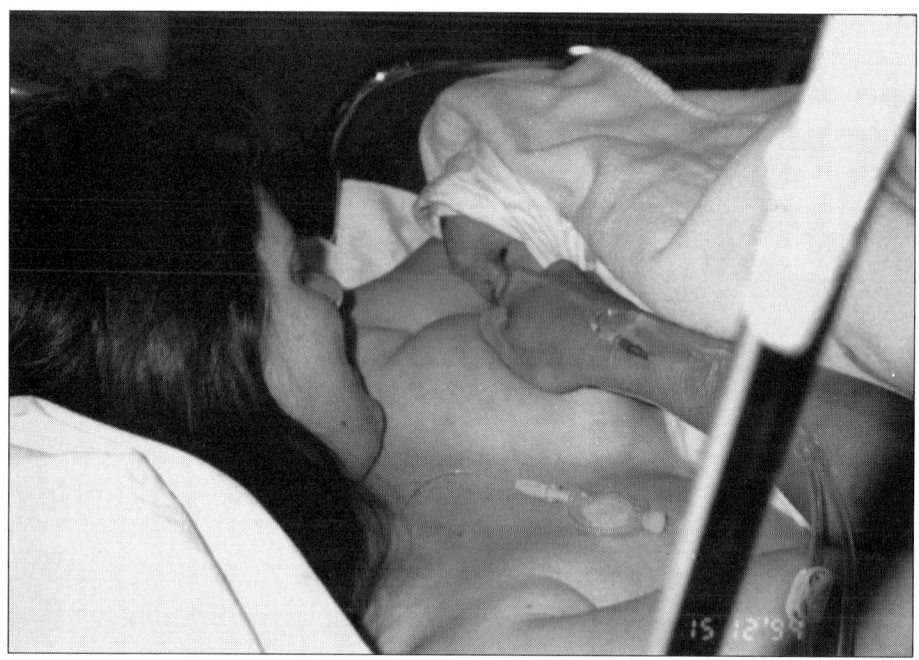

Photograph courtesy of Publications Unit

It may help you to focus on the positive rather than the negative. Today, as women have fewer children, the focus has switched from the survival of the children (which these days is much greater) to the birth experience.

A positive birth experience is rewarding and valuable, but should not overshadow the real purpose of birth, which is the delivery of a healthy baby.

You and your baby may have got off to a difficult start, but by breastfeeding him you will be giving him the best nourishment and comfort available. Many women report that breastfeeding after a caesarean helped restore their self-esteem. Talk about your feelings to your partner, friends who have also had caesareans or your NMAA Counsellor or support group.

ASKING FOR ADVICE

It is difficult to be assertive when you are leaking from almost every orifice, exhausted and suddenly responsible for a very demanding little human being. In fact most women feel particularly vulnerable after the birth of a baby.

Just when you need help most, it seems it is most difficult to ask

> 'Breastfeeding is a little bit more important (after a caesarean) because you feel you missed out on that close contact when he was born. If you are unable to express milk yourself, the midwives will express it for you. If you haven't had kids before and you haven't been through that, it's a bit of a weird thought – the fact that someone is going to do that to you. But it's a midwife's job. They learn how to do it and teach you how to do it.'
> – Carolyn, mother of Hannah, seven, and Paul, two, both born by Caesarean section and both breastfed.

for it. For a start, you may feel extremely emotional. In the first few days and weeks after giving birth, your hormones will be rampant and you will find that your moods will swing from euphoria to depression and back again in a surprisingly short time.

It is also a shock to find that while you may be extremely competent in other things, you feel extremely incompetent in dealing with your own baby. Even if you have been familiar with babies, each baby is different and you and your baby will be learning about each other now. This can be like learning to dance. Sometimes it is hard to get the synchronisation right, even if you know the steps.

Hospital and medical bureaucracies can also be intimidating. Hospital routines, while necessary, may feel intrusive and staff may seem busy and impatient.

It may help to make a list of your priorities and wishes to take to hospital with you before your baby is born. That way, if you are feeling unable to cope, your partner can ask for assistance for you keeping in mind the priorities you both set before your baby was born.

Many hospitals today employ lactation consultants who are paid to advise you and help you to establish breastfeeding. You will find that most are knowledgeable and sympathetic and many of course, are mothers themselves and know exactly what you are going through.

If you need to ask for help yourself, try to remember that the staff, however busy, are there to help you. That is their job, and as long as you ask in a polite and friendly manner, they should respond as quickly and reasonably as possible.

If this does not occur for some reason, you are within your rights to ask to see the staff member's supervisor or another person in charge, or to get someone such as your partner to ask on your behalf. Keep the basic principles of conflict resolution in mind. Do not start with accusations, but with how you feel. 'I feel upset at the way the nurse treated my baby and would prefer that ...'

If hospital policy means that your wishes cannot be accommodated, perhaps you could suggest a compromise that would make both of you happy.

Remember, too, that asking for advice does not obligate you to take it. You may canvass a range of opinions about one aspect of care for your baby, try the ones that you think will suit you and discard others that do not work.

If you are asking advice from relatives and friends, help them to understand that you are trying to learn what suits you and your baby. While you welcome their opinions, what worked for their children may not work for yours and so they should not feel offended if their advice is not taken.

If the advice you have been given by friends, relatives, doctors, NMAA Counsellors or lactation consultants has not helped, do not be discouraged. Every breastfeeding relationship is unique and sometimes it takes a little time and patience to find the right solutions for you. Sometimes it is a team effort. If you feel that something is wrong and that you are not being listened to, trust your own instincts and seek other opinions. You are the one who knows and understands your baby best. Listen to the 'experts,' but listen to your own heart, too.

However, asking for advice is seldom necessary when you become a parent. It is the only thing that is given out free and in abundance – not just in the first few weeks, but for the next 20 or so years.

DEALING WITH CONFLICTING ADVICE AND INFORMATION

While breastfeeding is now more widely promoted than it was 30 years ago, much of the promotion consists of conflicting information. Sometimes this is because there is still a lot of ignorance about how breastfeeding works.

Many people, including health professionals, are still trying to regain and reclaim the knowledge that has been lost about breastfeeding and in doing so, they may receive information from various resources and studies that is contradictory or inconsistent. Some conflicting information is the result of changes in attitudes due to new research.

Until new research is publicised and accepted, practices based on old research may still be applied. One example of this is the length of a feed. Even 10 years ago, women were being encouraged to begin breastfeeding slowly, feeding one minute on each breast per feed on the first day, three minutes on the second day, five minutes on the third day, gradually building up to 10 minutes on each side for each feed. It was thought that this would help prevent the mothers getting sore and cracked nipples.

However, later research has shown that this procedure just delays the time when nipples are sore. It was also recognised that good positioning was important in preventing sore nipples and that longer feeds in the early days help stimulate the milk supply and prevent engorgement.

This is just one example of how information and advice can conflict or change over the years.

So how do you cope with all this conflicting information in preparing yourself for successful breastfeeding?

It is an old adage that knowledge is power and this applies to breastfeeding. The more you know about it from your own research, observation, and later, experience, the more confident you will be and the more likely to be successful.

This book is a great start. There are also many other publications covering specific aspects of breastfeeding that may interest you, from the history and politics of breastfeeding to more practical concerns such as breastfeeding a baby with a cleft palate.

The Nursing Mothers' Association of Australia produces a series of booklets aimed at specific aspects of breastfeeding, covered in more detail than this book allows.

Contact your local NMAA Group. A list of current telephone counselling numbers is listed at the back of this book. There is also a reading list which you may like to refer to.

Another important way of dealing with conflicting advice, as well as for preparing for breastfeeding is to talk to mothers who are breastfeeding, or have breastfed and to watch them feed their babies. They can tell and show you what worked for them.

You may have close friends or family who are breastfeeding and whom you can watch and talk to, or women who have breastfed in the past. Pregnant women are also welcome to attend any of the coffee mornings, discussion meetings or information sessions provided by NMAA. These are held in suburban homes, community centres, halls or whereever is convenient, by local NMAA Groups all over Australia.

Attending these informal get-togethers will give you a first-hand look at breastfeeding couples, will provide you with information and support in your decision to breastfeed and may also provide friendships with other mothers who share your views.

If this is your first breastfed baby, watching and talking to other breastfeeding mothers will help you see first-hand how convenient and easy breastfeeding can be.

If this is your first baby, this experience of watching other mothers and children together will be like opening a window into a very special private world that is sometimes hidden from those involved in the more public hustle and bustle of paid work. Whether you decide to return to paid work early or later or never, your decision to have a baby will mean that this will be your world too, perhaps full-time for now and part-time later.

CHAPTER SIX

The learning period

- How lactation progresses
- Changes in breastmilk, breast size, bowel motions, sleeping habits, frequency of feeds, range of normal sleep
- Do I have enough milk? How to tell
- Increasing supply, too much milk, weight gains
- Out and about with a breastfed baby
- Travelling
- Feeding in public

HOW LACTATION PROGRESSES

One of the many miracles of breastmilk is that as your baby grows and his needs change, so will your milk. In fact your milk not only changes over the days and months to meet your growing baby's needs, it changes throughout each feed.

The composition of your milk depends on your stage of lactation.

While it may seem a little technical and bamboozling to talk about the precise nutritional aspects of breastmilk at each stage of lactation, a brief description will help you understand how perfectly your body is geared to providing just the right amount of nourishment for your baby.

The fact that infant formula is especially created from cow's milk by scientists in a laboratory and its contents can be analysed and measured has contributed in part to its status among mothers in both the developing and developed world. Sadly, people are sometimes more convinced by figures than by the evidence of a thriving, healthy baby.

The difference between 'man's creation' in the scientific laboratory and 'woman's creation' in her breast is that a woman does not need an expensive laboratory with special equipment. She simply needs to maintain her own normal diet. Nature will do the rest.

Knowing this will give you confidence while you are breastfeeding and will enable you to inform others who may express interest in, or doubt about, the composition of your milk.

So here is a description of how your milk changes to meet your baby's needs and what your milk contains.

In the first days, your breasts will produce colostrum. This is a rich, creamy yellow colour (due to B carotene). Colostrum is high in protein, immunoglobulins, lactoferrin, sodium, and chloride, zinc, and low in lactose and fat.

When milk production begins, colostrum mixes with the 'new milk', known as transitional milk, until mature milk is established. How quickly your milk changes to mature milk varies, depending on you and how frequently you feed.

Mature milk has higher concentrations of lactose and fat than colostrum, but lower concentrations of immunoglobulins, lactoferrin and total protein.

The average concentrations of lactose, protein and lipids remain relatively constant throughout lactation, as do iron and sodium levels. There is a gradual fall in zinc, copper and potassium levels.

Total and secretory IgA, lactoferrin and lysozyme levels also remain constant into the second year of lactation. Breastmilk does not lose its nutritional value over time, so if you continue to feed past the first year, you need not be deterred by suggestions that your milk will have 'gone off' or 'lost its nutritional power'.

During weaning, as milk production decreases, milk composition begins to resemble colostrum again, with an increase in sodium, protein and immunoglobulins and less glucose and lactose. This may also occur during breast infections and may result in less milk being produced.

Your milk composition is also affected by the length of gestation – in other words whether your baby was full-term or not. Miraculously, pre-term milk (milk produced before the normal 40 weeks of gestation), has a higher protein, sodium and chloride level and lower levels

Colostrum **Foremilk** **Hindmilk**

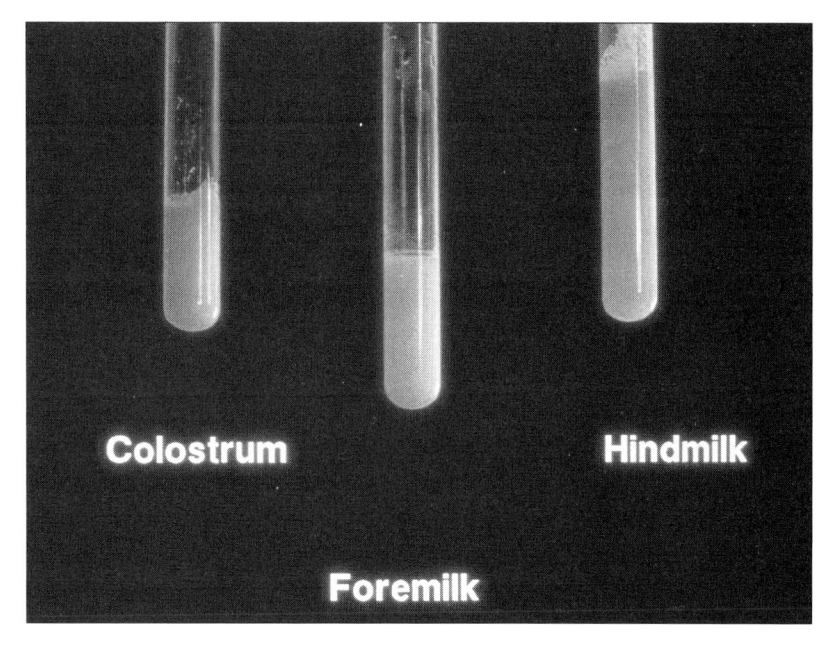

of lactose and is geared specifically to needs of the premature baby.

Milk composition also varies between women. Some women produce large quantities of low-fat milk while others produce smaller quantities of high-fat milk. Whether the baby is attached properly and how often he feeds, can also determine the fat content. This in turn, helps to determine the length of each feed.

The stage in the feed also affects milk composition. How quickly each individual baby extracts milk from its mother's breast varies greatly. Some babies manage to scoff the lot in three to five minutes, while others take their time.

At the beginning of the feed, the baby receives the foremilk, which is lower in fat and kilojoules and higher in water content. As the feed progresses, fat is forced out of the alveoli causing the fat content of the milk to rise. This fattier milk is called hindmilk.

Recent data suggests that the foremilk of the second breast has a higher initial fat content than that of the first breast, possibly caused by the let-down reflexes experienced while the baby was feeding from the first breast.

In hot weather, your baby may want short, frequent feeds to ensure he receives more fluid intake without the higher fat concentration in the hindmilk.

If your baby seems to feed well, but fails to gain weight, he may be getting adequate fluid, but inadequate hindmilk for his energy requirements due to reduced sucking time, an ineffective suckling technique or a slow let-down of milk. These babies often have wet nappies but infrequent bowel movements. Talk to your medical adviser if this is the case with your baby.

Your diet also subtly affects the composition of the milk. While your body always makes it a priority to ensure that your baby is well supplied with nutrients even if your diet is inadequate, the composition of fat in your milk is influenced by your diet.

If you are eating enough for your own energy requirements, the fatty acid pattern in your milk will resemble that of your diet. Some vitamin concentrations may be lower in the milk of mothers who eat poorly or follow a vegan diet containing only plant products. There is little difference in the protein content in the milk of well-nourished mothers compared with that of malnourished mothers.

You do not need to follow a special diet to maintain a good balance in the composition of your milk, but you do need to eat sensibly.

Eating poorly will not put your baby or milk at risk, but it will make you feel tired and less able to cope. You will feel better and your baby will thrive more easily if you maintain normal eating habits. You should also eat well simply because you matter as much as your baby, and eating well is a good way of taking care of yourself. Rapid weight loss through dieting is not advisable at this stage. If you need to lose weight, wait until your baby is older and breastfeeding is well-established. Otherwise you may put your own health, your milk supply and the health of your baby at risk.

YOUR BABY'S CHANGING NEEDS

The only thing that you can be sure of when you have your baby is change. It seems that no sooner do you become accustomed to your baby's habits and likes, than he develops new and different ones. Your baby is not doing this to deliberately irk you. Babies are people too, and like grown-up people, their behaviour changes according to their needs.

This can be a bit of a shock at first. That tiny sleepy bundle that seemed content to sleep and eat in hospital, may seem to metamorphose when you return home into a ravenous and ranting monster. Suddenly, he seems to cry more often, even after he has been fed and changed, and you may feel distressed, helpless or even angry at your inability to comfort him.

Don't worry. Your baby is growing rapidly. In his first year, he will grow at a greater rate than at any other time. This growth, the change of environment, your own feelings of anxiety, the need to adapt to a new routine and the noise and interest of other family members can make it difficult for both of you to feel settled.

Sometimes even a change in temperature can make your baby want to feed more, as he requires food for warmth and comfort.

At home, you may also have to resume other responsibilities and your baby may miss that 'cocooned' time in hospital when he was your only responsibility and you were able to meet his needs without delay.

Continue to offer the breast whenever he seems hungry or distressed, and try to satisfy his need for closeness and your need to attend to other duties at other times by using a Meh Tai sling or other baby carrier, by rocking and talking to him in soothing tones and just letting him know that you are nearby.

It may be difficult to believe at first, but as you get to know each other and his system matures, your baby and your life will become more predictable.

FREQUENCY OF FEEDS

By the time your baby is about six weeks old, provided you have been feeding whenever he seems hungry, your breasts should have adjusted to meet his needs. For some mothers, it can take longer, especially if they have a lot of milk in the early weeks.

However, between the ages of one and two months, usually at around six weeks, you may notice that your baby is restless before his usual feed times, particularly in the afternoons.

At this age, babies often need more food. You can provide this simply by feeding more frequently for a few days to build up your supply. This may mean putting other household tasks or appointments on hold in order to spend extra time with your baby at your breast.

You may feel that this is easier said than done if you have a toddler or other older children. However, if you can concentrate on your baby for just a day or two, you will find that it will be an investment in a smoother-running household anyway, as your baby will be more content and you will be freer to attend to other duties and activities.

If you can enlist help from a relative, friend or neighbour, this may take the pressure off and allow you to build up your supply without feeling anxious or worried about meeting your other responsibilities. If you cannot do this, then reading to your toddler or encouraging some quiet play nearby, or even allowing a day of television or videos can be a temporary alternative.

Sometimes you only need to give two or three extra feeds a day to increase your supply within a few days. You may find you need to boost your supply by extra feeding when your baby is around three to six months of age, or indeed, any time that you feel your baby needs more.

Only your baby can tell you how often he needs to feed. Usually, this will be whenever he is hungry, which may be every three or four hours, or as often as one to two hours, depending on his age, health and even the weather. In the early weeks, most babies need at least eight to 12 feeds a day, and will use the breast for comfort as well as food.

A baby that sleeps for four hours or longer between feeds may appear content, but, sometimes, babies like this are not getting enough kilojoules to have the energy to wake up and cry. The lack of stimulation to your breasts will mean your supply will dwindle, and the cycle of sleeping/starving will result in a loss of your milk.

THE WITCHING HOUR

If your baby remains unsettled despite more frequent feeding, he may be suffering the effects of what author and lactation consultant Maureen Minchin dubbed 'the six-o'clock starvation syndrome'. She found that some women seemed to 'run dry' by late afternoon or early evening – just at the time when mothers are often busy preparing dinner or bathing other children.

Other people call this afternoon/evening period when the discontent of a baby or toddler clashes with the mother's needs to attend other family responsibilities the 'witching hour'. At this time, it seems everyone is tired, grumpy and hungry – including your baby.

If your breastfed baby is unsettled at this time, it may help to increase your supply for this demanding period by having a nap after lunch.

Experienced mothers know that the witching hour is not exclusive to breastfed babies. All young children seem particularly demanding at this time, as their need for food, comfort and attention after a tiring day clashes with the needs and feelings of other family members.

The best way of coping with this, whether breastfeeding or not, is to prepare as much as you can in advance and establish a routine.

Make meals ahead if possible, when baby is sleeping or happy to be left in a bouncinette or on a rug on the floor. And keep it simple. (*See chapter 7 on 'Looking After Yourself.'*) Meals that can be frozen and reheated later are easier.

Enlist the help of older children, explaining that the sooner the baby's needs are attended to, the sooner you can try to meet theirs. Discourage visitors at this time, whether yours or theirs. It is difficult and stressful enough to try to attend to your baby at this time, without having to conduct adult conversations at the same time or worry about whether visiting children are to be picked up or taken home.

It is important to know that although your breasts may be low on 'reserve' milk, they are actually in the process of maximum production at this time.

HOW TO TELL IF YOU HAVE ENOUGH MILK

'Not enough milk' is the most common reason cited for giving up breastfeeding. However, inadequate milk supply is a rare problem if uninhibited, exclusive breastfeeding is allowed. In these very rare cases, where a mother is not able to produce enough milk for her baby, it can be a case of some human milk being better than more. Many mothers in this situation choose to feed their babies as much milk as is available and complement with infant formula.

While a low supply can be a very real problem, particularly when your baby is obviously distressed and hungry, this can be quickly redressed by early intervention and frequent feeding for a few days.

In some cases the real problem is a mother or her advisers not being properly informed about how to judge if a baby is getting enough. The following checklist is a good guide. If your baby shows two or more of the signs below you probably do have enough milk.

- **At least six to eight very wet cloth nappies in 24 hours, provided no other fluids or solids are being given.** If you are using disposable nappies, particularly those containing 'moisture absorbing gel', you may use less than six nappies in 24 hours. However, the nappies should feel heavy to hold after use.

A very young baby will have two or more soft bowel movements a day for several weeks. Infrequent (ie not daily) bowel motions in a young baby suggest he needs more breastmilk.

An older baby is likely to have fewer. Small quantities of strong, dark urine, or formed bowel motions do suggest that the baby needs more breastmilk.

- **Good skin colour and muscle tone.**
- **Your baby is alert and reasonably contented for some periods in the day.** Your baby may still wake for night feeds. Some babies sleep through the night at an early age, while others wake during the night for quite some time.
- **Some weight gain and growth in length and head circumference.**

Other points to consider:

- **Racial and family patterns.** Slow weight gain is more likely in a family where the parents are of small stature. However, a baby must show consistent growth over the first year.
- **Some babies are very undemanding and need to be woken for feeds so that they will continue to gain weight.** Most new breastfed babies feed between six and 12 times in 24 hours.

A good rule of thumb is to make sure an undemanding baby feeds at least three-hourly during the day, and at least once during the night.

- On the other hand, **some colicky babies seem far from content, yet continue to gain weight steadily.** Colicky babies can be miserable and want to feed constantly.

IS YOUR MILK SUPPLY REALLY LOW?

There are times when you can mistakenly believe that your milk supply has decreased:

- When the early engorged feeling passes and your milk settles down to match baby's needs
- When your newborn baby needs more feeds than you were giving in hospital.
- When your baby grows stronger and becomes expert at emptying the breast efficiently – often in just a few minutes.
- In later months when you find your breasts are smaller
- When your baby is older and you may not feel the milk 'letting down' any more.
- When the weather is hot and your baby is feeding more often to quench his thirst
- When your baby is unsettled even after being allowed to breastfeed for as long as he wants. Are you mistaking discomfort or even illness (an ear infection, thrush, teething?) for hunger?
- When a baby who has gained large amounts of weight in the early weeks (common in breastfed babies) suddenly changes to a slower gaining pattern, or a large baby's weight gain slows temporarily. It is common to see a plateau in weight gain around three months. The charts in clinics are derived from a mixture of bottle-fed and breastfed babies and do not truly represent a breastfed baby's pattern of weight gain.
- If test-weighing has shown that your baby is not getting much. Test weighing is not recommended as it can be very misleading and undermining. Unless the weighing is done over a full 24-hour period or even longer, on reliable equipment, the results can be extremely variable and inaccurate.

Breastfed babies take very different quantities of milk at each feeding. The volume of milk may not be an adequate measure of how well your baby is being nourished. The content of your milk changes throughout the feed, continuing to become much richer in fat towards the end.

The baby who has drained the breast will therefore be shown to have received more calories than one who was given a routine time and then test-weighed.

- If you have taken all these possibilities into account and you are still concerned, talk to your medical advisers.

There are some rare physical conditions which can prevent a baby from utilising breastmilk fully, or which can prevent your baby from sucking efficiently, or more usually the baby has some problem unrelated to milk supply.

REASONS FOR A LOW SUPPLY

Getting the supply and demand right is a matter of give and take. You and your baby need to get the giving and the taking in correct balance before his needs are met. If you do not think this is happening, there may be a reason, such as:

• **Inadequate stimulation of the breasts** due to too few feeds, too short feeds or incorrect positioning. Your breasts need the stimulation of your baby's sucking to make milk. The more often he sucks, the more milk you will make. A baby who is fed on a schedule may not be stimulating the breast to make enough milk.

• **Changing sides before your baby has finished the first breast.**

• **Incorrect attachment or poor sucking technique** of the baby at the breast.

• **A baby who has not learned to milk the breast correctly** may not adequately stimulate milk supply or many not get most of the milk available in the breast. This will cause inadequate fluid intake, fewer wet nappies, slow weight gains, a falling supply and possible sore nipples. This can happen with some newborns, weak, sick or sleepy babies if they are not put to the breast early and often, or if the baby does not have to work for the milk because of your strong let-down or oversupply. It may also happen if your baby has been confused about how to suck at the breasts because he has been given bottles or dummies in the early days.

If you think this is your baby's problem, talk to your NMAA Breastfeeding Counsellor, lactation consultant or child health nurse or doctor. They can help you learn how to encourage correct sucking techniques.

• **Tension, pain or overtiredness** which can inhibit the efficient let-down of milk.

• **A physiological reason.** Only very rarely is there any physiological reason for a mother not to be able to produce enough milk for her baby. However, there are rare occasions when insufficient glandular tissue (which has nothing to do with the size of the breast), hormonal disturbances, or some types of previous breast surgery may result in failure to produce enough breastmilk.

• **Use of a hormonal form of contraception** which may cause your milk supply to drop. These days breastfeeding mothers are usually only prescribed the mini-pill (progesterone only). However some mothers have reported that even this has caused problems with their supply. Others say that this has made their babies irritable. Frequent feeding is sometimes enough to offset the initial drop in supply. If not, you may need to discuss alternative methods of contraception if you wish to continue to breastfeed successfully.

• **Regular use of complementary feeds.** By reducing your baby's demand for the breast, you will reduce your supply of milk. If you have been frequently using infant formula when leaving your baby, or to 'top up' after breastfeeds, your supply may have decreased.

Mothers who return to paid work sometimes notice a drop in their milk supply if they use infant formula to complement or replace expressed breastmilk (EBM). More frequent feeds in the evenings and/or at weekends can overcome this.

• **Early introduction of other foods.** Your baby's demand for breastmilk will diminish if solids or fruit juices are introduced too soon and your supply will drop. Breastmilk alone is the only food that your baby needs for at least the first six months. It is also the most nutritious. All other foods are less suited to your baby's digestive system.

• **Hormonal change.** When the balance of hormones in your body is undergoing change, your baby may want to feed more often. Sometimes, a baby will refuse to feed altogether at these times. Don't worry. He will usually make up for it when your hormones settle down again. Specifically, these times may be:

- Just before your monthly period and sometimes during ovulation, your baby may be fussy and even refuse some feeds. Try to stay calm and relaxed. Feed more frequently if you can and things will usually settle down in a few days. (*See your NMAA Counsellor if you are concerned.*)

– If you become pregnant your supply may decrease and your baby may become temporarily fussy at the breast. Some mothers like to wean at this time. However, with adequate diet and plenty of rest you may continue feeding if you prefer. It is important to let your doctor know that your are breastfeeding during pregnancy. (See NMAA booklet 'Breastfeeding Through Pregnancy and Beyond'.)

• **Many drugs both prescribed and off-the-shelf,** can affect breastfeeding, either by passing through the milk to your baby, or by affecting the process of lactation itself. Make sure you tell your doctor or pharmacist that you are breastfeeding and discuss the affects of any medication you are prescribed.

Research has shown that excessive amounts of alcohol, nicotine and caffeine (in tea, coffee, cola drinks, chocolate etc) may affect the let-down reflex and the production of milk or make your baby irritable or restless. Try to reduce your consumption of these drugs while you are breastfeeding.

• **If you have been ill,** your milk supply may be lower. Try to get plenty of rest and feed your baby frequently both during your illness and after and your milk supply will increase again.

HOW TO MAKE MORE MILK

REMEMBER: SUPPLY EQUALS DEMAND

Make sure your baby is correctly positioned, and feed more frequently. Offer the breast every two or three hours for a few days, or express between feeds if he won't come to the breast more often.

If your baby does not settle after a feed, wait 20 to 30 minutes and offer a top up.

Let your baby finish the first breast before switching to the second.

Let your baby decide how long he will feed. Some babies are very efficient, others are more leisurely and may take up to 20 minutes to finish one side.

Alternatively, it may help to change sides several times during a feed whenever your baby's sucking slows. Some mothers find this encourages the baby to suck more strongly and stimulates a good let-down reflex.

Offer little snack feeds when your baby is awake.

Offer the breast as a comforter for a few days instead of a dummy or thumb.

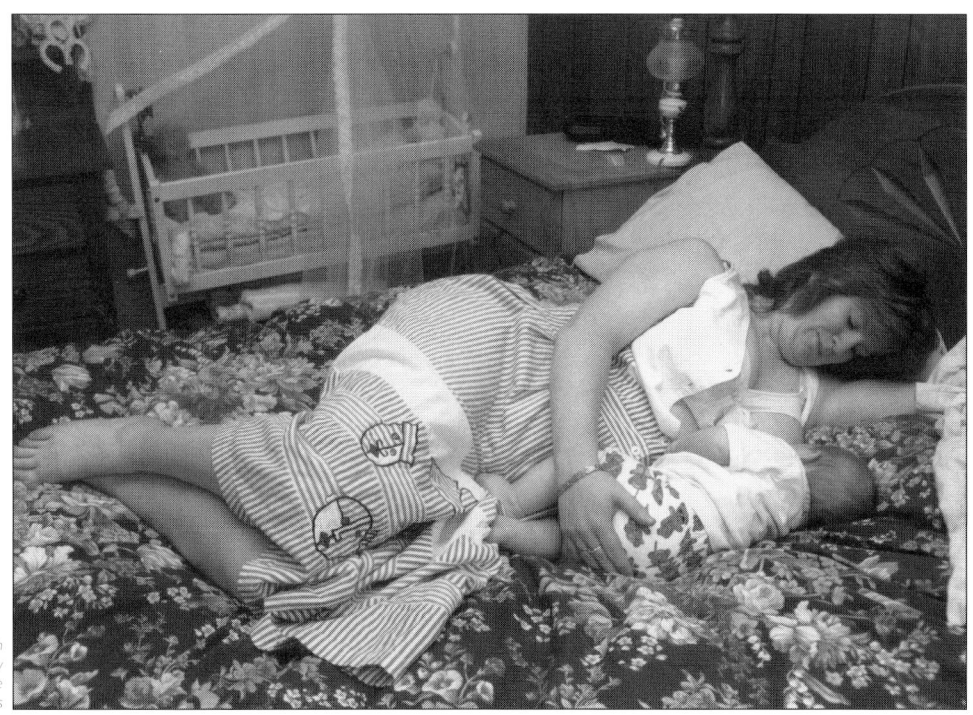

Photograph by Dianne Griffiths

Try stroking the breast towards the nipple on all sides as baby feeds, taking care not to dislodge the nipple from his mouth.

Go with the flow. If your baby is hungrier and wants to feed more often, do so. This is nature's way of increasing your supply to meet his changing needs.

Most mothers find they need to feed at least six times a day to maintain their supply.

Eat well so that you do not get tired or run down.

Seek support from your partner and others who can give it.

Rest whenever you are able. Try not to become stressed. Your health and well-being are important. Be kind to yourself. A day in bed or with the telephone off the hook makes a big difference. (*See Chapter 7 on Looking After Yourself.*)

Do not give water, juice or any other complementary feeds, unless there is a medical reason. This will lessen your baby's interest in breastfeeding and your supply will dwindle. In most situations where a mother has had to give complementary feeds due to a low supply, with support and information from a NMAA Counsellor, the mother is able to boost her supply and return to full breastfeeding. Some mothers who have weaned their babies have also been able to return to full breastfeeding.

Some women find a NMAA Supply Line, which allows the baby to stimulate the breast and obtain either artificial formula or expressed breastmilk from a tube at the same time, helps build up a low supply. With the Supply Line, a special container is worn around your neck. Fine tubing carries expressed breastmilk or formula from the container to the nipple. When your baby suckles the breast, milk is drawn through the tube into his mouth.

Cleaning and disinfecting the Supply Line is time-consuming and some women find it awkward to use, but it can be invaluable in encouraging a baby to suckle while his mother's breastmilk supply builds up.

TOO MUCH

While many mothers worry about whether they have enough milk for their babies, there are some mothers who worry about having enough baby for their milk. If your breasts are behaving as if you have produced triplets and are still large and uncomfortable and leaking profusely six weeks after birth, or your baby splutters and gasps whilst feeding, you may have an overabundant supply.

It usually takes about six weeks for your breasts to adjust to the job of producing the right amount of milk for your baby at each feed, but occasionally a mother can have continuing problems with too much milk. It is as if her breasts have become taps which she cannot turn off.

Sometimes this is accompanied by a let-down reflex which is excessively fast, causing your baby to gag, splutter, or pull off just before milk starts to flow, resulting in milk spraying from your nipples, sometimes as far as a metre.

This is caused by the pressure of a lot of milk in the breast combined with an extremely efficient let-down reflex.

If you have too much milk there are several things you can do to reduce your supply.

REDUCING YOUR SUPPLY

- **Let your baby finish the first breast before switching sides.** In the early days your baby may prefer to have the second breast two or three hours after the first. Your breasts make milk according to the amount of milk your baby takes from them, so giving only one breast will reduce your supply. (Make sure, though, that you start the next feed with the second breast, not the first, or you may risk engorgement or blocked ducts.)
- **Ensure your baby is positioned to suck effectively.** (*See positioning and attachment Chapter 4.*) This will allow him to drain the breast efficiently, reducing the risk of engorgement.
- **Express only when necessary** for your comfort or to help your baby attach properly if your breast is too full or hard.
- **Drink to satisfy your thirst, but don't overdo it.** Some mothers find increasing their fluid intake exacerbates an oversupply of milk. Reducing your fluid intake too severely could lead to urinary tract infections or blocked milk ducts.
- **Try to avoid any extra stimulation to the breasts and nipples** as this will tend to increase your supply.
- **Feed whenever you need to** as this will help your supply settle to match your baby's needs.
- **Alternatively, you may like to try scheduled feeding to help your baby go longer between feeds and reduce the stimulation your breasts receive.** NMAA does not ordinarily recommend schedule feeding and some babies can never be coaxed to accept it. If your baby does not accept this, try other methods of reducing your supply.
- **Don't give your baby extra fluids** as this will complicate your supply problems.
- If your baby is colicky from too much milk, he may be wanting to suck very frequently. In fact you may have thought he wasn't getting enough as he always seemed hungry. **For two or three hours, feed him on one side each time he wants to suck.** Use the other breast for the next two-three hour period, and so on. This might help reduce your supply and reduce your baby's colicky symptoms.
- **Don't give solids to babies under the age of six months** as this is unnecessary and won't help your oversupply problem.

- **Trigger your let-down reflex by hand or pump** before you put your baby to the breast, catching the most forceful flow of milk in a nappy or disinfected container. This will stop your baby from gagging and spluttering and will encourage him to feed and empty the breast.
- **Try feeding your baby while lying on your back** with your baby on your tummy so that he is effectively sucking uphill, finishing the feed sitting up so the breasts are drained properly. This 'posture' feeding will help your baby cope with the fast flow of milk. Make sure your baby is attaching well, as this can be tricky in unusual positions.
- **Persevere.** These suggestions or a combination of them will need to be tried for a few days before you notice any real change.

LEAKING

The phrase 'having a leak' is a peculiarly masculine term in Australian culture, but perhaps it should be reapplied to breastfeeding women!

Leaking breasts, especially in the early days when your milk comes in, is a common problem for many nursing mothers. This usually settles down as the sphincter muscles at the tip of each nipple develop and exert more control over the outflow of milk when your body becomes more accustomed to breastfeeding.

Meanwhile, there are several things you can do to reduce the discomfort and inconvenience of having milk stream onto your clothes, bedding and furniture.

- Try bathing your breasts several times a day alternately in very warm and cold water. This sometimes increases the blood circulation to the breasts, improving their tissue tone so that leaking lessens.
- Cover your nipples with nursing pads tucked into your bra. Make sure your bra is comfortable enough for this. You can buy washable nursing pads, or disposable ones, or make your own from old towels or linen. Use plastic-backed pads only for special occasions or for short spells as they can trap moisture against the skin, resulting in soggy nipples which may become sore or cracked.
- Use a clean nappy or other soft natural fibre cloth to catch any milk that pours out of one breast while baby is on the other. Don't use tissues or other synthetic fibres as these can be abrasive.

Alternatively, you can catch this overflow in a disinfected container and freeze it for baby later, but this must be done carefully and hygienically. (*See Chapter 10 on Expressing and Storing.*)

• Wear your bra and nursing pads to bed, and perhaps use a mattress protector if you are leaking during the night, or you may prefer to place nursing pads or other absorbent padding inside a closely-fitting vest, singlet or T-shirt.

• If you need to prevent the overflow of milk in certain circumstances, (such as breastfeeding away from home), press firmly on your nipple with your hand or forearm for several seconds after the let-down reflex starts. But be careful, sometimes this can cause blockages in the milk ducts.

WEIGHT GAINS

Most babies lose weight after birth and regain it within anything from a few days to several weeks. If your baby is slow to regain his birth weight, this is not an indication that your milk supply or quality is inadequate. All babies are individuals and their growth rates are as variable as their personalities.

Although the emphasis on weight gains is not as obsessive these days as it was in the past, regular weighing and measuring is still one of the most accepted and common ways of monitoring your baby's growth in the first few years.

This can be helpful, but too much emphasis on weight gains can cause unnecessary anxiety for parents.

While attitudes to babies' weight gains have become more relaxed and less regimented than they were in the 1940s and 1950s, at the same time, our society seems to have become more obsessive about adult weight. These past and present ideas about weight gains often combine to paint a confusing picture for parents. On the one hand, you may be praised when your baby gains well, but on the other, if he is chubby, you may be warned that he is getting too much and that you should watch his diet!

A baby who is being fed breastmilk alone for the first four to six months, may sometimes appear chubby, but will not be obese, as there are no empty calories in breastmilk.

A breastfed baby's pattern of weight gain is very different from that of a bottle-fed baby and should not be compared. In the breastfed baby, at around four or five months, the monthly rate of gain is often less than it was in the first three or four months.

However, you may find that some of the charts and other methods of working out averages used by maternal and child health nurses, doctors and hospitals are still largely based on the patterns of bottle-fed babies who tend to gain weight more quickly and steadily on cow's milk based formulas, which are designed to provide a given amount each day rather than being regulated by the baby's appetite.

For an accurate picture of how your baby is growing, it is best to look at gains over the period of a month, rather than a week. Weekly gains may vary from 50 grams to 250 grams, depending on his rate of growth, hunger, or any illness, such as a cold. Some babies may gain as much as 400 grams a week, but on average, a gain of 500 grams a month is considered a good indicator of healthy growth. However, keeping your eye on charts and figures, rather than your baby, can sometimes be misleading.

If your baby is fully breastfed, is obviously growing well in length and head circumference, is alert and has good skin tone, then do not be too disturbed if he is not gaining weight according to averages.

Weight gains are one indicator of how well your baby is growing and being nourished, but they are not the only indicator.

Inheritance plays a big part in determining our baby's size and growth rate. Your baby's birth and birth weight may also be factors in assessing weight gain.

A baby who was sick or premature may gain more slowly. On the other hand, a large baby may only make small but steady weight gains after birth and a premature baby may make up for a slow start with enormous weight gains.

To make matters even more confusing, your baby's physical development now is not necessarily a good indicator of how he may look as an adult. All well-nourished babies have fat deposits on their cheeks (facial and otherwise), arms and legs and abdomens. This fat deposited during the relatively inactive time of babyhood is laid down in preparation for the very busy toddlerhood, when your baby will probably be interested in tasting everything, including sand, teabags, etc, but eating little. Before long, you will find that those charming little pork-sausage arms and legs have grown into long thin frankfurters as your child progresses from baby to toddler to young child.

Breastfeeding is the best prevention against weight problems in later life. Breastfeeding mothers seldom get caught in the trap of trying to force their baby to finish a bottle or worrying about how many millilitres he has had. And if you wait until he is six months old to introduce solids, your breastfed baby will be a more active participant in the feeding process and you will get a better indication of when he is hungry and what he enjoys.

> 'My first child was double his birth weight at three months, instead of the usual six, and it was often assumed that he was being stuffed full of food other than breastmilk. 'It must be all that spaghetti you're giving him!' people would joke. However, he showed no interest in anything other than breastmilk for the first nine months of his life, and the only reference to spaghetti we get now is his arms and legs, which are long and lean.' – Kate

SLEEPING HABITS

For some babies, sleep, long and sound, does become a habit very early, but this is rare. While all babies sleep, most take quite a while to turn it into a habit, that is, something done at a regular and predictable time and for lengthy periods.

Apart from feeding, sleeping, or more correctly the lack of it, is a big issue for most parents. Perhaps this is because in our culture babies are still expected to fit in with adults rather than the other way round.

The general acceptance of bottle-feeding in the past may have also affected our expectations of when a baby should sleep and for how long. The curds formed from cow's milk formula are much tougher and more difficult to digest, which meant that bottle-fed babies usually slept for longer.

Breastmilk is so ideally suited to the infant's gut that it is easily absorbed. A newborn baby's stomach is very tiny (only six centimetres long) so it does not take long for breastmilk to be digested and the tummy to need refilling.

The notion that a 'good' baby is one that is undemanding also affects parents and society's expectation.

Soon after you return home, most people who ask after the baby will ask 'Is he sleeping?'

Having to confess that your baby wakes frequently, even after the three month period when you were told he would 'settle into routine' may make you feel guilty, embarrassed, frustrated and angry.

Whoever penned the favourite nursery rhyme, 'Rock a Bye Baby' was probably a new mother who felt that both the bough and her patience were at breaking point.

Rather than focus on these feelings it is best to remember that babies' sleeping habits change as they mature. Today's good sleeper may be tomorrow's teething and tossing baby.

Remember too that baby's sleep patterns are different from an adult's. There are two basic types of sleep; quiet sleep, when the breathing is slow and regular and the body hardly moves, and active sleep.

Very young babies usually sleep a lot as they need to conserve energy to grow, but about sixty per cent of this is Rapid Eye Movement (REM) sleep, the more active sleep when breathing is faster and more irregular and there are lots of body and facial movements. Rapid eye movements indicate that the person is dreaming.

As your baby grows, the proportion of quiet sleep gradually increases to about 80 per cent of sleep time and REM sleep decreases to 20 per cent as the brain matures. Large amounts of REM may provide the brain with extra stimulation to help it develop. These two types of sleep alternate to form a cycle. One cycle of quiet and REM takes about 90 minutes in adults but is much shorter in babies and children. The problem may not be baby, but that his sleep patterns do not match yours.

Some say that the pregnancy, which causes many women to be nocturnal, what with frequent urination and indigestion, is a kind of dress rehearsal for parenthood.

You may be surprised – if a little depressed – at how much sleep you can do without.

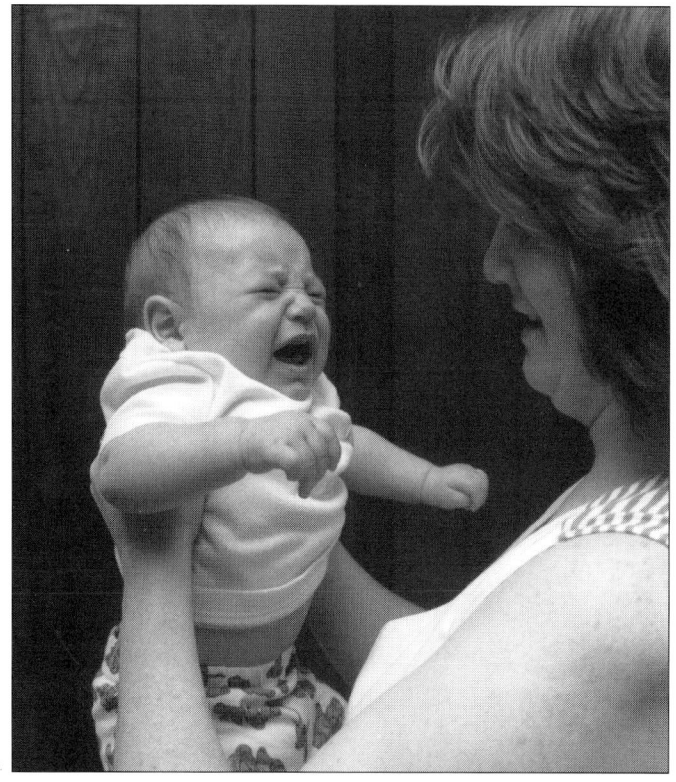

Photograph by Dianne Griffiths.

Sometimes it is a matter of coming to terms with the reality of babies compared to the fantasy. If other people's expectations and inquiries are making you feel pressured, a little white lie may be in order. Just nod and smile to inquiries about whether he is a good sleeper. For a baby, he probably is.

SOME POSSIBLE REASONS:
Sometimes, however, there are good reasons for your baby's wakefulness.
- **Is it your first week at home?** Newborn babies are often unsettled for a few days after birth, and after they arrive home. Time, a relaxed attitude and patience will solve this.
- **Hungry?** If your new baby wakes one to two hours after his last feed, he is probably hungry. Feeding is usually the quickest and most effective remedy.
- **Uncomfortable?** Perhaps he is too hot, too cold, needs a nappy

change or would prefer to be more or perhaps less snugly wrapped. It may take some time to find out your new baby's preferences. Perhaps he has been woken by a sudden sound and is frightened. Babies who sleep through daytime noise may become unsettled when the house is quiet. Try a soft tape or the radio on low.

• **Lonely?** Babies, particularly newborns, are reassured by physical contact and may prefer to see you or be near you.

Some babies cope better with solitude than others. Trying to teach him a lesson by resisting comforting him will only make a sensitive baby more insecure.

Most parents of babies like this find it is more effective to attend to them quickly and quietly.

• **Unwell?** A sudden change to your baby's feeding and sleeping habits may indicate that he is ill. Check with your doctor. If medication is prescribed, ask about side affects as some medicines affect sleep.

• **Something you ate?** Some breastfed babies are affected when their mothers eat or drink certain foods, or are taking medication. Discuss the problem with your doctor, child health nurse or NMAA Breastfeeding Counsellor to help find the cause.

• **Teething?** If your baby seems upset, is dribbling, drooling, has slight cold symptoms, seems to want to chew often and has swollen gums, he may well be teething.

Teething symptoms sometimes appear for weeks before teeth erupt. He may be soothed by something cold rubbed on his gums, something to chew on, or if he is very distressed or ill, by medication. Consult your doctor before giving baby any teething medicine.

CHANGING SLEEP PATTERNS

Sleeping and eating are two things that you cannot force your baby to do. However, sometimes it is worth trying to alter sleep and waking patterns in an attempt to ensure that he sleeps more during the night. Cut or shorten his daytime sleep, or you could try keeping him up later, so that he is more tired, or sleeps longer.

Unfortunately, many parents report that this results in overtiredness, leading to an even more disturbed night and an irritable baby the next day.

CRYING IT OUT

Sometimes well meaning friends and relatives will advise you to let your baby cry it out in the hope that he will learn to go back to sleep himself.

Remember, though, that crying is your baby's only means of communication. He is not crying to wreck your evening, but because he needs something.

Meeting your baby's needs will not 'spoil' him. On the contrary, he will learn more quickly how to tell you what he wants and that the world is a secure and loving place.

He is the helpless one, not you. Without you to come to his aid when he cries, he will not survive.

Before you decide to let him cry it out consider this.
- **Is there an obvious reason for his crying?**
- **How do you feel about listening to it?**
- **How important is it to you to comfort your baby when he is scared or lonely?**
- **Will ignoring his cries solve or worsen the problem?**

Older children sometimes respond to a program of controlled crying. However, this must be handled sensitively and the parent will need professional support. This is not suitable for babies under 12 months.

A night-time routine. A set routine of bath, story, breastfeed, a favourite toy and a song or, tuck-in or kiss can help settle a baby or child. Usually, this is not effective until the baby is 12 months old.

Other ways of helping your baby sleep are rocking, or carrying in a sling. The motion, warmth and comfort of your body often helps your baby drop off to sleep. A walk in the stroller or pram or a drive in the car may also help, although many babies usually wake once the car or pram stops.

Background noise is also helpful. Hum or sing a favourite song over and over, or use a radio, tape or loud ticking clock.

If you have tried all this to no avail, you might find some small comfort from the fact that wakeful babies usually reach their milestones earlier as they receive more stimulation, and are generally good company at a relatively young age.

Try to remain calm, share the burden of getting up to a wakeful child, try to organise time for yourself when you can catch up on sleep, perhaps taking it in turns to go to bed early, eat well and seek support from people you know will be sympathetic.

Accept any help you can get with other chores. Reduce other stresses in your life if possible.

Be reassured that sleep patterns change and this is usually only a temporary stage.

CRYING AND SLEEPLESSNESS

Your baby's crying can be worrying and distressing for both of you, but a baby who does not cry is more of a worry. Crying is your baby's way of communicating with you, and while all babies cry, some babies are better communicators than others.

Crying is your baby's language and one that you will quickly learn as you get to know him.

It is normal for your baby to cry and normal for you to feel distressed by this. This is nature's way of ensuring that you attend to his needs and that he survives.

It is also normal for your feelings of love and devotion to turn to despair and even anger if his crying is prolonged and, despite all your efforts, you are unable to comfort him.

If you feel like this and fear that you may harm your baby, leave him safely in his cot for a few minutes and leave the room, or even the house if necessary while you regain your equilibrium. A few minutes crying alone is less harmful to him than your feeling that you may not be able to control your despair at not being able to resolve the situation.

This is a good time for your partner, another relative or friend to step in to support you while you try to deal with your feelings as well as whatever is bothering your baby.

If your feelings of anger towards your baby and your role as a mother do not pass after a break from your baby or support from your partner or others, you may need to seek professional help.

Photograph by Dianne Griffiths.

THE FAMILY BED

The idea that babies must not interfere with the marital bed comes from a combination of Freud's ideas that this is unhealthy for both the psychological development of the child, and the sexual relationship between husband and wife. However, Freud may have been the father of modern psychology, but he was never a mother. There are others today who consider it is equally unhealthy for a tiny baby, newly emerged from the warmth and security of his mother's womb, to sleep alone.

The human animal is one of the few whose young sleep alone, and while this is in part because modern housing and heating means that the infant does not need the warmth of his mother's body to survive the cold nights and predators, there is no doubt that many mothers and babies enjoy the special closeness and security this brings (But this is not recommended if you have a water bed).

If you choose to sleep with your baby for some or all of the night, do not worry about rolling on him or suffocating him. As long as you do not drink alcohol or take drugs that may affect your normal responses, most mothers find that they are aware enough of their baby's presence to be careful. You may find that his presence and the fact that you are now more tuned into waking to attend his needs, means that you do not sleep as deeply as you used to. Despite this, some mothers find this preferable compared to the effort of getting out of bed and attending to their baby in a separate room several times a night.

To ensure that your baby does not roll out of bed, make sure he is placed in the middle of the bed, between you and your partner, without pillows. If he is on one side, push the bed against the wall or a large piece of furniture. If you continue to sleep with your baby as he begins to learn to roll, you may like to consider placing your mattress on the floor.

If you find that the baby's presence in your bed is depriving you and your partner of loving time together (not just intercourse, but cuddles and chats), the three of you may like to start off in bed together, then move baby to his own cot when he is more deeply asleep.

For many, this is easier said that done. If your baby won't move happily, perhaps you and your partner could go to another room? The arrival of a new baby is a challenge to any couple's sex life, but it is not just a new baby that causes coitus interruptus. Babies grow into toddlers who grow into children. The privacy that you once enjoyed in the bedroom in some ways has gone for ever. Maintaining a good sex life will require you both to think laterally, rather than horizontally.

OUT AND ABOUT WITH YOUR BREASTFED BABY

One of the 'virtues' of bottle-feeding that is often promoted is that it gives a mother freedom because it allows her to leave her baby to be fed by someone else. But a breastfeeding mother does not need to leave her baby to have her freedom. She can take her baby with her anywhere and breastfeed him anytime, without having to worry about whether she has disinfected bottles, measured formula powder or has access to clean water and bottle-warming facilities or has briefed a baby-sitter. Of course, breastfeeding mothers also need to take breaks from their babies. However, there is a difference between breaks that are desirable and those that are necessary. Baby sitters can give both you and your baby a change of scene, enabling you to catch up with your partner, friends or leisure. Very few mothers have cheap and easy access to a baby sitter all the time, so most find that for everyday activities baby must come too.

Your breastfed baby will adapt very easily to normal, daily events such as shopping, visiting friends, picking up other children, picnics in the park, attending meetings etc. All he needs is a change of nappies, and possibly clothes, and you. And all you need is a chair and the chance to sit down.

When you are learning to breastfeed you may prefer privacy and may not feel like venturing out. However, later, both you and your baby will enjoy socialising. (*See Chapter 3 on What to Wear.*)

If you are out and your baby needs a snack or a meal, it is a good idea for you to enjoy a break and a bite, too. For safety's sake, it is best not to have hot drinks close by while you are breastfeeding. By all means, eat while your baby feeds, but enjoy your coffee when he is safely back in his pusher.

TRAVELLING WITH YOUR BREASTFED BABY

> 'Generally, I found it more convenient to breastfeed. We went back to England and I was able to breastfeed my baby on the flight over and back. At least I didn't have to wash bottles.'
> — June (mother of James, aged 14 months.)

Breastfeeding gives your baby a distinct advantage while you are travelling. His meals are always available, at just the right temperature and are not influenced by the climate or surrounding environment or any problems with hygiene. Travelling as a family can be exhausting, as well as exhilarating, so not having to worry about your baby's meals is a big bonus. It also saves money.

However, if you are travelling somewhere hot, make sure that you drink plenty of fluids as your baby will be thirstier and you do not want to risk becoming dehydrated yourself.

If you are travelling overseas and need to be immunised

Baby Care Room

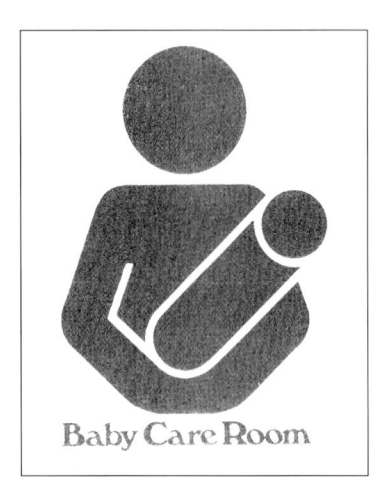

yourself, or to take preventative medications, make sure you tell your doctor that you are breastfeeding and discuss any affects these medications may have on your baby.

You will also need to discuss any special protection that your baby may need, although your breastmilk will be an important aid in boosting his immune system.

If you are travelling by plane, it will be more comfortable for your baby if he sucks during take off and landing when the air pressure changes inside the plane, so offer your breast. If your baby is unsettled by the changed environment and being on the go, your breasts will provide important comfort.

Airports and train stations these days often have a parents' room, if you would like to feed in private or to change a nappy. Look for the NMAA and 'Australian Parents' Magazine symbol, (illustrated on this page). This indicates that the facilities have had to meet strict standards. However, if there is no room available and you prefer not to use the ladies toilets, ask if there is an office or other spare room which you could use briefly.

If possible, it is wise to plan ahead. Try to find out what facilities are available for you and your baby before you embark on your trip. If you have friends or acquaintances who live near places where you are travelling, you may be able to arrange a quick detour for feeding or nappy changing and a cup of tea or snack for yourself and your partner. If friends will not be home, they may be happy to leave a key so that you can still use the premises. These breaks will make the journey longer for you, but they will make it easier on your baby and any other children, and more pleasurable for all in the long run.

If you are travelling by car, NEVER feed your baby while the car is moving. This is extremely dangerous for both of you and illegal. It is much safer and more pleasant to stop and have a bite to eat or a drink yourself while you feed your baby, perhaps at a roadside stop or picnic spot. It may be a good idea to carry an umbrella for shade as well as rain, plenty of extra drinks for you and plenty of extra nappies, cloths for wiping and changes of clothes. Car air conditioners can sometimes cause dehydration, so your baby may need extra feeds. If your car has no aid conditioning, you baby can get quite hot in the back seat. Try to ensure he is always shaded from the back and side windows and offer him frequent feeds.

PESTICIDES

Occasionally, you may read a newspaper report or hear a radio report about high levels of pesticides in breastmilk. Although this may sound alarming, breastfeeding is still recommended. A build up of organochlorins – such as dieldrin, aldrin, chlordane and other related compounds – are found in body fat, in various foods and in animals. Breastmilk is tested because it is the only non-invasive method of measuring levels of pesticides in the bodies of all the population. These residues are accumulated just by living in our environment.

Weaning your baby from the breast to a bottle will not protect him from other contaminants in the environment. Artificial milks are also higher in aluminium and radioactive substances and heavy metals tend to accumulate more in the milks of grazing animals. There is no evidence that any of the levels found in breastmilk in Australia pose any danger whatever to babies. Levels have in fact dropped fairly dramatically in the past decade. Weaning your baby from the breast would not only be misguided but would deprive him of important protection against infection that can only come from your breastmilk.

To avoid building up pesticides in your body fat and that of your family, avoid having your house treated with insecticides and eat a wide range of foods, preferably peeled but at least well-washed.

CHAPTER SEVEN

Surviving the early weeks

- Looking after yourself
- Diet during lactation
- Hormonal changes
- The return of ovulation
- Postnatal depression
- Drugs and breastfeeding
- Sex and relationships

Photograph by Dianne Griffiths.

LOOKING AFTER YOURSELF

Throughout your pregnancy, especially if this was your first baby, you probably felt very special. Your partner, family, friends, and even strangers may have constantly asked about your health, your feelings and plans. When your baby finally arrived, though, the focus of attention probably, and rightly, moved to him.

Now it probably seems there is no one more important in the world – or your world at least – than your baby. The emotional and physical time he requires from you may leave you little time to care for yourself.

However, caring for yourself is just as important as caring for your baby. If you are tired and run-down and feeling frustrated you will be less able to cope and may even risk your health. Feeling lousy will also affect your relationship with your partner and your baby as you will not be able to enjoy this precious time. Your breastfeeding relationship will also be affected as you need good nutrition, rest and positive feelings to help you establish and maintain a good milk supply.

Learning to breastfeed and to care for your new baby, as well as care for yourself and your home and any other children you may have, on far less sleep than you may be accustomed to, is a lot to expect of anyone. You will probably feel overwhelmed and exhausted at times. You may also find yourself in tears for no apparent reason. This is partly caused by the changing hormones in your body and is perfectly normal.

Don't be surprised if you find yourself sitting nursing or breastfeeding your baby, or walking the floor with him for most of the day while the dishes and the washing pile up, the beds and dinner go unmade.

You may be lucky enough to have a baby who sleeps well between feeds, but even so, small babies need frequent feeding – sometimes every two to three hours. You will probably find that when your baby sleeps you will want to grab the chance to catch up on the housework, especially the nappies.

This will be tempting – we all like to be organised – but if you do this all the time, as well as get up in the night to attend your baby, you will quickly become exhausted and this may affect your milk supply and your health.

YOUR NEW LIFE

Everyone tells you that things change after you have a baby; that you will have less time for other activities, and particularly less time for yourself. But few of us believe it. Most new parents don't really believe that much will change. It is common to hear a woman who is newly pregnant say confidently: "This baby is not going to change my life. He will have to learn to fit in with me." You may even be regarding this as "time-off" from paid work, and be planning to do lots of gardening and maybe start a diploma or degree that you'd always wanted to do. In some ways you are right. This will certainly be a learning phase. Babies have a way of teaching their parents and the first lesson is usually that baby comes first.

The second lesson is that managing all this will be a lot easier if you also look after yourself. The third lesson is that to do this, you will need help. The fourth is take any help that is offered and if none is offered, ask.

In the first few days or weeks, you may find it difficult to even get out of your dressing gown before lunch. This is common. Babies are very time-consuming and mothering, unlike paid work, is a 24-hour job. You will need time to get used to the idea of being a mother, to get to know your baby and to bounce back physically.

Now, particularly if you are feeling that "nesting" instinct coming on, is the time to cook and freeze meals in preparation for those first busy weeks at home with your baby. Now is also the best time to enlist the help of those offering – even if it is offered by people you don't know very well. Bearing and caring for children often brings together women who would otherwise find little in common with each other, and this is a time when even acquaintances sometimes offer to pitch in.

Don't be afraid to ask for help and take advantage of the experience of others. There are few mothers who do not know what you are going through right now. Most of us muddled through with the help of others and along the way learned a few tricks and shortcuts to make things easier.

Mobiles and booties are lovely gifts, but home help, arranged privately or through your local council if that service is available, or through the help of a relative or friend will be far more appreciated by any new mother. So too will the gift of a nappy wash service for a few weeks or months, or the offer to cook a week's worth of casseroles, or to be available to pick things up from the supermarket when necessary.

Some newly pregnant women feel quite offended at offers of help as they see it as a presumption that they will not cope. Don't take offence, take the offer. This is really a time when mother, any mother, knows best. Their offer of help is recognition of the fact that you will have a more important job to do, learning to mother your new baby.

This period of intense need is very brief. It is far more important for you to relax and enjoy your new baby than to have a clean and tidy home and a meal on the table. Of course, the housework still needs to be done. Just try to make sure it is done by somebody else.

This is not meant to sound glib. You cannot expect to come home from hospital with a new baby and do everything you did before. If your partner or other family members or friends cannot help at this time, if you can manage it, you may like to consider paid help, or a serious reorganisation of your priorities for the time being.

YOUR DIET

It seems the wider the choice of food in a society, the harder it is to choose the right food. However, choosing the right food for you and your family will make a big difference, not only to your budget, but to your sense of well-being. A healthy and varied diet is important anytime, but particularly when you are pregnant or breastfeeding and catering for the needs of two. This does not mean that you must eat for two, just that you must take responsibility for two.

Nature will ensure that your baby will not miss out on nutrients if you eat cola and chips and chocolate biscuits, as your body will still produce excellent milk – but you will miss out and will risk your own health and well-being.

Most women store extra fat during pregnancy to be used up while breastfeeding. Some lose this extra fat quickly and easily after birth, others find it much more difficult to shake. If you are still a few kilograms overweight, but otherwise healthy and are eating a nutritious diet, try not to worry to much about the extra weight until your baby gets older – no matter what your partner or mother says! Research has shown that the time mothers take to return to pre-pregnancy weight varies, but is definitely sooner (without dieting) in breastfeeding mothers than in those who bottle-feed.

Doing more exercise is probably a better alternative than a strict diet, and certainly easier as your baby will enjoy walks in the pram or pusher and will probably be highly amused watching you "work out" with an aerobics video or class. Take care that this "work out" is suitable for postnatal women.

Now is not the time to go on a crash or fad diet. Diets like this which are not nutritionally balanced are unsuitable for pregnant and breastfeeding women.

Anyway, feeling hungry all the time will probably make you irritable and less able to cope with everyday chores. It could also affect your let-down reflex and your breastfeeding relationship with your baby. Lack of important nutrients at a time when your body is making extra demands could also affect your long-term health.

EXERCISE

If you are eating well, have lost weight, but still can't fit into your pre-pregnancy clothes, you may need to tighten and tone a few muscles that have been stretched during pregnancy. This can take time and patience, and may never result in the slim girlish figure of your youth. Be realistic about what you can achieve and you are more likely to maintain both a good exercise routine and a healthy diet. Remember, Elle Macpherson is a supermodel, not a role model.

However, you may find the type of exercise that you enjoyed before now cannot be done without a baby sitter. You may be lucky enough to be able to arrange this by either leaving your baby with your partner, parents or a friend or hiring a sitter. If you can't arrange this, try walking with your baby in a pram (or sling) to the shops, the park or a neighbour regularly, or try an aerobics class at home courtesy of the local video shop. Many recreation centres hold special classes for mothers, with a creche provided.

Exercise is important for your health and pleasure. Regular, moderate exercise will give you more energy, a sense of well-being and will help you cope better with the demands of being a mother, and protect you against osteoporosis and heart disease later in life.

However, check with your doctor before beginning an exercise program. This is especially important during pregnancy and the first two months after giving birth. Postnatal exercises, those usually recommended by a physiotherapist, are worth the time and effort, in order to avoid problems later in life with incontinence and prolapse of the uterus, and to regain your desired shape.

YOUR MILK SUPPLY

Research into the effects of exercise on milk supply has shown that moderate exercise presents no problems. Some women report a decrease in supply after vigorous exercise. Others feel that it boosts their supply. Overall, moderate exercise is beneficial. If you are worried about your milk supply, you may need to feed your baby more often. How much milk you make depends on how much stimulation your breasts receive from your baby. Feeding baby before you exercise is a good idea, so that your breasts will not be so full and heavy. A good supporting bra, properly fitted, will help you exercise more comfortably and will help avoid blockages. Avoid tight clothes which flatten the breasts. You may find exercises which involve lying on your stomach uncomfortable. Check your breasts regularly for lumps caused by blockage of the milk ducts, particularly underneath and near the armpits. Be careful not to bump or bruise your breasts.

Dancing, skipping, bike riding (with an approved safety seat for your baby) and playing ball are all good and enjoyable ways to get exercise with or without your baby. Remember to take a shower afterwards, as some babies don't like sweat with their milk.

SOME PERSONAL TIME

One of the rarest commodities once you become a mother is personal time. Even the most private acts, such as going to the toilet, become public as toddlers are fascinated by and like to be included in absolutely everything their parents do. That's why it is important to insist on some personal time for yourself right from the start.

After giving birth you may feel a little bedraggled. Your hair and skin, which glowed in the middle trimester of pregnancy, may have dulled due to changed hormone levels, your tummy may feel flabby, you may feel and look tired at first, and you will probably feel less than glamorous.

Even if it is only for an hour, you may feel better if you can visit your hairdresser or beauty parlour or masseur – anywhere where you can be looked after for a change.

Or perhaps you are longing for an uninterrupted phone conversation, bath or coffee or some social contact with someone who knew you before you were a mother?

Many mothers who have had a hobby or sport before their babies, try to make a regular time to free themselves of parenting responsibilities to continue it. However, others are not happy being separated from their babies. If you are happy to leave your baby, and if money is short for baby-sitters, perhaps you could arrange a swap with another mother? Or better still your partner can have some precious time with his baby on a weekend or evening while you do something for yourself.

Sometimes you may not want to do anything. You may simply want to have the house, or the bed to yourself for a few hours. Even achieving something as simple as this needs organisation and help. You may need to express milk if you need more than a few hours off and it may seem like a lot of trouble to organise for someone else to care for your baby for even a few hours, but it will be worth it. This time out will help you to relax and feel cared for and will make you feel happier to return to your mothering role.

SMOKING

If you are or have been a smoker you are probably well aware of how harmful this can be too your health. But are you aware of the harm it can cause your unborn child or those living with you?

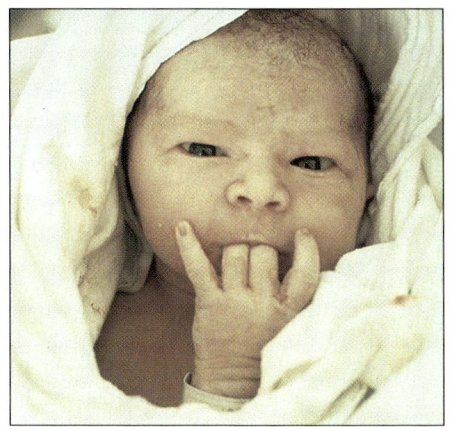

ABOVE: Newborn babies have a strong sucking instinct and start as soon as they are born.
Picture: PRUE CARR

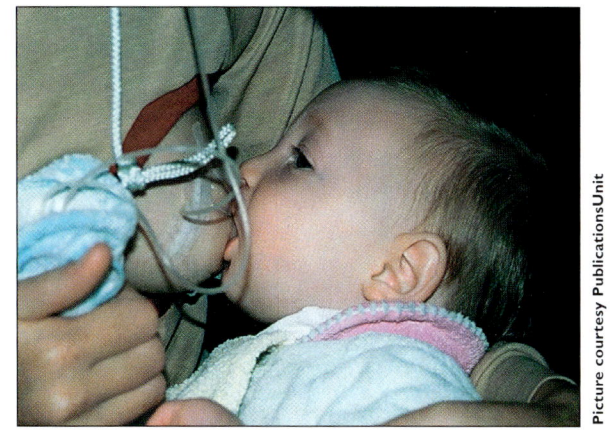

ABOVE: A NMAA Supply Line enables babies to receive extra milk at the breast rather than by bottle. The extra stimulation of the breasts also increases the mother's milk supply.

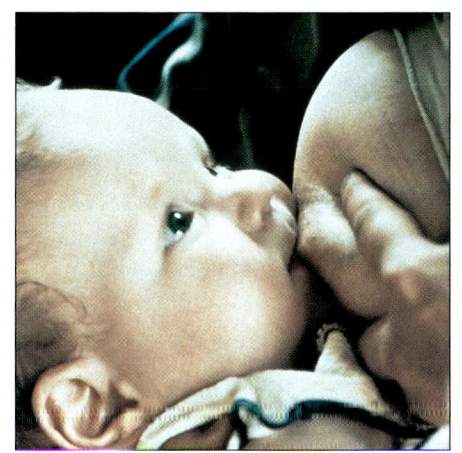

Picture courtesy PublicationsUnit

ABOVE: Babies can bite and damage the nipple if not well attached. Pressing too hard can also cause blocked ducts. **Picture: PRUE CARR**

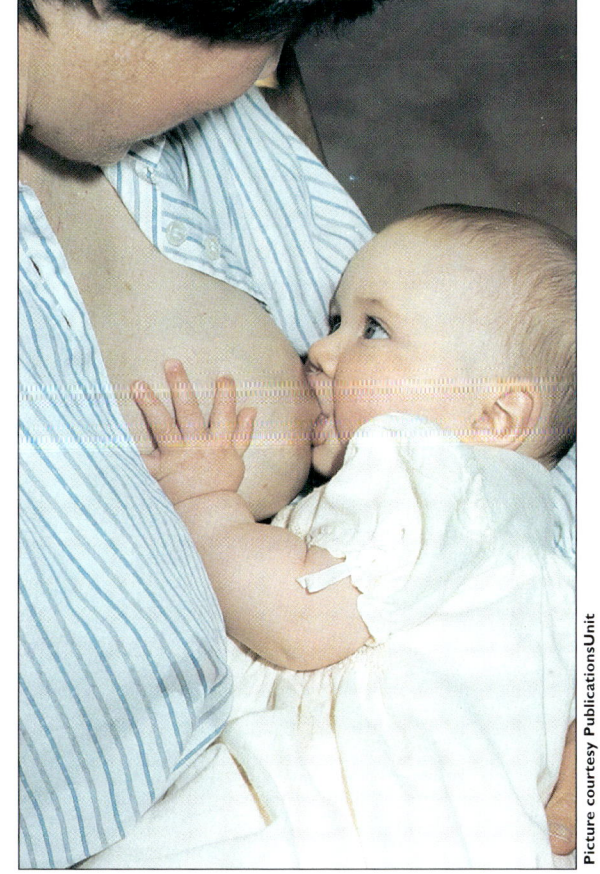

RIGHT: A baby's sucking starts the whole system of milk production and delivery. Notice the flanged lips and the tongue just visible.

Picture courtesy PublicationsUnit

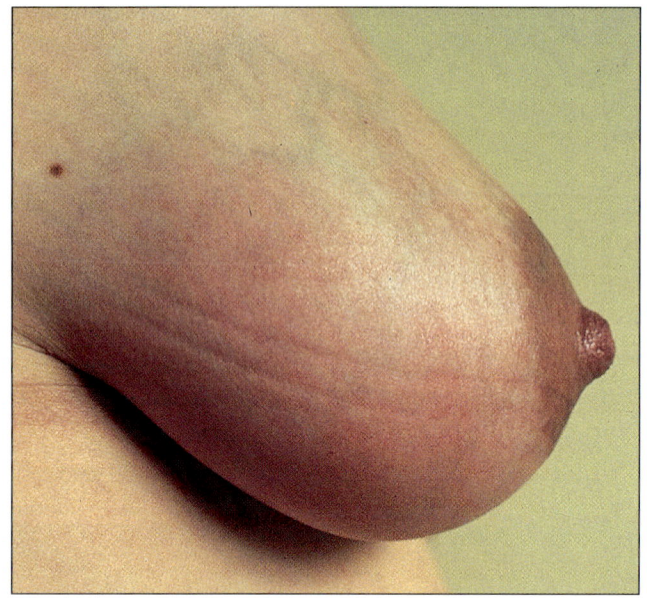

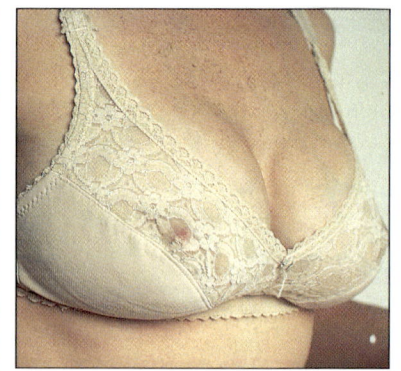

Redness on the breasts (left) is an indication that there is a blockage in the duct system leading to the nipple. If left untreated, the blockage might develop into an infection, so it is important to attend to it as soon as it is noticed.

One of the causes of a blocked duct can be a bra which is too tight (above). This will restrict the flow of milk by pressing on the duct.
Pictures: PRUE CARR

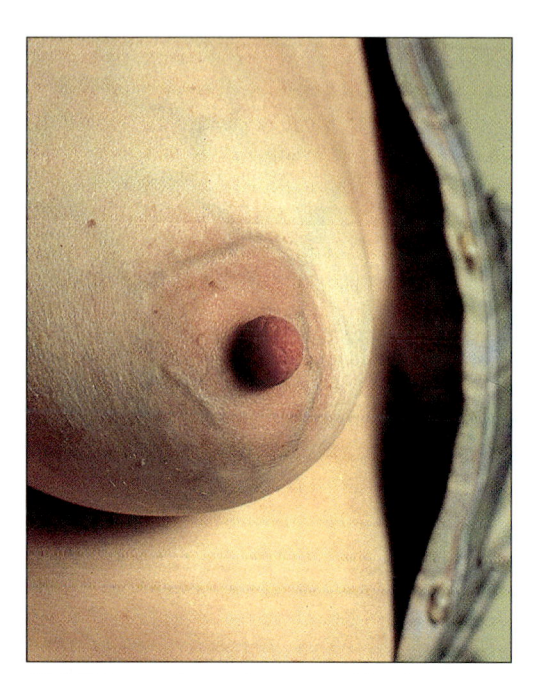

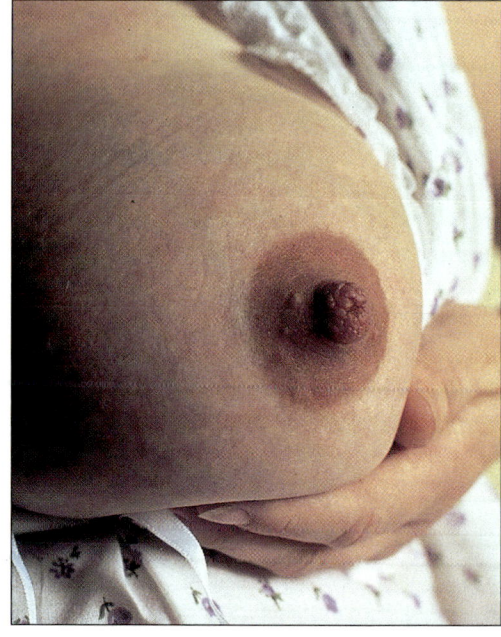

ABOVE: Sore nipples can be very painful and need immediate treatment to prevent further damage. **Pictures: PRUE CARR**

Once you have learned how to position and attach your baby, you will find a variety of feeding positions comfortable.

Pictures: YVETTE O'DOWD

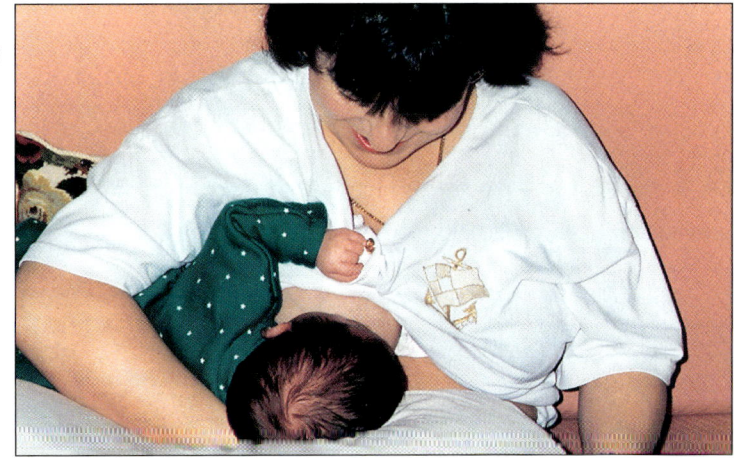

ABOVE: As your baby grows, your breastmilk changes to meet his developing needs. Breastfeeding also provides comfort and a special closeness as your baby gains increasing independence. **Picture: DIANNE GRIFFITHS**

ABOVE: Friendship and support is important to all new mothers as they learn about caring for and feeding their babies.
Picture: DIANNE GRIFFITHS.

IF YOU SMOKE DURING PREGNANCY:

- Perinatal mortality (death of an infant just before, during or just after birth) rises sharply;
- Your baby may be an average of 200 grams lighter.
- The blood flow in the umbilical cord, which carries nutrients to your baby, slows minutes after you start to smoke, and this can last up to an hour.
- Your baby could be shorter and is more likely to have learning difficulties
- The risk of your baby dying of Sudden Infant Death Syndrome (SIDS) is greater.
- In his first year, your baby has a much higher risk of developing pneumonia or bronchitis.
- At preschool age your child is likely to spend twice as many days in hospital.

IF YOU SMOKE DURING BREASTFEEDING:

- The chemicals from the cigarettes pass through the milk to your baby.
- The chemicals in your bloodstream inhibit your let-down reflex and also reduce your milk supply.
- Your child has a greater risk of developing respiratory illnesses and colic.
- Your child may have long-term health problems caused by passive smoking, and may even take legal action against you in the future.

WHY YOU SHOULD STOP:

- Stopping smoking can benefit the health, lifestyle and the pockets of both you and your family within weeks.
- There is more support for people who want to stop smoking than for smokers. Your doctor, child health nurse, community health centre and the anti-cancer organisation in your state, are waiting to help you quit.

ALCOHOL

Alcohol, although widely considered socially acceptable, is a drug which is quickly passed to your baby via the placenta while you are pregnant and via your breastmilk when you are breastfeeding. Drink it in moderation (one or two standard drinks a day at most), preferably only occasionally.

OTHER DRUGS AND BREASTFEEDING

If you are ill and must take drugs in the short term or you have a condition for which long-term drugs are necessary, ensure that your doctor is aware that you are breastfeeding. There are forms of most types of drugs, such as the contraceptive pill, that are safe for breastfeeding women. Others may need to be avoided. Never take any drug that is not prescribed particularly for you by your doctor with his or her full knowledge that you are breastfeeding. Something that your sister may have found invaluable from the naturopath, or that your aunty or mother has had in her handbag or cupboard may do you and your baby more harm than good.

Be aware also, that tablets bought across the counter from your health food shop or chemist should also be checked by your doctor before you take them or ask the pharmacist about their use.

SEX AND THE BREASTFEEDING WOMAN

For some new mothers, this very title is a contradiction in terms. Many couples find that becoming parents strains and puts extra tensions in their relationships. Sex can be tricky at the best of times.

We are all affected by tiredness, other commitments, tensions in the emotional side of the relationship, and of course, hormones. Add a new baby and all the extra work he entails and you may wonder how any couple ever manages to have a second child. The fact that there are so many families with two three or more children is proof that lack of interest in or opportunity for sex after the birth of a baby is usually temporary.

Talk to your partner about your feelings and ask about his. Talking to other sympathetic friends or family and consulting appropriate books, or talking to your doctor may be helpful.

It is natural to have fears and questions about making love after the birth of your baby. It is also natural for patterns of lovemaking to remain disrupted for some time. Most couples don't enjoy intercourse for at least two months after the birth, and sometimes much longer, depending on the amount of healing needed after the birth. Even by the baby's first birthday, many couples find they are making love less often than they did before the pregnancy.

If you have had a vaginal tear or stitches after the birth due to an episiotomy, or other damage to the vagina, you may be experiencing extreme pain which will naturally kill any sexual desire. You may find that your vagina is very dry and intercourse is no longer pleasurable. It is also difficult to relax and enjoy lovemaking knowing that the climax is likely to be a crescendo of screams from the nursery. Babies seem to know when romance is in the air. Perhaps it is part of their survival mechanism – an ancient instinct to prevent the possibility of any sibling rivals on the scene too soon.

You may find though, that it is breastfeeding, rather than your baby that is blamed for your lack of libido. Some people believe that breastfeeding is "draining" on the mother, or that the intense intimacy a breastfeeding mother shares with her child displaces the need for intimacy with her husband. This is both true and false. Studies comparing the sexual behaviour of breastfeeding women with women who are not breastfeeding vary in their conclusions. Some say there is no difference, others say breastfeeding women are more sexually active, and still others say the opposite. One American study found that women who were not menstruating while breastfeeding were more likely to have a lower libido. Overall, responses may vary widely but breastfeeding women on average have reduced libido, less intercourse and fewer orgasms than bottle-feeders until the baby is weaned.

PHYSIOLOGICAL FACTORS RELATED TO BIRTH

They say that sex is all in the head – that is, your mental attitude has more to do with your sexual feelings than anything else. However, there are several physiological reasons why you may feel less interested in making love right now.

Firstly, for up to six weeks after the birth you will have a vaginal discharge (lochia), and this puts some people off sexual intercourse. As long as your doctor has not advised against it, there is no reason you cannot still have intercourse. However, you may prefer to wait anyway.

Secondly you are probably exhausted. Tiredness is the most common cause of abstinence in the first weeks or months. This can affect your whole outlook on life and is thought to be a major contributor in postnatal depression.

Thirdly, you may no longer feel "sexy". Changes in body shape can also affect your feelings about your sexuality. Your breasts, hips and thighs are probably bigger than before. Some spreading and fanning of the outer part of your vagina after the birth is normal, too. The lips of your vagina (labia) may also seem larger and hang down further.

Less obvious will be the change in the strength of your abdominal muscles and your pelvic floor (the region of your anal, vaginal and urinary openings). Weak stomach muscles will prevent you from fitting into your favourite figure-hugging clothes and may lead to some alarming jokes about whether you are still pregnant. This can be rectified by attention to diet and exercise. But weak pelvic floor muscles are no laughing matter, especially if they cause you to wet your pants when you laugh or cough, or your tampons drop out. As you get older, weak pelvic floor muscles can also cause uterine prolapse. You will enjoy sex more and be more easily aroused and reach orgasm more often and more easily if your pelvic floor muscles are strong, so now's the time to start doing those invisible push ups.

PHYSIOLOGICAL FACTORS RELATED TO BREASTFEEDING

As women, rightly or wrongly we are all used to having our moods blamed on our hormones. During pregnancy, the levels of two reproductive hormones oestrogen and progesterone rise and then fall rapidly after birth. Women who do not breastfeed return to their "normal" hormone levels, ovulate (produce an egg) and menstruate within about three months.

However, breastfeeding women generally do not regain pre-pregnancy hormone levels, ovulation or periods until much later. This delayed fertility is caused by hormones related to breastfeeding indirectly suppressing the release of oestrogen and progesterone. How long this lasts varies from mother to mother. Rarely, some breastfeeding women become fertile four weeks after delivery and a few could conceive within 12 weeks of giving birth; but for most women, ovulation occurs much later.

There are wide variations in the length of postpartum amenorrhea, but it is agreed that perhaps 98% protection from pregnancy is possible in the first six months after birth, provided women remain amenorrhoeic and the baby is exclusively breastfed.

Low oestrogen levels are generally thought to cause the vaginal wall to become thinner and less elastic and to reduce lubrication. Many mothers find they need to use a lubricant like KY jelly for a while after birth when having sex. Dry skin and acne may also be caused by changed hormone levels. Depression, fatigue, the baby blues, feelings of emotional vulnerability and loss of libido are also suspected to be caused by hormone changes.

Having full or leaking breasts can also be uncomfortable or off-putting during intercourse for some people. It is common for milk to leak from the breasts during arousal; so is experiencing some sexual arousal (even orgasmic sensations) while suckling your baby. The reason for this is that the same hormone – oxytocin – triggers both letdown and orgasm. There is no need to worry about this. Breastmilk is vital for your baby. Any good feelings that encourage breastfeeding are to the baby's advantage.

RETURNING TO FERTILITY

An Australian study has shown that breastfeeding women who give no other solids or liquids to a baby before six months, who do not offer a dummy and who use the breast for the comfort of the baby as well as nutrition, on average do not have a menstrual period for 14.6 months. Ovulation can occur though, before menstruation, so unless you know the signs of ovulation, you will not know for sure that you have returned to fertility until you have your first menstrual period after the baby. About 80 per cent of breastfeeding women are not fertile until after the first period – leaving 20 per cent fertile. That leaves you with two choices. Take a risk, or take or use a contraceptive knowing that it is probably 80 per cent unnecessary.

The most widely used oral contraceptive for breastfeeding mothers is the progesterone-only pill (the mini pill). The other most common methods are the intrauterine device (IUD), the diaphragm, condoms, spermicides, or ovulation awareness methods, such as Billings, Temperature or Rhythm). The combined oral contraceptive is not recommended for breastfeeding mothers as it has been shown to deplete milk supply and contains oestrogen, which may pass to your baby. It is best to consult your medical adviser about any oral forms of contraception. Your Family Planning doctor will be able to help you decide what is best for you and will tell you all you need to know about natural planning methods and the use of aids or medication.

PAIN

Pain is a big turn-off, unless of course you are a masochist, which it is presumed you are not. The mere thought of intercourse is more likely to make you wail like a police siren than be a sex siren if you have tear or a cut (episiotomy) at the opening of your vagina due to the birth.

Even if you have no tears or cuts, your vagina may be unusually dry and this can make intercourse painful. If you have had stitches, these may prickle for a few days and then as the wound heals you may have a bump of tender tissue. Don't worry, though, that intercourse will cause the scar to open again. Providing your partner is reasonably gentle, this is unlikely.

How long it hurts depends on the size of the wound, the position, the type of repair, how well lubricated you are. Most pain eases after a while, but in rare cases an operation is needed. Report any pain or difficulty to your doctor at your post natal visit.

PSYCHOLOGICAL FACTORS

As if pain, fatigue and hormones, were not enough to make you take a detour on the road to sexual fulfilment, there is a positive minefield of emotional problems also set to way lay you. First of all there's fear: fear of pain, pregnancy, or not being sexy; jealousy; of your baby, your partner whose body or lifestyle has not changed as drastically; of others who seem to be coping better; protectiveness of the baby and reluctance to share yourself further; anticlimax; the big event is over as far as you're concerned; disappointment, with the baby, the birth, yourself, your partner; guilty for not instantly loving your baby, for yelling at your toddler again, about not feeling sexy or giving time to your partner; anxiety, over money, not coping, health problems, about not being a good mother and not getting enough sleep; resentment over the constant demands, sadness over the loss of your previous relationship with your partner, your work friends, your old life, control and freedom, boredom, spending too much time at home, feeling trapped, thinking about your own childhood, feeling depressed because of all or some of the above.

Depression may be both the cause or the result of some of the other emotions. Identifiable depression occurs in more than 50 per cent of pregnancies, most frequently in the first two weeks after birth.

Most times these feelings resolve themselves, but for about 10 per cent of women, depression develops into a deepening self-perpetuating crisis.

Symptoms include fatigue, mood swings, irritability, loss of libido, changed personality, anxiety, frustration, fear, feelings of violence, guilt, lack of awareness, being unable to cope, feeling resentful. If you are feeling like this and nothing seems to help, you may need professional advice and certainly should talk to your doctor about how you feel. PANDA, the Post Natal Depression Association is a self-help non-profit support group for women and their families who are experiencing this.

PLANNING FOR SEX

People often explain their first sexual involvement with someone using the words, "It just happened". Well, once you become parents, sex seldom "just happens" unless you plan for it.

This might mean planning to make love at 7pm, just after the baby falls asleep, rather than sitting up watching telly and falling into bed at 11pm, when the baby is likely to wake. It might mean having a passionate picnic on the bed at home while a neighbour or grandparent looks after the baby for an hour. It might mean setting up your toddler and older child with a video and some munchies while you and your partner have a shower together. Remember how creative you had to be when you were courting and had nowhere private to kiss and cuddle? Well, now is a good time to revive some of those exciting, if furtive, times again – even if the back seat of the car is now crowded with capsules and baby seats.

GET A TUNE UP
A positive attitude, a flat tummy, a sexy nightie, a good diet, a good laugh, perfume, a massage, will all help you to feel sexy. Also, make sure you are comfortable with your method of contraception. The risk of another pregnancy while you are trying to adjust to a new baby is definitely a turn-off.

COMMUNICATION
Let your partner know how you feel, physically and emotionally. If your breasts are sore, or your vagina is dry, tell him. If you don't feel like sex, but would love a cuddle, tell him. If you have had a good night's rest and found yourself fantasising about him while you were doing the dishes tell him, too. If watching a sexy movie made you feel sexy, tell him that. Even if you don't have intercourse, it will help both of you to realise that you are still sexual people and that there are many ways of relating sexually. Loving each other does not have to be restricted to making love. Touching, bathing together, or those three important words, "I love you" are sometimes all that is needed to create intimacy.

Take your time, don't expect too much of yourselves and be reassured that your sex life will resume, in one form or another, eventually. However, this does presume a certain mutual understanding and acceptance. Some partners find lack of interest in sex extremely difficult to accept. If you or your partner are out of balance regarding sex and you are both feeling angry and resentful, it may help to talk to other parents, your local NMAA Counsellor or to seek professional help.

WILL WEANING HELP?
Sometimes, it can feel as if you are now married to your baby, rather than your husband. This may cause you to wonder about weaning early. There is no easy answer to this. Breastfeeding is only one fac-

tor affecting your sexuality at this time, but it often wrongly gets the blame. Whether you wean depends on you, your relationships, how important breastfeeding is to your self-esteem and what other pressures you may be under.

Breastmilk is the perfect food for your baby and breastfeeding will help your uterus return to its normal size earlier. Bear in mind, too, all the other benefits of breastfeeding, not only for your baby, but also for you, such as reduced risk of breast and cervical cancer.

You are also more likely to have more bountiful breasts, and to lose weight more easily after the birth. You may also feel more womanly, and your partner may enjoy this, your fertility will be reduced, reducing the risk of pregnancy and your breasts may be more sensitive now. You and your partner may also find it sexy to see milk flowing from your breasts during lovemaking.

On the other hand you may have a dry vagina, a lower libido, your leaky breasts may be a turn-off, you may feel exhausted, confused over the role of your breasts now and becoming a mother may have made you feel less sexy, or your partner may lose interest in you sexually.

Overall, having a new baby and a sex life is a balancing act, whether you are breastfeeding or not. Whether the scales are still tipping in favour of breastfeeding for you, is an individual matter. If you are considering weaning for this or other reasons, remember that artificial feeding has its own disadvantages, and that while you may be feeling a little more like heading for the bedroom, you may need to spend some extra time in the kitchen first washing and disinfecting bottles and measuring infant formula.

CHAPTER EIGHT

Common problems

- **Sore nipples**
- **Mastitis**
- **Crying and sleeplessness**
- **Colic**
- **Gastric reflux**
- **Lactose intolerance**
- **Allergies**
- **Breast refusal**
- **Sucking problems**

> 'After my new baby was born, I suffered from epidural headaches for four weeks, had cracked and bleeding nipples, nipple thrush and numerous bouts of mastitis – in fact every time my baby awoke I dreaded the thought of latching him on, for the pain was unbearable. I tried everything and the only thing that worked was time, patience and experience (for both of us!) I persevered for six hellish weeks and now, after seven months, I'm so glad...we both love our breastfeeding relationship and he is thriving. It's the best thing I could have done.
> - Karen, East Brighton, Vic

COMMON PROBLEMS AND HOW TO DEAL WITH THEM

The best way to ensure successful breastfeeding is to get the right information and support to prevent problems or to help resolve them quickly. Sometimes, even with the best care, problems persist. This can be distressing and discouraging and may even lead you to consider weaning. If your breasts or nipples are tender or hurting as you read this, if feeding your baby has become an endurance test rather than an enjoyable experience, you may be wondering whether it is all worth it. Fortunately, most problems can be solved, but you may need some patience and perseverance as well as the correct support and advice.

By perseverance we do not mean continual suffering. If you are in pain, then something is wrong and should be addressed. This chapter aims to provide some suggestions on how you may treat problems and more importantly prevent future ones, so that breastfeeding is a positive and rewarding experience for you, as well as for your baby.

Just as natural childbirth has come to be seen in some circles as an endurance test for mothers, breastfeeding is sometimes seen as something mothers 'must' do to earn a 'good mother' badge.

This is not the NMAA view. Breastmilk is the best food for your baby but it is not something that you should pursue at the expense of your own health or sanity. Doing so will not be good for you as a woman, a mother, nor will it be good for your baby as your negative feelings about breastfeeding may affect your relationship with him.

In most cases, problems can be solved quickly and easily, but sometimes lack of support, other demands, your own exhaustion and your baby's distress can mean that it makes more sense to consider an alternative method of feeding.

If you have exhausted all solutions – and yourself – and breastfeeding is not a rewarding and happy experience for you, then weaning may be the answer. (*See Chapter 11.*)

However, in some cases weaning is not really the best solution to your problem. Sometimes the solution is far more simple.

Often weaning is seen as a quick fix and is represented to mothers as the only option. Many women report feelings of intense sadness at having weaned before experiencing a happy breastfeeding relationship. For example, if you have mastitis, weaning will exacerbate the problem and could make you ill. Your breasts need to be kept as empty as possible to clear the inflammation and this is best achieved by your baby's sucking. Early weaning for other less severe problems may also exacerbate your feelings of anger and disappointment as you may feel that the people who were supposed to support you let you down, or that you let your baby down.

Weaning to infant formula also brings its own frustrations and problems as it is less hygienic and less convenient and takes more time to prepare correctly.

This is why it is important for you to look at alternative solutions first.

Sometimes the solution to your problem can be as simple as feeding your baby more often – or applying cold cabbage leaves to ease engorgement. At other times you may need to try several different suggestions before your problem is resolved, such as if your baby seems to be 'fighting' the breast.

If you do eventually decide to wean early, you will feel better about it if you know that you thoroughly canvassed possible solutions to your breastfeeding problems. You then will know that you have tried your best for your baby.

It may help you to know that there are many mothers who breastfeed successfully for months or even years but who began with similar problems and felt equally discouraged. Their perseverance was helped by the support of other experienced breastfeeders who had overcome similar problems and who could advise them and also reassure them that, in most cases, such problems are temporary.

You will find that in your local NMAA Group, or among relatives and friends, other mothers are keen to tell you how they overcame any problems they may have had. These stories are meant to encourage and inspire you, not intimidate you. Becoming a mother for the first or even the fifth time can be an exciting, but stressful experience. Breastfeeding should be one of the joys, not one of the stresses.

SORE NIPPLES

Breastfeeding should not hurt, but it does take a little while to get used to the strong sucking of a healthy baby. Also, your nipples will be more sensitive for a few days after the birth, so you can expect some nipple tenderness in the early days.

Sometimes mothers are advised to limit the feed times to start with, to minimise this early discomfort. However, research now shows that this merely delays the soreness. Restricting your baby's time at the breast can also lead to a build-up of milk and increased engorgement, which may result in further soreness. Taking care in getting your baby on and off your breast, some simple first-aid treatment, and a little time and patience are all that is needed to solve the problem.

Many mothers find that sore nipples improved quickly once they learned how to attach their babies correctly to the breast.

When your baby is properly attached, his tongue will have come forward to take a good bit of the underside of the areola as well as the nipple in his mouth, his head will be tipped back a little so that his chin is touching the breast and his bottom lip will be turned out rather than sucked in. (*See Chapter Four on Positioning and Attachment.*) A baby who is attached properly should not hurt you as he feeds. If it does hurt, break the suction by placing a clean finger in the corner of your baby's mouth, and try again.

Remember, chest to chest, chin to breast.

BEFORE FEEDS

One way of reducing soreness is to feed your baby more often, as he will be less ravenous when he comes to the breast, and will suck more gently.

If you find that your nipples hurt most at the beginning of a feed, before your milk lets down, you may find it helpful to gently massage your breast and express some milk beforehand. This will get the milk flowing and soften the areola so that your nipple is easier for your baby to grasp. The milk will also lubricate the nipple allowing it to slide more easily in to your baby's mouth. If you find you are dreading each feed, try to relax and make yourself comfortable to help you cope with the pain. Your doctor may be able advise you about suitable pain relieving medication. Make sure you are comfortable and bring your baby to you breast. Do not move forward to put your nipple into your baby's mouth. Once your baby is attached properly and the milk starts flowing the pain usually disappears. If it doesn't, you may have a problem, such as thrush, which needs treatment. (*See Medical Problems.*)

WHILE FEEDING

Feed from the less sore side first. This will take the edge off your baby's hunger and make sure that your milk is flowing freely when your baby comes to suck from the sore nipple.

When you take your baby from your breast, check your nipple. You may notice a line of swelling and redness across the nipple, a white area or even a small stripe of blood under the skin. This is a sign that your nipple is stressed by your baby's sucking. Check that your baby is taking your breast correctly. Changing the baby's position for part of the feed may help. Try feeding lying down, on your side or use the twin position, holding your baby under your arm against your body on the side from which he is feeding, his head facing your nipple and his feet behind you. (A pillow beneath him will lift him up and reduce the strain on your arms and back.) You still need to check that your nipple and a good portion of the underside of your areola are well in and your baby's chin is close to your breast and his lips are turned out.

While your baby is small, it may help to support him with extra pillows. This helps keep the nipple in his mouth and prevents him pulling back and stretching it.

Babies have three different types of sucking. The first is the ravenous hungry suck which occurs before the let down. When the milk is let down from the back of the breast, the suck changes to a deep nutritive suck and swallow action. As the feed progresses, your baby may swallow less frequently and pause from time to time. Comfort sucking occurs towards the end of a feed and is faster and more gentle, with occasional swallowing. Most babies need to comfort suck and it helps to remove the very nourishing hindmilk from the breast. However, if your nipples are sore you may like to shorten his comfort sucking time by letting him satisfy this need by sucking on your finger. You could also try rocking, cuddling and patting him. If this does not work, another short feed half an hour or so later will probably settle him.

AFTER FEEDS

Authorities generally agree these days that the best ointment for sore nipples is not the one you get over the counter, but the one you get under the T-shirt. Research has shown that colostrum or breastmilk itself relieves sore nipples. Just express a few drops at the end of the feed and smear over the nipple. Allow it to dry by leaving your bra open for a few minutes. This hindmilk is high in fat and has many anti-infective and healing properties. Some mothers also find dry heat from a heater, or a hair dryer set on low, held at arm's length can help. Take care not to burn your sensitive nipple skin.

Specially designed breast shells (available from NMAA) can be worn inside your bra to allow air to circulate around your nipples while protecting them from clothing that may rub.

THINGS TO DO

- Feed your baby often – don't put off feeds
- Before feeds: Relax, make yourself comfortable
    - Massage your breasts gently
    - Apply warmth
    - Express some milk to soften areola and get the milk flowing
- During feeds: Offer the less sore side first
    - Make sure baby is properly positioned and attached
    - Try different feeding positions
    - Restrict comfort sucking while nipples are tender
- After feeds: Check your nipples for problems
    - Express a few drops of hindmilk and smear on your nipple
    - Let your nipples dry in the fresh air, or expose them briefly to warm, dry heat
    - Use breast shells to stop clothes rubbing and to allow air to circulate

THINGS TO AVOID

- Using anything on your nipples which may damage nipple skin (eg tinct benz, methylated spirits, soap, shampoo, harsh towels, toothbrushes etc.)
- Wearing poorly fitted bras and plastic-backed nursing pads
- Using breast pumps incorrectly or inappropriate breast pumps.
- Using nipple shields
- **SEE YOUR MEDICAL ADVISER IF SORENESS PERSISTS**

It may sound bizarre but some mothers have found that tea strainers inside their bras can also help the air circulate and stop clothes from rubbing.

Use plastic-rimmed strainers so the handles can be cut off, and which have a firm metal mesh which will not cave in when clothing presses on it.

Make sure your bra is large enough so the strainers rims do not press into the breast as this can cause problems such as blocked ducts.

NOT AGAIN! SORE NIPPLES WHILE FEEDING AN OLDER BABY

Sore nipples can occur at any time during breastfeeding. If this occurs when your baby is older, follow the advice above but also check that your baby is attached correctly.

Heavy babies held loosely on the lap can drag on the nipples. Acrobatic and inquisitive older babies may turn and twist the breast without letting go, stretching and twisting the nipple. Babies who sleep at the breast and hold onto the nipple sometimes bite to catch it if they feel it sliding out.

Teething babies can sometimes bite to relieve gum tenderness. Give your baby something hard and cold to chew on before a feed. Some mothers feel that changes to the acidity of their baby's saliva during teething can irritate their nipples.

Try rinsing the nipple area with a little bicarbonate of soda dissolved in water (about one teaspoon to one cup), bathing in salty water, or a swim in the sea.

Hormonal changes, caused by menstruation, ovulation or pregnancy can also cause nipple tenderness.

MEDICAL PROBLEMS

The sudden onset of sore nipples when feeding an older baby or prolonged nipple soreness at any stage should be checked with your doctor. If your nipples are red, itchy or sore to the touch, or if the skin on the nipple and areola looks scaly or flaky, it may be a sign that there is a medical problem.

THRUSH

Thrush on the nipples is always a possibility, especially if you have a cracked nipple or if your baby has thrush too. You may feel severe pain, throughout and between feeds, sometimes radiating through the breasts. Your medical adviser will recommend treatment to solve the problem and prevent cross-infection without harming your baby.

DERMATITIS

This can occur after an allergic reaction to a nipple ointment or to soaps, shampoos or detergent residues in clothing. Stop using the suspect substances. Try washing your bras with pure soap and rinse well. If soreness continues after a day or two, consult your doctor.

WHITE SPOT ON THE NIPPLES

Occasionally, a small white blister may appear on the nipple. Often the area around the spot is inflamed and red and painful, usually throughout the feed. This is a fairly rare condition which often resolves itself. Position your baby carefully to avoid pressure on the sore spot.

If it persists, apply warmth to the area and hand express to clear the spot. Sometimes the skin can be removed, but take care to avoid infection. It is best to check with your doctor.

CRACKED NIPPLES

If sore nipples are left untreated, they can develop fissures, or cracks. This can be caused or made worse by medical conditions such as thrush or dermatitis, or by using inappropriate breast pumps

Sometimes you can see the crack on the tip of the nipple or where the nipple joins the areola, but sometimes it is too fine. Feeding is usually very painful and may cause bleeding. Healing usually occurs quickly if the baby is properly attached.

You can continue to feed your baby. However some mothers find this too painful or that the crack worsens in the next 24-48 hours. If this occurs your baby may be taken off the breast temporarily. Express your milk by hand to rest the nipple until it begins to heal. Using a breast pump may only worsen the problem. You can feed your expressed milk to your baby by cup. Make sure you drain the breast well, as bacteria can enter through the crack and infection may follow. Smear some hindmilk on to your nipple after expressing.

After 24 hours, or when the crack has healed, gradually reintroduce the breast. Start each feed on the good side.

Check your sore nipple after each feed. Continue to express from that breast and use the milk to top up your baby until you are back to full feeding.

ENGORGEMENT

Engorgement, when your breasts are very full and hard, can occur with the early rush of milk, and usually subsides as the breasts become more efficient at producing milk. It is caused by increased amounts of blood and other fluids as well as milk.

You can avoid engorgement by feeding your baby frequently from birth (at least 6-8 times in 24 hours – 10-12 times is quite normal) including at night. If you do become engorged, feeding your baby is the best remedy.

However, if your breasts are so swollen that he cannot grasp the nipple, try gently massaging the breasts and expressing some milk before the feed to make them softer. Be gentle, as engorged breasts bruise easily. Express enough only to soften the breasts. If you express too much, your breasts will simply make more milk which will worsen the problem.

However, some mothers find that one complete expression with an electric breast pump solves the problem.

Cabbage is an age-old remedy for engorgement, but don't worry if you hate cabbage. You don't need to eat it, just wear it.

Thoroughly washed and dried crisp cold cabbage leaves, changed about two hourly or when they become limp, can help. Stop using them as soon as your engorgement is relieved or your supply will be reduced.

Engorgement can lead to one of the ducts that carry milk to your nipple becoming obstructed.

This can then lead to mastitis. If you find a tender lump or a swollen or reddened patch on your breasts or if you start to feel unwell, take action immediately.

TO RELIEVE ENGORGEMENT

- Feed your baby frequently from birth. Do not limit sucking time
- Take your bra off completely before breastfeeding
- Avoid giving your baby other fluids
- Wake your baby if your breasts become uncomfortable
- Use warmth to soften breasts before feeds
- Express a little milk before feeds to help your baby latch on
- Massage your breast gently while feeding
- If necessary, express after feeds
- Use cold packs after a feed to keep you feeling comfortable
- Use cold washed cabbage leaf compresses
- See your doctor about pain relief if you need it

BLOCKED DUCTS

If you have a lumpy or engorged area on your breasts, you feel sore or the area is red, you may have a blocked duct.

Sometimes a duct which carries milk from the glands in the breast becomes compressed or narrowed and blocked. Milk then banks up behind the blockage, a lump forms and your breast begins to feel sore.

Start treatment immediately as otherwise your breast may become inflamed and you may begin to feel feverish. See your medical adviser if this occurs or you cannot clear the blocked duct within 12 hours.

WHAT TO DO

- Start treatment immediately
- Rest as much as possible
- Feed frequently to keep the affected breast as empty as possible
- Apply warmth before a feed
- Feed from the affected breast first when your baby is sucking vigorously
- Gently but firmly massage the lump towards the nipple during and after feeds
- Change feeding positions to help empty the breasts
- Hand express if necessary
- Use cold packs after a feed to relieve pain

- **See your medical adviser if you cannot clear the lump in 12 hours**
- **See your doctor immediately if you begin to feel unwell**

MASTITIS

The term mastitis is often used loosely to describe a wide range of breast problems, including engorgement, blocked ducts, breast inflammation and infection.

Generally, it means breast inflammation. Fortunately, with prompt treatment, it can be cleared up quickly.

If you begin to get the shivers and aches, as if you are getting the flu, and your breast is painful or has an angry red patch on it, you may have mastitis, or 'milk fever', as it is sometimes known.

When there is a blockage in a milk duct, some of the milk banked up behind it can be forced into the surrounding breast tissue, which becomes inflamed.

At this stage, although you feel unwell, there may be no infection present. However, stagnant milk in the glands and duct behind the blockage and in the surrounding tissues can easily becomes infected.

Bacteria may enter your breast through sore or cracked nipples. Start treatment as soon as you suspect a breast problem and see your doctor quickly if the problem does not solve itself in a few hours. You may need antibiotics. Untreated mastitis can lead to a breast infection, although some mothers feel no early signs and seem to get a breast infection 'out of the blue'.

The infected breast looks similar to a breast inflamed due to a blocked milk duct. The breast is usually red and swollen, hot and painful. The skin may be shiny and there may be red streaks. You will feel ill. Learning to recognise the early signs of a breast problem will help you to solve it more quickly. Start treatment as soon as you feel a lump or sore spot.

Treatment for mastitis is similar to that of a blocked duct: draining the breast efficiently, applying warmth and gently massaging during feeding, relaxing, changing feeding positions, hand expressing when necessary, and cold compresses to reduce swollen tissues and relieve pain.

Rest is also extremely important. To achieve this, you will need the support of your partner, or a relative or friend for a few days. If you have a breast infection, you should stay in bed if possible. Take your baby, his nappies and other needs, and your own food and drink with you so that you don't have to keep getting up. If you have other children, you may find it easier to lie on the couch so they can play near you while you rest and breastfeed.

THINGS TO DO
- Follow suggestions for blocked duct
- Consult your doctor immediately
- Go to bed, if you can, with your baby
- Breastfeed frequently

PREVENTION
If you have had a breast or nipple problem, the most important thing to do after treatment is to work out why, so that you can prevent it happening again. Tiredness, stress, worry, tension, shock, poor nutrition, particularly diets high in sugar, poor drainage of the breast caused by hurried feeds or a baby who is not attached well or is ill, a breast obstruction caused by a tight bra, nightie or even the way you lie in bed can all contribute to breast and nipple problems.

Here are some tips for prevention:
- Avoid hurried or interrupted feeds
- Keep your breasts from getting overfull
- Avoid pressure on your breasts
- Look after yourself
- Feed frequently for well-drained breasts
- Ensure your baby is positioned correctly
- Watch out for soreness or lumps and start treatment immediately
- Join NMAA

BREAST SURGERY
If you have had breast surgery you will need to be particularly careful to check for blockages while breastfeeding. If you are worried about how your surgery will affect your ability to feed, talk to your

medical adviser. Your ability to feed your baby will depend on the size and location of the incision and any scar tissue. Many women who have had surgery are able to feed successfully. If one breast cannot be used, a baby can be fed successfully from the other.

BREAST ABSCESS
This is a serious and painful condition that requires immediate medical attention. It is usually the result of untreated breast infection. However, by following all of the above suggestions, it is usually easily avoided and rarely seen these days.

COLIC

> *... Peine in the belly is a common disease of chyldren ...The childe cannot rest, but cryeth and fretteth itself ... Moreover the noyse and rumblying in the guttes, hither and thider, declareth the child to be greved, with wynde in the belly, and colyke ...'*
> Thomas Pharie's 'Boke of Chyldren' – 1545.

We may have come a long way, baby, but not so far that doctors have been able to find a cause or a cure for colic in babies. The term 'colic' is used to describe a wide range of abdominal pains, but should not be confused with 'wind'. Although both include pain and crying, colic causes much more intense crying and in severe cases may require medical treatment.

The term 'wind' generally refers to the bubble of air brought up during or soon after a feed. The baby can be calmed by gentle burping and soothing. Unless the flow of milk is too fast, a baby can safely swallow and breath alternately about once a second. In most babies, a bubble of air precedes every swallow down the oesophagus from throat to stomach. During the feed, the accumulated air distends the stomach and the baby may stop feeding, squirm or show other signs of discomfort. Hold him upright and the excess bubble or wind will rise from the stomach.

To help your baby bring up wind, hold him comfortably against your shoulder so that the upper part of his tummy fits into it. Gently rub or pat his back. You may also lie your baby on his back, his body flat on your knees for about a minute, then raise him gently to sitting position, keeping his back straight. Another popular position for burping is to sit baby on your lap, supporting his chin with your hand, and with your other hand on his back.

Some babies will reward you with an adult size burp, others will never seem to bring up much wind. Everyone swallows air when they eat, and this is not always a problem.

In fact, in some cultures burping babies is seen as an eccentric and unnecessary practice.

Babies often make strange faces and seem to be considerably uncomfortable and surprised by their digestive systems. This is entirely normal and doesn't necessarily mean your baby is in pain or has colic. He is just getting used to these new sensations as his digestive system springs into action.

Colic is a painful condition in young babies, who for some reason, seem to have great difficulty in expelling swallowed air or intestinal gas. The trapped gas is thought to be in various locations in the bowel at different times.

You will know if your baby has colic because he will have muscular spasms, accompanied by a tightening of his abdomen. He may begin at first to squirm and fuss, desperately sucking at his hands and showing all the signs of hunger, yet when you put him to the breast, he will nurse eagerly for a few minutes, then stop and scream. He may settle for a short while, only to wake again screaming.

During these attacks, his face will probably redden, his brow will furrow and his pupils may dilate as if he is frightened. He doubles up and draws his legs to his abdomen, crying with sharp, shrill yells. Picking him up seems to offer little comfort. He stops crying only when the spasm ends.

Each attack may last four or five minutes, and although the baby may drift off to sleep he is soon woken with another attack. This may be repeated many times, causing distress and exhaustion for the whole family. Sometimes the symptoms are accompanied by loud tummy gurgles, frequent burping or breaking of wind. This may give him some relief, as does passing a bowel motion or sucking. The desire to suck sometimes leads mothers to misinterpret colic as hunger. No one knows what causes colic. One theory supported by recent research suggests that the baby who is switched to the second breast too early may take in large amounts of foremilk, and little of the fat-rich more satisfying hindmilk. This means his stomach has too little fat and more lactose than can be broken down. The excess lactose moves from the small bowel into the large bowel, and the bacteria in the large bowel ferment the lactose to produce gas which causes colic, wind and frequent loose and sometimes explosive bowel actions. The fat in breastmilk acts by slowing down the gastric emptying time and gut transit time. A baby who takes low fat feeds may still be hungry, demanding more feeds and so exacerbating the problem of colic, ie if your baby is getting too much, too fast.

Other research shows that some babies seem to react to the cow's milk products in their mothers' diets. When the mothers changed their diets, these babies no longer suffered crying. If you do this for a prolonged period, consult your doctor or dietitian to ensure you maintain a balanced diet.

Some mothers report that if they eat certain foods in excess, this upsets their babies. Some babies are particularly sensitive to caffeine, which is found in tea, coffee, chocolate and cola drinks.

HOW TO COPE
First of all be reassured that this will pass, and that most colicky babies seem to gain weight well. Rest assured too that your breastmilk is still the best food for your baby. Infant formula is not as easily digested as breastmilk and formula-fed babies suffer with colic too.

As your baby grows, his digestive system will mature, as will his ability to concentrate on other things going on around him. Meanwhile you can distract him gently from his pain by offering comfort.

Try to encourage quiet daytime feeds to encourage your baby to relax. Pick him up before he gets upset.

Walk with him, as this rocks him naturally. Crying colicky babies are seldom reported in countries where babies are carried around until they can walk. A NMAA medically-approved Meh Tai sling will allow you to carry your baby and keep your hands free. Being taken for a ride and watching you go about your business will also distract him from his pain. Wrapping him snugly in a warm, softly-textured material, such as cotton or light wool can help comfort him. Colicky babies prefer being upright and/or to have pressure on their tummies.

Some colicky babies cry in their sleep without waking. Wait to see if he drifts back to sleep before you pick him up, but don't let him get distressed. It is probably best to have him sleep near you so you can watch and assess whether he needs to be left alone or comforted.

A dummy can help a baby who gets his main comfort from sucking, but whose constant suckling is causing an overabundance of milk. However this will not work if your baby is hungry, and while it is a good substitute for the breast in this circumstance, it is not a good substitute for you. He will still need the comfort of your arms, even if he has a dummy. Sucking is good for colicky babies as it helps expel the gas by moving it towards the bowel.

If your let-down reflex is very strong, your baby may not be able to swallow fast enough and may choke. It may help if you express some milk before a feed, waiting until the flow has subsided before offering your baby the breast.

Posture feeding, or feeding so that the baby is sucking against gravity, is one way of stemming the flow. Some mothers say an early morning posture feed helps ease colic. You can do this by attaching the baby as usual while sitting then lying back on one pillow with your baby on your tummy. Remember to finish the feed sitting up, though, so that all the milk ducts are drained.

OTHER THINGS TO DO

- **Raise the bassinette at the bed head. This helps the bubble of wind to rise. Let baby kick on the floor for a while, or you can exercise his legs for him with a gentle bicycle action. A gentle massage also helps**
- **Warm the room, but avoid overheating**
- **A warm bath often helps baby relax at any time of the day. You don't need to use soap each time as this may dry your baby's skin**
- **A change of scenery, a stroll in the garden or around the block can relax you both**
- **Gentle movement in a bouncinette, pram or pusher. Roll the**

pram back and forth as you sit or stand. Providing a slight 'bump' such as folded towel to roll over sometimes help, or use a doorway where there is a change in floor coverings – the join will provide a gentle bump
- Noise and movement provided by a drive in the car
- Rhythmic, continuous noise, such as the drone of the washing machine or a vacuum cleaner can help lull your baby to sleep.
- Music – put on a record that has a soft melody or gentle beat, or sing to your baby

Be easy on yourself. This period will pass, but until it does, focus on your baby's needs and your own needs rather than those of the household. Enlist the help of others for meal preparation and shopping, fight fatigue by resting whenever you can, try to find some time to relax or do something you enjoy. Your local NMAA Group will also rally around, providing moral and physical support, when you become a Member.

Share your responsibilities. Your baby needs lots of Tender Loving Care at this time and so do you. Your partner should not be surprised to find both you and the baby in tears when he arrives home, the washing in the laundry, the dishes in the sink and dinner nowhere to be seen.

Understanding, teamwork and optimism is necessary now, not criticism. By comforting you both and cheerfully cleaning up and cooking dinner or getting take away food, he will help restore order, sanity and your feeling that you can cope with another day of colic.

Try not to feel guilty if the beds are unmade and toys clutter the floor. Having a new baby, especially a colicky baby, means that your responsibilities and expectations may have to change.

Leaving your baby for a short while with a trusted person may give you some personal relief.

If colic continues, have your baby checked regularly by your doctor to ensure that he is growing well. Most colicky babies thrive and the colic passes. Meanwhile, focus on soothing your baby and getting as much support and encouragement for yourself as possible.

Photograph by Dianne Griffiths

GASTRIC REFLUX

Nearly all babies bring up a little milk now and again. This 'posetting' or regurgitating, is often accompanied by a burp, and is the baby's way of coping with overflow. Apart from the fact that it usually occurs on somebody's shoulder just after they have changed into something clean or special, it poses no problem. Although it may look as if your baby has just thrown up his dinner, this is not vomiting.

However, there are some babies that seem to have a fountain inside. What goes down, does not stay down for long and inevitably seems to come up. If your baby does this, you should take him to a doctor to check whether he is simply regurgitating, has gastric reflux or another condition known as pyloric stenosis.

Some babies are 'happy chuckers' while others will be quite distressed. Gastric reflux, also known as gastro-oesophageal reflux, is sometimes confused with colic as some babies suffer heartburn as the stomach acids rise in the lower part of the oesophagus. Not all babies with gastric reflux vomit, some arch their backs to cope with the pain of heartburn, but vomiting is the most common symptom.

Sometimes the milk oozes up, while at other times it seems to be projected with the force of a hose. The baby may vomit milk long after the end of a feed, after being asleep for some time.

Babies with gastric reflux may also be poor sleepers, waking easily and frequently, sometimes screaming after being laid down. Crying and irritability, especially during feeding or after a feed is another symptom, as are feeding difficulties, either frequent feeding or breast refusal, snuffles, a dry cough and hiccoughs.

Apart from the distress and mess this can cause, in occasional babies the amount of milk lost can cause weight loss and failure to thrive. In severe cases, an operation is sometimes performed, but mostly gastric reflux is mild and disappears as the baby matures, settling down by six months of age. By the age of 12-18 months, most babies show no symptoms.

If your baby is diagnosed with gastric reflux it is better for both of you if you continue to breastfeed. Babies fed on infant formula risk the possibility of allergy if they inhale traces of cow's milk properties after vomiting. It is also easier to treat this condition if you are breastfeeding as these babies need smaller, more frequent feeds.

A number of different medications can be prescribed. These can be given to a breastfed baby. Consult your doctor for a proper diagnosis before giving your baby any medicine.

Some practical suggestions.

- Settle your baby before feeding. Irritable babies are more likely to vomit.
- Keep him upright while awake by using a baby sling as this helps keep the gastric contents down.
- Prop his bed at a 30 degree angle.
- Prop him on pillows to keep him relatively upright while you change his nappy. Avoid pressure on the stomach with tight nappies or pants. Short periods in a reclining baby chair may help.
- Ask for support from family and friends and health professionals if necessary. The constant cleaning up and washing, accompanied by the distress of your baby, frequent night waking, worry about his weight gains and the need to carry him upright to help him keep his feeds down, will take its toll on both your and your partner.

LACTOSE INTOLERANCE

This is a condition where the lactose in your milk – the main carbohydrate component in all mammals' milk – cannot be digested by your baby. The main symptoms are watery, acidic diarrhoea, wind, a distended abdomen and failure to thrive.

While, rarely, some babies are born not being able to digest lactose, most cases of lactose intolerance follow a bout of gastroenteritis, especially the rota virus infection. The virus sometimes damages the lining of the small intestine so it is unable to produce enough of the enzyme lactase, which is necessary to break down the lactose.

Lactose intolerance should be medically diagnosed and treated. If your baby is diagnosed with this condition, you may have to stop breastfeeding at least temporarily. Most paediatricians recommend that the baby be fed a lactose-free formula instead.

Sometimes, the doctor may recommend that the lactose-free formula be given for a short time and then breastfeeding resumed, or that the baby have a combination of breastmilk and lactose-free formula. It is important to maintain your supply by regular expressing (*See Chapter 10.*) for when you are able to continue breastfeeding your baby.

If your baby must continue with the lactose-free formula, you may decide to wean. However, in most cases lactose intolerance is temporary and will last for less than a week, when breastfeeding can be reintroduced.

Many breastfed babies produce multiple, loose bowel motions and this should not be confused with lactose intolerance. A baby who is switched from one breast to the other without the chance to drain the first breast may sometimes show symptoms similar to lactose intolerance. Allowing the baby to drain the breast usually overcomes this.

ALLERGIES

Food allergies have received a lot of media attention in the past few decades and studies quoted in the media and in professional papers often result in conflicting and confusing conclusions.

Parents who suffer from allergic conditions themselves, such as asthma, eczema or milk allergy may fear they will pass the condition on. This is both true and false. Although the tendency to allergies is inherited, a mother cannot actually transmit her allergy directly. However, many studies show that exclusive breastfeeding in the first few months, particularly babies at risk, helps decrease or delay the risk of allergic symptoms.

Contrary to popular belief, soya-based or goat's milk baby formulas do not necessarily protect against allergies. Soya protein is as foreign as cow's milk protein and can also cause an antibody response.

Some babies are sensitive to particular foods, even through their mothers' milk. Sensitisation can occur both before and after birth as antigens can cross the placenta. Before the age of four months, your baby's gut is immature, allowing foreign proteins to transfer into the body more easily. This can increase the risk of sensitisation. That is why giving babies formula complements soon after birth is thought to predispose those at risk to cow's milk allergy, even if they are later fully breastfed.

If you suffer from allergies, it is best if all foods which cause a reaction are avoided during pregnancy and breastfeeding. However, the popular concept of babies being unsettled because of a reaction to something the mother ate recently is less common than most people think. Weaning usually makes the baby's condition worse.

If you need to prepare special food for your baby this can cause extra work and cost. Seek a referral to a specialist who can help you get the right advice etc.

Sometimes the support of others who are going through the same thing is the most vital. Allergy Association of Australia, PO Box 298 Ringwood, Victoria, 3134. Phone: (03) 9888 1382.

BREAST REFUSAL

All the books tell you that babies love breastfeeding, that they instinctively root for the breast and seek the nipple. So what if your baby refuses to suck and in fact seems to fight the breast every time you offer it?

If your baby refuses to suck at the breast, you will naturally feel very distressed. You may already be feeling apprehensive, and perhaps not very confident, so if your baby screams and turns away when you offer him your breast, you may misinterpret his reaction and feel that he is rejecting you as a mother, or that he doesn't want you, need you or even like you.

In this situation, you may feel that you have no alternative other than to wean. Fortunately, this is not so. Breast refusal is usually a temporary problem and there are ways in which you and your baby can be helped through this problem so that you can breastfeed successfully.

A baby may refuse the breast at some or all feedings, at any age. Reasons for this vary with his stage of development.

He may suck for a few minutes, then break away with signs of distress and may refuse to continue. He may refuse to even begin sucking, although he is obviously hungry.

Sometimes, your baby may not actually refuse to feed, but will be very fussy and difficult to feed.

He may seem unwilling to start sucking or take a long time to get going. Once started he may feed well, yet seem to receive little satisfaction.

He may suck for a short while, then break away, finishing after lots of stops and starts. He may be easily distracted and restless during the feed, perhaps pushing you away with his feet or fists. When he stops he may still seem restless and fidgety.

A baby like this needs calm and patient handling. This can be difficult for you as it is easy for you to feel stressed by his behaviour. However, the best way of overcoming these problems is to concentrate on remaining calm yourself.

If you found your antenatal breathing exercises worked for you, you may like to try them in this situation. You could also try rocking your baby gently, or carrying him around either in your arms or in a Meh Tai baby sling.

By remaining relaxed you will help your milk flow readily, helping your baby receive milk as soon as he latches on.

If you cannot remain calm about feeding, try something else, such as a game or a walk to distract him, or ask your partner or someone else to take over while you have a break.

It may be tempting to try to attach your baby while he is crying, as his mouth will be wide open. This is best avoided as while he is crying his tongue will be drawn back in his mouth and if he is attached to the breast with it in this position, he may learn to put it in the wrong place. Try to calm him first then get him to gape properly with his tongue forward before attaching.

NEWBORN BABY REFUSING

Sometimes a baby refuses to feed because he is tired, particularly after birth. He may like to just nuzzle and lick. Forcing him to the breast before he is ready will upset him and make it appear as if he is rejecting your breast and you. Encourage him by expressing a little colostrum into his mouth. If he still refuses, don't worry. He will show more interest when he is more awake.

Clothing around his neck and chin can also interfere with his natural 'rooting' reflex. When you touch his cheek, your newborn baby will automatically turn and lift his head towards the side that your nipple or finger touches. Holding his head or grabbing both cheeks will confuse him and may cause him to fuss, shake his head or appear to refuse the breast. A baby who is uncomfortable will not feed contentedly. If his nose is covered by his top lip or the breast, he will not be able to breathe. If your breast is very full, lift it up slightly with your free hand. If your breast is impairing his breathing, wrap him round your tummy more. Don't press on your breast with your finger to create an air passage.

Breast refusal can occur if the baby is having difficulty attaching. This sometimes happens after the milk comes in and your breasts are very full. Try to express a little milk before you feed so that the areola is soft enough for your baby to latch onto.

Your baby may also have difficulty attaching if your nipples are flat or inverted. (*See Chapter 3.*) Ideally, it is best for your baby to learn to breastfeed before your milk comes in and your breasts become very full, as the nipples may be difficult to draw out when the breast is full. However, if this occurs, soften the breast by hand expressing or using a breast pump, helping to draw the nipple out before feeding.

Breast 'rejection' may also occur if your baby is having difficulty coordinating sucking, swallowing and breathing. Time and patience will overcome this. If rejection persists and he appears to be losing 'weight' try not to be too alarmed. All babies lose weight after the birth so a weight loss combined with breast refusal will not put your

Photograph by Dianne Griffiths.

baby at risk if it is temporary. If he is angry and upset at being offered your breast, try to calm him by doing something else before offering it again.

BREAST REFUSAL IN A BABY AGED THREE TO SIX MONTHS
Your baby may also fight the breast if he is overtired or over stimulated after a lot of handling, as he may be too agitated or tense to feed. Try a more settled daily routine. Between feeds, cuddle him against your bare breast without offering it to him, to help him associate breast contact with comfort as well as food.

Your older baby may refuse the breast if he has had bottles or cups of infant formula, boiled water and fruit juice, as his appetite will be diminished, and your supply will drop. Your baby may also prefer the different sucking action of the bottle. Try extra breastfeeds rather than bottle-feeds.

Babies sometimes also refuse one breast. If your baby has fallen asleep after one breast, he has probably had enough. Feed from the second breast first next time to avoid becoming overfull or lopsided. Many babies prefer one breast rather than the other. You may need extra patience to encourage him to take the least-preferred breast.

A baby who has a sore leg or arm after immunisation may suddenly refuse to feed on one side because he is lying on a sore spot. Try changing sides. A baby with an ear infection may also refuse the breast as lying down exacerbates the pain. A baby with a blocked nose may find it difficult to breathe and feed and so may refuse. Also, a baby with gastric reflux may be fussy when laid down flat to feed. Ask your doctor to check your baby.

Teething discomfort can also cause your baby to refuse to feed, although this may occur weeks before any gum or tooth eruption. Try rubbing ice on his gums before a feed.

Between the age of four and six months, babies are very easily distracted. Feeding in a quiet room may help.

Finally, perhaps your baby is just not hungry? Feeding patterns do change. A ravenous feeder may start to be more interested in his surroundings than your breast. Most babies have longer breaks between feeds as they grow older.

BREAST REFUSAL IN OLDER BABIES

If there is no apparent reason for baby refusing to breastfeed, and you have had your breasts checked for any medical problems, and your baby is becoming more independent, he may want to wean.

This may come as a shock as you may have planned to wean him slowly later. Your may feel very disappointed and take a while to accept that your baby no longer wants to breastfeed.

This does not mean that your baby no longer wants you. He will still want and need those special moments that you enjoyed together while breastfeeding, including lots of cuddles and reassurance when he is tired, sleepy or sick.

If your baby weans suddenly you will need to express some milk occasionally to ensure that your breasts do not become overfull and uncomfortable. (*See Chapter 11 on Weaning.*)

SOME SUGGESTIONS
- Check that baby is comfortable and correctly positioned. He will need to be unwrapped, lying on his side
- Make sure that you are comfortable and relaxed yourself. Before feeding, practise the relaxation techniques you may have learned at antenatal classes

- Offer the breast as soon as your baby begins to wake. He will usually respond better if he is not upset or crying. Change his nappy after the feed or before the second breast
- If necessary, help your baby take the breast into his mouth. If you have large nipples, try to shape the breast between your thumb and fingers so that it is easier for your baby to grasp. If your nipples are very small, try to pull them out gently just before your offer the breast
- Express your milk until it begins to flow easily so that your baby will get something as soon as he starts to suck.
- Express a little milk on the nipple to encourage your baby to begin sucking.

OTHER REASONS FOR BREAST REFUSAL

- **Gushing flow** which makes your baby gag and become frightened. Express a little before the feed until the flow settles down. If your baby pulls away during a feed because of fast flow, allow the flow to subside before starting again.
- **Low milk supply.** Your baby may be frustrated if his appetite has increased and your supply has not adjusted. If he has not had at least six to eight pale thoroughly wet cloth nappies in 24 hours, and no other fluids or foods have been given, he may be hungry.
- **Fast flow settles down.** If your baby has been used to milk just pouring into his mouth, he may not have learned to milk the breast efficiently, so doesn't take enough milk, and may become fussy and irritable if your supply goes down.
- **Slow let-down.** If your let-down reflex takes a few minutes to get going,(and this may happen if your supply is diminished), your baby may be sucking without reward and may become angry and frustrated. Try to trigger the let-down before a feed by gentle massage or expressing, so that baby is rewarded as soon as he comes to the breast.
- **Are you stressed or overtired?** This can affect your let-down, frustrating your baby. Relaxation is the key here.

Moving house, holidays, visitors, your partner's work stress, can all affect your breastfeeding relationship. Consciously trying to relax with music and a special routine, such as a comfortable chair, a drink for you etc. will help trigger your let-down.

- **Last night's take-away?** A sudden change in diet can affect the taste of your milk and the smell of your body, causing your baby to refuse to suck.
- **You smell different.** Even a new perfume, spray deodorants that have strayed to your nipple, strong detergents that affect the smell of your bra, chlorine from a pool, or salt from the ocean can all cause baby to refuse. A quick shower will usually solve this problem.
- **Are you menstruating or ovulating?** Hormone changes can affect the taste of your milk. For some women this is an early warning that their period is due. Patience and gentle handling for you both are the best answers to this. Pregnancy can also sometimes cause a drop in the milk supply or a change in the taste.
- **Oral contraceptives.** Some of these have a marked affect on milk supply. Make sure your doctor is aware that you are breastfeeding before an oral contraceptive is prescribed. Even some oral contraceptives which are routinely used in breastfeeding women, affect the baby's feeding behaviour. If you continue with this method of contraception, you may need to build up your supply, or you may need to consider an alternative method of contraception. (*See Chapter 7.*)

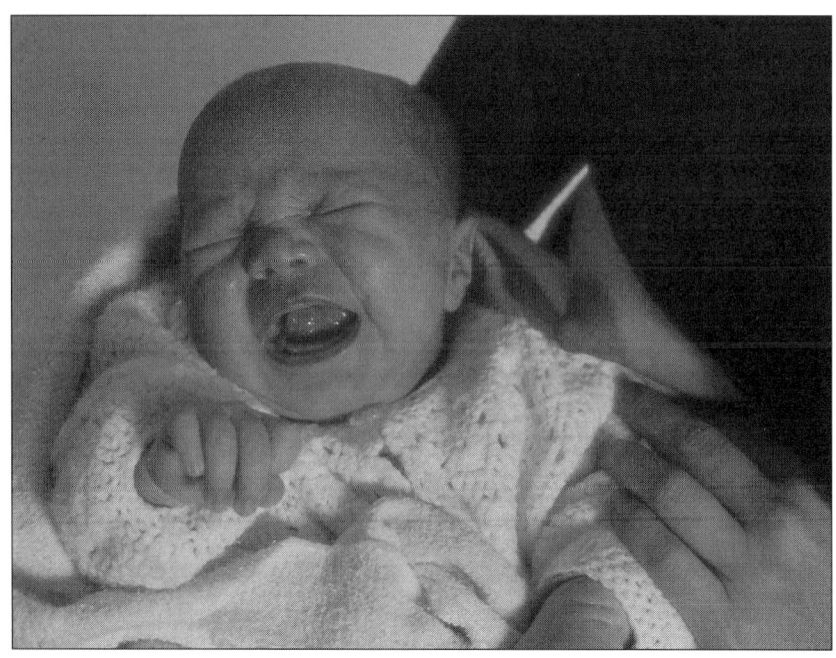

Photograph by Prue Carr.

SUCKING PROBLEMS

In most babies, the sucking reflex is instinctive. However, a small proportion may need help to learn to suck effectively. This is more common in premature babies born before 34 weeks gestation when the suck/swallow instinct is not well-developed.

Sucking problems can cause crying, fussiness, slow weight gains and a failure to thrive in the baby, and nipple problems and low milk supply in the mother.

In most cases, positioning the baby properly at the breast will solve the problem. A baby who sucks his thumb while in the womb, or who is ill, premature or has mouth problems may be at risk of developing sucking problems.

Occasionally, babies have sucking problems because of a poor rooting reflex, or because they have poor mouth closure (mouth breathers), are affected by maternal medication given to the mother during labour or were subject to birth trauma.

One cause of poor sucking is 'tongue tie' where the fold of skin that anchors the tongue to the mouth is so long that the tongue is not free or mobile. Babies' tongues are anchored by the central thin tissue (frenulum) for a much longer proportion than the tongues of adults, and this does not impede sucking or speech development, as long as the baby can extend his tongue over his lower gumline. By the end of the first year, most babies' tongues have grown so that they are fully mobile. True tongue tie where this does not occur is quite rare and tends to run in families.

In some cases, where sucking problems persist and this is related to tongue problems, a snip to the frenulum can solve the problem.

In a few cases, 'suck training' may be done by a medical adviser using a finger.

However, most cases of poor sucking are caused by giving bottle-feeds, separating mother and baby at birth so that breastfeeding establishment is delayed, the use of dummies and medication that interferes with the baby's ability to suck when he first comes to the breast after birth, or the inappropriate use of nipple shields. Patience and attention to correct positioning and attachment will usually overcome these problems.

GOOD AND BAD BABIES

There is little difference between a 'good' baby and a doll because good babies are often required to be as undemanding as dolls. Your baby may look as pretty and perfect as a doll, but if he is healthy and normal, he will not behave like one.

In Western culture, much of our concepts of how babies behave is based on the text-book behaviour of a bottle-fed babies, whose digestive systems took longer to cope with the larger, tougher curds formed by cow's milk and which stayed in the stomach longer. The bottle-fed baby therefore slept longer between feeds and so appeared less demanding.

In the past 100 years, there has been a sharp rise in the number of experts and books directed at educating mothers about the care of their children. This rise occurred at the same time as the rise of the medical profession and many scientific 'breakthroughs' and improvements in communications which made the common person much more aware of and impressed by the work of 'experts'.

Once a natural function, parenting soon became a series of problems that experts (usually men) were required to solve. With the increasing mobility brought by the motor car and with the growth of more affordable outer-urban housing estates, young people became increasingly isolated from the support of extended family.

This isolation, and the increasing public validity and reverence given to science, combined with women's lack of equality and status, generally led mothers to doubt their own instincts, bodies and knowledge, and that of their foremothers.

Much of what had been considered essential knowledge about maternal and child welfare began to be dismissed as 'old wives tales'. This, and the power of radio, and later television, to promote images of 'ideal' babies, supposedly thriving on the artificial milks and rigid routines of the day and who always appeared to be out of the way, meant a decline in breastfeeding and maternal confidence.

The more constant needs of a breastfed baby, which are vital in ensuring the breast is stimulated in the early days to create a good supply of milk, were seen as 'bad' and a mother who eagerly met these demands as 'soft' and spoiling.

Mothers who were breastfeeding and whose babies were feeding one-two hourly rather than four-hourly were therefore encouraged to 'put the baby on the bottle' to make it conform to society's notion of how a good baby should behave.

The wide acceptance of artificial feeding, and medical intervention in birth (appropriate for some, but not all), has diminished women's knowledge, understanding and confidence in breastfeeding.

The separation of mothers and babies at birth and at home, with the promotion of separate rooms for young babies, also impeded successful breastfeeding, which depends on frequent stimulation to maintain supply.

The emancipation of women and their economic need to seek paid work outside the home and the lack of support for nursing breaks at work, also encouraged bottle-feeding.

This is not an argument for women to stay home. In our society, women work outside the home for both economic, social and psychological reasons. Separating a mother from her mental and social stimulation so that she may not be separated from her baby, only swaps one problem for another.

What this book argues is that a woman who chooses to breastfeed should be supported in that choice, whether she works in the home or outside it, or both. Rather than label babies or mothers 'good' or 'bad' and try to make them both conform to some impossible ideal, we should be examining how both paid work and family life can be adapted to suit the real needs of real people. It may help you to think about this next time someone asks if your baby is a 'good' baby.

CHAPTER NINE

Breastfeeding and paid work

- **When to return**
- **Negotiating with your employer**
- **Expressing and storing at work**
- **Child care options**
- **Choosing a caregiver**
- **Staying at home**

YOU CAN CONTINUE

There is no reason why you cannot continue to breastfeed your baby when you return to paid work, with the right knowledge, equipment and support.

Breastfeeding your baby will not only be best for him, but best for your employer too, as studies have shown that breastfed babies are healthier. Babies who are breastfed are one third less likely to be hospitalised in the first two years. This means fewer doctor's visits and less time off work for you. It is cheaper for you, too, especially if you are having to return to work for financial reasons.

Breastfeeding will also contribute to your health by reducing the risk of breast and ovarian cancer and, for some women, by increasing the space between pregnancies.

Breastfeeding your baby will also help you feel closer and less anxious about separating from him. If you can breastfeed during your work day by either visiting your baby at a creche on site or nearby or by having someone bring him to you, this will allow you to maintain contact with him during your work day.

It will also give you an irreplaceable identity, letting him know that while he may have a loving caregiver, his mother has a special nurturing role.

Alternatively, you may leave expressed breastmilk for your baby's caregiver to feed to him during your absence.

Today, many more employers in Australia and overseas are implementing family-friendly work policies that help ease the transition from home to work. These policies are not just a public relations exercise to give the company a good image. This makes sound economic sense.

Many women are choosing to have their families later in life and these women may have spent many years establishing themselves in their work or profession. Whether you are a salesperson, a tradesperson, or a professional, your employer has probably invested quite a lot of time and money into training you, formally or informally, over the years.

One of the key findings in 'The Family Friendly Front – A Review of Australian and International Work and Family Research', by Kate Spearritt and Don Edgar, of the Newlinks Workplace Project at Monash University in Melbourne, was that the cost of losing a valued employee and training another was far greater than making a few concessions to help parents juggle work and family life.

In 1990, Australia signed an agreement to support the International Labor Organisation Convention on Workers with Family Responsibilities. All of these changes mean that family-friendly workplaces are increasingly seen as a right, not a privilege.

With this knowledge, you should approach your employer with the confidence that what you are seeking is not only to your advantage, but to the company's.

However, there is no Australian breastfeeding policy for women wanting to return to work. This means that the issue of breastfeeding and work is largely still left up to individuals to negotiate.

Few informed people would argue about the benefits of a mother in paid work still continuing to breastfeed, however, it is important to be realistic about the amount of understanding and empathy you are likely to receive.

Some Australian companies, such as Esso, Australia Post and Alcoa, are exemplary, making policies that actively support breastfeeding and working. Many others are yet to be convinced.

Whatever your employer's stance, good communication is the key to good relationships, whether at home or work, and it is this that will ensure that both you and your employer understand each other.

Whether you are fortunate enough to be employed by a family-friendly workplace or not, it is vital that you talk to your employer about your needs and desires, well before you go on maternity leave. This will help you both plan for the future.

You will also feel more confident if you can discuss these issues face to face and without the demands of a newborn baby to distract you.

You may be surprised at what can happen with the right approach. A company which has had no set family-friendly policies may respond to requests for support if approached in a positive manner and if it is made clear that the benefits are mutual.

Find out your entitlements, either through the company's Human Resources Department (otherwise known as personnel or staff) or through your union.

Find out, too, whether the company is providing any other benefits, not necessarily required by law, but which may have evolved through dealings with other employees having babies.

For example, a company may not have a written policy on working from home, but may have come to some agreement with another employee whose job allows such flexibility.

Think about how your paid job and your unpaid job of caring for your family may be better integrated to allow you to do both well, such as part-time work, or working from home for a while.

While you may have more interruptions to your work day when you are breastfeeding and working at home, you will be able to still provide optimum nutrition for your baby while your caregiver attends to his other needs, and you will cut travel time and expense.

Talk to other employees with children about their experience of returning to work and breastfeeding. Company policies may change as the needs of the workers change. A company which suddenly finds a large group of women seeking maternity leave may decide to set up a special room for nursing mothers to express and store their milk if the employees point out that this will encourage mothers to return to work on schedule and will help making nursing breaks more efficient and relaxed.

If there is resistance to this, you could suggest an in-service seminar for both employees and executives with a NMAA Counsellor as a guest speaker.

Perhaps you could also include a representative from another company which has implemented breastfeeding friendly policies.

With the benefits properly explained, what company could resist helping to create happier mothers and workers and to ensure a healthier and smarter workforce in the future?

Photograph courtesy of Publications Unit

WORKPLACE REQUIREMENTS FOR EXPRESSING AND STORING BREASTMILK

- A private room (not the toilet area) with a comfortable chair.
- A fridge to store expressed breastmilk (EBM).
- A place to store your manual breast pump, or an electric breast pump and other equipment.

- Facilities to wash hands and wash or disinfect equipment.
- Time allowed for expression of milk during lunch break or other breaks if necessary. If extra time other than normal entitlements is needed, an agreement could be made that this time be made up in other ways.

Consider all options, be creative, persistent and positive.

Consider also buying or renting an electric breast pump to make expressing at work quicker.

Be aware that expressing may seem difficult at first, but most mothers in paid work say the benefits are worth the initial effort.

WHEN TO RETURN

Nobody knows how they are going to feel after the birth of a child, particularly a first child. Much depends on the type of birth you have, your age, the physical and emotional support you have, and of course, your own character and personality and that of your baby.

Many women, sadly, are forced back to paid work early through eco-

> 'We ask them to give us a plan before they leave. In most cases people come back when they say they will part-time, but extend out full-time.
>
> 'I think its really important to set goals around maternity leave. No one would hold you to it. It is important to think about it before you have the baby. I sit them down and talk to them: they can work from home, they can reduce hours. In our experience people change things and that's fine. Talking about it first helps get your head around what options are . When you've been at home and then you've got to come back and negotiate that sort of arrangement its much harder. It's easier to have a plan first than come back. If you do it later, your confidence and self esteem is not as great. To negotiate this stuff you have to be feeling good about yourself and that you're valuable and after having a baby you sometimes question that.' – Fiona Kautrill, Esso EEO officer.

nomic circumstances rather than choice. If you are lucky enough to have a choice, it is wiser not to make any firm commitments until your baby arrives.

Of course, you must still discuss your intentions with your employer, whose needs must also be respected. But try to make an arrangement that can be flexible.

If you are entitled to take 12 months leave, ask your employer if you can take the full entitlement with the option of returning to work earlier, should you need or want to.

Everyone is different. Some women who, during pregnancy, could not imagine staying home with a small child, find that the rewards of their paid work are not as enticing as the rewards of mothering full-time, despite the economic disadvantage.

Others who may have intended taking the full 12 months, find themselves climbing the walls after three months and aching for the intellectual and social stimulation of paid work.

Others who believed that they were financially secure enough to take the full 12 months may suddenly find economic circumstances changed at home. They may then be forced to renegotiate their leave at a time when they are feeling particularly vulnerable.

While some women return as soon as six weeks after the birth, most women choose not to return before the baby is three months old. Some prefer to come back before their 12 months leave expires believing it is easier to settle a younger baby into child-care.

The first year of a child's life is exhausting both physically and emotionally for his mother. It can be very difficult to juggle this and the demands of paid work, as many women find. However, there are others who thrive on this combination.

There are others too, that enjoy mothering full-time and thrive on the network of supports, such as Nursing Mothers' and the playgroups, (contact the Association in your state), that are part of home and community life. There are also those who like to keep a foot in each door, by combining part-time paid work with the work of caring for children and the home.

Much depends on the type of work you do and the support you receive at work and at home. Much also depends on the type of person you are and the type of baby you have.

> '*I set this goal where I wanted to breastfeed. Part of it was coming back to work. I wanted to give my babies the best food, which was breastmilk, and the immunity, because I new they'd be in creche. I was determined.*' – Lisa, mother of two children.

Whatever you decide, the challenge of maintaining your supply of breastmilk while you try to juggle the conflicting needs of your paid work and family should not be underestimated.

If you do intend to breastfeed when you return to paid work, it is important that you do not return to paid work until breastfeeding has been fully established.

This may sometimes take three months. Maureen Minchin, writing in ALCA News Vol 5. No 1, April 1994, of the campaign by the ACTU for three months paid maternity leave said: *'Three months is simply too short a time for both mother and baby to benefit from maternity leave. In the postpartum period, it takes time for a woman to adjust to the reality of motherhood and the first three months are not always easy.*

'Colic, sleepless nights, tiredness, sore breasts or nipples, the emotional roller-coaster these involve: often the reality that precedes what has been described as 'the reward period' when the baby is between three and six months, and much more settled and responsive and enjoyable. By three months, breastfeeding has become familiar and easy, even pleasurable for many women.'

Ms Minchin said published studies already indicated that six months unpaid maternity leave after birth resulted in better breast-feeding rates than 45 days paid leave.

Having a baby is a profound life-changing experience that must be respected as such. It is not the same as taking long-service leave, or study leave. However, it is difficult for women to acknowledge the monumental effect the birth of a child can have on them when this brief need to nurture and be nurtured has been turned against them throughout post-industrial history to exclude them from so many fundamental rights, such as the right to paid work.

It is also difficult to acknowledge this when maintaining the right to work means competing with others who do not need this 'time out'.

Australia has ratified the United Nations International Labor

Organisation Convention 156 upholding the right to parental leave, but women need reassurance that taking up one right will not cost them another.

Many women worry that if they take up the right to maternity leave, it could cost them promotion or even their job. While the law offers some protection against discrimination, exercising these legal rights is also stressful and often costly.

Some women also worry about whether they will get bored or go stale if they choose to stay at home for the full leave period.

Whatever your decision, try to make a flexible arrangement before your baby arrives and keep the lines of communication between yourself and your employer and colleagues open during your maternity leave. This will make it easier should you need or want to renegotiate your leave and it will also keep you abreast of work news and changes and keep your employer aware of your intentions to return to work and your continued interest in your job.

Good planning will play a big part in maintaining your milk supply and your job. Talk to your employer, husband, caregiver and any one else whose support you can enlist before you return to work.

Learn as much as you can about expressing and storing breastmilk. (*See Chapter 10.*) It is important to learn to express by hand comfortably, but you may also like to invest in a breast pump to help you express more quickly and conveniently, or to hire an electric one from NMAA or a pharmacist or hospital.

Express and freeze as much milk as possible before you return to work so that you will have your own personal milk bank and will not feel as pressured to keep up with your baby's demands.

> '*I started working at home two days a week when she was six weeks old, doing 16 hours over the week whenever I chose to. I could have (taken longer leave) but it didn't suit me. I had a couple of projects I wanted to keep going and the last time, with my first baby, after three months I was ready to come back. If you're going to stay home in the long-term you get involved in other things. That was my choice, this was my social network.*' – Karen, bank officer, and mother of two

This is important in case of work or home crises, too.

In preparing to breastfeed and do paid work, consider your own situation, your coping abilities, the support you can count on, and what you can realistically expect of yourself and others before you take the plunge. Be prepared, too, to change your plans if things don't work out as you planned. If you decide to give up paid work, or to give up breastfeeding, this should not be seen as failure but just a recognition that you as a person, have limits, and that these limits have been reached.

YOUR BABY AND GOING BACK

Your return to work will also be influenced by the age and stage of your baby. Returning to work before your baby is six weeks old is not easy. You may find you need this long to completely recover from the birth. New babies need feeding very frequently and not necessarily at regular intervals. It can take six weeks or more for breastfeeding to become well-established. Some lactation experts believe three months or even six months is more realistic.

At this stage, if you are committed to breastfeeding your baby, the only work arrangements likely to be compatible are those where you can work from home or take your baby to work. Your supply depends on the stimulation of your baby's sucking, so being there is important in the early days.

If you do need to return to work very soon after the birth, a major aid to success is feeding or expressing frequently during the day. If you can do this at least six to eight times a day, your are more likely to establish and maintain your supply. While this may be tiring at first, it will be worthwhile and easier in the long run if you can establish a good supply and continue to breastfeed.

This arrangement might be more workable than you expect. Without you around constantly reminding him of his dinner, your baby's feeds will tend to be more regular and less frequent. His caregiver can keep him entertained and make sure that any unhappiness is really due to hunger.

If the baby is unsettled because he misses the extra comfort of sucking, you may consider using a dummy at unsettled times.

> 'From my experience here, the first week of coming back is really hard, it doesn't matter whether you've had 12 months or not.' – Fiona Kautrill, ESSO EEO, who returned full-time at three months and continued breastfeeding, and whose husband took three months long service leave to care for their baby when Fiona returned to paid work.

If you are only at work for few hours, your baby may manage on only one feed, with some frozen expressed breastmilk as a backup, or some cooled, boiled water occasionally.

If you work a full eight hours, your baby will need at least two feeds in this time. This will probably mean juggling your baby's own natural schedule to fit in with your work schedule.

For example, if he usually feeds at around 5.30am and 8.30am, and you need to leave at 8am for work, offer him his feed at 7.30am instead.

EXPRESSING YOUR MILK AT WORK

If you cannot manage to feed your baby during the day yourself, you can still express your milk during your breaks and providing that it is stored properly in disinfected containers at work, you can take it home with you to freeze so that your caregiver can give it to your baby while you are at work.

You may also find expressing a little at night to freeze for later will help maintain your supply.

You will probably find that you need to express your milk for your own physical comfort as well as to provide milk for your baby and to maintain your supply.

It is important to learn to express as soon as possible. This will give you a chance to try both hand expressing and expressing with a breast pump.

Learning to use a breast pump and learning how to trigger the let-down reflex is helpful at this stage. Hand expressing is a knack and with practice most mothers find it very efficient and convenient as less equipment is needed.

See chapter on Expressing and Storing Breastmilk.

TRIGGERING THE LET-DOWN REFLEX

Rushing out during your work break to express milk for your baby while thinking about the work piling up on your desk, or whether your supervisor will be anxious for your return, is not the best way to ensure successful expressing.

For a start, anxiety inhibits the let-down reflex, which is necessary for the breast to release the milk.

The let-down reflex is a hormonal response to your baby's sucking, and it is this that you will need to trigger artificially when you are expressing milk. The best way to do this is to relax – easier said than done when you are in a different environment and have limited time. To help you relax, try a warm drink or snack, deep breathing exercises and even looking at a photograph of your baby. You may also use imagery. Think of milk flowing and a warm, pleasant place.

Ways to encourage your let-down reflex:

Sit comfortably. Your body needs to be well-supported.

Relax. Practice deep-breathing exercises. Listen to the NMAA audio cassette 'Softly, Softly,' which was designed especially to help encourage the let-down reflex, or any other relaxing music of your choice.

Warmth. Apply gentle heat from a warm face-washer.

Massage. Lightly massage your breast towards the nipple before and during expressing.

Stimulation: Gently roll your nipple between your fingers.

Think about your baby while expressing or look at his photo.

BREAST AND NIPPLE CARE

You may choose to express just enough to remain physically comfortable and avoid engorgement (uncomfortably full breasts). If you have been unable to express at work and your breasts feel engorged, you may need to feel for lumps. This lumpiness may indicate the beginning of a blocked milk duct which if not cleared over a six to 12-hour period may lead to mastitis. Massage any lumpy areas towards the nipple and express a little milk whenever possible.

Breastpumps can be harsher on your nipples than your baby's sucking and may cause temporary soreness as you learn to regulate the suction of the pump. To help prevent nipple soreness, centre the nipple in the cup of the pump and ensure that the vacuum is applied intermittently to your breast.

Breastfeeding mothers also need extra fluids, so remember this when you are at work. Rather than drinking extra tea and coffee, which may make both you and your baby wakeful at night, keep a jug of water nearby. This will ensure that you get extra fluids, but no extra calories.

GIVING YOUR MILK TO YOUR BABY

You do not need to introduce your baby to a bottle just because you are returning to work. Expressed breastmilk may be given in various ways, depending on the age and preference of your baby.

In the early days, some babies can become confused by the different methods of sucking needed for breast and bottle-feeding. This is known as nipple confusion and can lead to problems, including sore nipples and a drop in milk production, especially if your baby is under four weeks of age.

Your baby may take your milk from a small cup or a bottle. If you do use a bottle, you do not need to introduce it until a few days before your separation. Some mothers have found that introducing a bottle can lead to breast refusal, but this problem is usually temporary. It is usually overcome as the child matures and learns to cope with differing situations and caregivers. (See chapter on Coping with Breast Refusal.)

Breast refusal may be due to a combination of factors, so do not misinterpret it as an outright refusal of breastfeeding.

CHILD-CARE OPTIONS

No other subject seems to cause such polarisation among parents than the issue of child-care. In most cultures, including our own, the ideal carer for an infant in its first six to 12 months of life is still considered to be his mother, especially if she is breastfeeding. But this does not mean that the mother must be the sole carer. Both babies and mothers benefit from shared care, whether the mother is absent for an hour, or for a day, because she must work outside the home, or because she is attending the dentist, the hairdresser, having a break, or doing anything where it is not appropriate or possible to care for a young baby.

Before industrialisation, babies and children were cared for by various people in the home. It is only after that, when fathers were forced to seek work in cities leaving mothers at home, combined with the economic and baby booms of the 1950s and 60s, that a mother at home as the sole carer has been considered the norm.

These days, many households need two incomes to function, and so whatever the 'ideal' or the fantasy, choosing a caregiver is often the reality for families.

Your choice in this matter will depend on your preferences and the age and character of your baby. You may find that what suits you both to start will change as your baby's needs change, so prepare to be flexible. Prepare, too, to think laterally. You may end up combining various types of care.

Make your choice according to the needs of your child and your own needs – not according to the views of others. Others may judge, but they do not have to live with the choice you make. Don't be afraid either to change your mind. If you find that your choice does not suit after all, be polite and firm but make no apologies.

The type of child-care you choose will depend on your personal views about the care of young children, your type of work, the age and temperament of your baby, the proximity of home and work and your budget.

After their maternity leave expires, some women are lucky enough to have partners who are able to take long service leave or extended holidays to swap roles. This can be an invaluable experience for fathers and their children. If you cannot arrange for your partner or another relative to take over, you may like to consider employing a nanny.

A young baby will especially benefit from the more one-to one care a nanny can provide. Make sure you choose from an accredited agency or nanny school. Child Care Assistance is not available for informal care arrangements (outside an approved centre) but if your nanny is registered with Medicare, you will be eligible for a rebate from the government which will help with fees.

If you cannot arrange care at home, work-based child-care, where you can take your baby to work with you, or to a nearby centre where your employer has booked a specific number of places, is ideal for the breastfeeding mother. Having baby close by means that you can feed him as he needs you.

This does not mean, however, that you do not have to pay for the child-care. Some employers arrange for cheaper child-care if you forfeit some pre-tax income (saving you tax and fees) while others provide a direct subsidy. Others offer no concessions other than the convenience of the centre on-site or close by.

Some employers who do not have work-based child care still can help you locate a suitable carer through their Human Resource Departments. Some have special referral services, which keep lists of places available at local creches, or may subscribe to a service which provides this.

If work-based child-care is not available, and your baby is still very young, you may prefer the more intimate style of care offered by Family Day Care. This is where a woman with children, or who has had children, cares for a small group of children in her own home. Her suitability and that of her home is checked by your local council, which administers these schemes. You will be given a choice of carers to interview and there should be no pressure on you to feel obliged to accept any of them unless you find one suitable.

Your council will notify the caregivers of your choice. Family Day Care fees are relatively low and Child Care Assistance and the Child Care Rebate are available for those eligible to help ease the costs.

If your baby is older, or you prefer the more structured program of a child-care centre where your baby will be cared for by a team of people who are supervised, then you should inquire about centres in your area or near your work. Your council will have a list of child-care centres in your area, or you could try one of the child-care centre associations for a recommendation.

Whether you choose a publicly funded centre or a private one, the same assistance – Child Care Assistance and the Child Care Cash Rebate still applies. Child Care Assistance is reimbursed to your account through the Department of Social Security and is means tested. The Child Care Rebate is not means tested and may be claimed at Medicare outlets providing you and your carer have registered.

The Federal Government's accreditation scheme for long day care centres means that both public and private creches must adhere to the same strict principles and high standards, so you can be assured that your baby is getting the best care available when you are not around. However, personalities cannot be dictated by governments and if you find that you are not comfortable with the caregivers, do not be afraid to change, even if this means putting your baby's name on a waiting list elsewhere.

Photograph by Elin Birks.

CHOOSING A CAREGIVER

Mary Poppins, Nana the St Bernard from 'Peter Pan,' Mrs Doubtfire, Alice from 'The Brady Bunch' ... popular culture abounds with images of caregivers, once known simply as baby-sitters. Some of these images can be very reassuring to parents when choosing a caregiver for their baby, others can be frightening.

How do you choose a caregiver who is the right person for both your baby and you?

If you are breastfeeding, it is important to ensure that your caregiver supports you in this decision. Better still, try to choose a caregiver who has breastfed herself. You do not want your caregiver topping up your baby with infant formula while you are at work.

Ideally, your caregiver will have breastfed herself or will be knowledgeable or experienced with breastfed babies, and will know how to support you in maintaining your supply, expressing and storing.

Do not be afraid to ask any potential caregivers about their attitudes to breastfeeding, and to change caregivers if you feel you are not being supported or are even being undermined. Even if your baby seems to get along well with someone whom you find unsupportive, it is better to upset him temporarily by changing caregivers than risking your breastfeeding relationship which will affect his health in the long term.

If you are interviewing people in your home and you are not sure about your decision it is a good idea to say that you have others to interview and will let them know of your decision later.

Don't be afraid to say no. Your feelings about your baby's caregiver will affect your feelings about returning to work.

If you are worried, you will not be happy and chances are neither will your baby. Trust your gut instincts on this one.

If you are looking at Family Day Care or a child-care centre, make sure the premises are clean. This is more important than tidiness, which may indicate that children are not free to make a mess.

Check, too, for safety. What is safe for a toddler may not be so for a crawling baby. Ask whether the carer has first-aid training and what her policy is in a medical emergency. Some councils provide this training for caregivers.

Make sure, too, that the premises has proper sleeping equipment and toys for your baby, and car restraints should the caregiver need to take your baby out. Do you need to provide nappies, meals or strollers? It may also pay to talk to other mothers who have returned to paid work about any feelings of guilt you may have, or feelings of jealousy towards your caregivers.

These feelings are natural and you should not be afraid to acknowledge them and discuss them. Breastfeeding while you are working will help you feel better about leaving your baby as he will still be getting the best food, and your breastfeeding relationship will help you maintain your closeness and remind him that you are the most important carer in his life.

STAYING HOME

It is obviously easier to establish and maintain breastfeeding if you do not have the pressure of having to return to paid work earlier. However, if you decide to stay home while your children are small, it is as equally important to prepare for this as it would be if you were returning to paid work.

In our culture, much of our identity is defined by our public life, rather than our home life. Although the distinction between the home as the private domain and the paid job as the public domain is blurring, it is still very difficult for those who are not in paid work to maintain their status and self-esteem. This is because work is too often defined only in relation to its economic remuneration.

How often do you hear a mother say: 'Daddy's going to work', as she waves him off at the door and returns to her own, unacknowledged work, of caring for their baby or toddler, washing, cooking, shopping, cleaning and nurturing. In this book, the distinction is made between paid and unpaid work, acknowledging that despite the lack of economic reward, caring for a home and family is definitely work.

In the battle to recognise both the demands of women's unpaid work, and the struggle they have to combine this unpaid work with their paid work, women often find themselves fighting each other rather than the system.

This puts an extra burden of stress on women whatever their choice. Each feels obliged to justify and rationalise their choice and in doing so, condemn the choice of those who choose differently.

There is no similar burden placed on men, who partly because of their biology and partly because of social expectations, are still less torn between their work and family obligations.

It may help to realise that part of the antagonism between women is due to the lack of support and resources available to both mothers in paid work and mothers working at home. Each in their own way feels unappreciated, and rather than band together to acknowledge that most women experience both roles at some times in their lives and to fight to change the unsupportive and unsympathetic system, they feel obliged to compete within it.

The truth is that while the 'women at home' and the 'women at work' are often pitched against each other in the media in the battle for recognition and limited resources, statistics show that most women move in and out of these roles according to family demands and ideally, many choose to do paid work part-time while children are small or at school. According to the Australian Bureau of Statistics publication "Australian Social Trends (1995)", the proportion of couple families with children where both parents were employed increased from 35 per cent in 1979 to 42 per cent in 1994. "In 1994, the father was employed full-time in 58 per cent of these families. In a further 38 per cent, both parents were employed full-time. Employed mothers were more likely to work part-time if they had young children, especially if they were under five years old." This means that both mothers and a small proportion of fathers are both 'at home' and 'at work' while the children are of preschool age, and sometimes until the end of primary school.

However, as more women enter the paid workforce for social and economic reasons, and benefit from the increased economic and social status, it becomes more difficult for those who choose to stay home to maintain their status and self esteem.

If you decide to be a full-time mother for a year or more of your child's life, you will need to ensure that you have the knowledge and support to help you enjoy this special time.

The model of the nuclear family where mother stays at home and father goes to work largely grew from the affluence of the 1950s and 60s where it was possible to live on one wage. The need for one adult to care solely for the children largely occurred because of the industrial revolution which took men away from the home as a centre for work and into the cities, leaving the women to care for the children.

This model has been both idealised and reviled in our culture. While conservatives cite the benefits of children being in the care of a loving mother at home, others quote studies showing increasing depression and drug dependency among women who found themselves isolated and economically and socially powerless. The mother who lives only for her children's welfare is an object of ridicule. But so, too, is the mother who is seen as a selfish careerist who places her children in an 'institution' so that she can get money and status. Women who choose to be mothers are therefore often caught in a no-win situation.

For women who choose to stay home with their young children, this is made more difficult by the fact that the dream no longer matches the reality. Today the cost of buying a home and supporting a family often means that choosing to stay home for a short time means choosing economic hardship. As more women enter the paid workforce, the woman at home may also find that it is difficult to make social contact with women in her position.

If you choose to stay home, you may find that your friendships are mainly made through work and that some of these friends may have little interest or time for young children. Others with young children may be working part-time and may prefer to catch up with home chores on their days off. Your parents or parents-in-law may live too far away to provide the emotional and physical support you need. There are many organisations and networks in the community that aim to support you in your job as a parent. NMAA is a good start. It is like an extended family, except the information is contemporary rather than conservative. It enables women to contact other women with a common interest – particularly important for first-time mothers. You can learn from other mothers' experiences. NMAA also provides a social connection if you move house or if other friends don't have children. There is also your child health nurse available through your local council. Apart from monitoring the development of your baby, she can put you in touch with new parents groups, parenting classes and other organisations that you may like to join.

Playgroups are also an excellent way to meet people and help your child gain important social and intellectual skills.

Your local library or swimming pool may also conduct special events for families with young children. Contact your local council for a list of other organisations, such as the library or toy library, which may help.

Many women are reluctant to go back to paid work after discovering the freedom of life at home raising children. They can't imagine how they had time to go to work in the past and how they would cope cooped up all day in an office or shop again.

Others enjoy one or several years of staying home, but see studying or working part-time as an important step to returning to full-time work if they choose to later. Mothering, while vital, is a relationship, not a career, as many women find when their children have gone. It is also a job with an element of built-in obsolescence. It is hard to imagine when your newborn is at your breast that he could need anyone else, but as he grows he will become more independent, physically and socially. And so will you. Maintaining your job skills and other interests is important to your emotional and financial welfare.

Women today are having fewer children, an average of 2.3, and are living longer. Even if you didn't start having your family until your thirties, by your late fifties you will have grown children and perhaps another 20 years of living to do. Having something of your own will ensure that these years are financially secure, independent and as rewarding as possible.

CHAPTER TEN

An expression of love

- **Expressing and storing breastmilk**
- **How to hand express**
- **Lactation aids**
- **Storage and thawing and feeding EBM to baby**

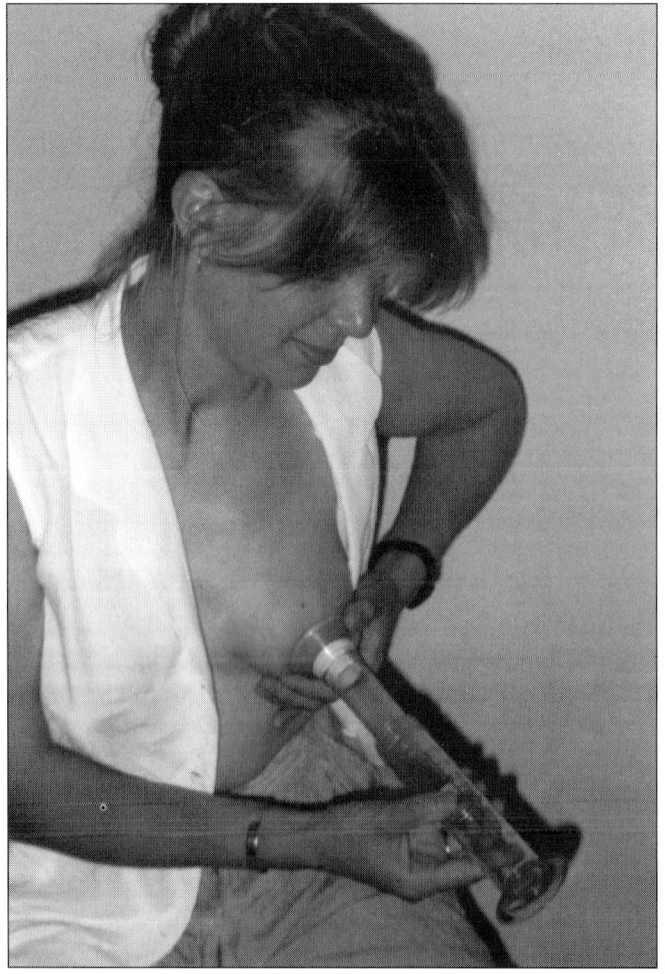

Photograph by Yvette O'Dowd.

MASTERING THE TECHNIQUES OF EXPRESSION

If you cannot be there to breastfeed your baby, he can still receive your breastmilk and all its benefits if you express and store your milk. Expressing and storing your breastmilk may seem a little difficult at first, but once you master these simple techniques, you will find it makes the ultimate convenience food even more convenient should you need to leave your baby for any reason.

However, on such occasions, you may be advised by well-meaning people to offer your baby a bottle of infant formula instead. "Why bother?" people may ask if they see you expressing at home, or taking nursing breaks to do so at work.

They, (and you), may wonder why you cannot breastfeed your baby when you are with him, and allow his caregivers to give him bottles of formula at other times. While you may choose to do this later when your baby is also sampling other foods and fluids, for a very young baby, the introduction of complementary feeds may only reduce his appetite for breastmilk and reduce your supply.

If you do not express your milk while you are separated from your baby, your breasts will get the message that less milk is needed and so will make less.

Not expressing may also put you at risk of engorgement and mastitis as your breasts may become overfull. This can be overcome by expressing for comfort. Your breasts will adjust after a while, especially if feed times are reasonably consistent from day to day.

By expressing your milk to give to your baby later, you will maintain and build your supply and help maintain that special and vital link between you. Consider it an expression of love, rather than a chore. It sounds corny, but in many ways, it is true, especially if your baby is sick or premature and you need to express to build up and maintain your supply. This takes emotional and physical energy as well as commitment, and you will need lots of support.

If your baby is sick or premature, your expressed milk may be vital to his survival. Research has shown that the milk of mothers of premature infants contains special properties to aid their survival.

You may also need to express your milk if you need to return to the paid workforce, study or other commitments, if you wish to go out without your baby or if your breasts feel full or uncomfortable. Whatever your reason, expressing and storing can be easier than mixing formula and disinfecting bottles, much cheaper and much better for your baby and a very handy skill for any breastfeeding mother.

THE LET-DOWN REFLEX

You are locked in your office with a photo of your baby, a breast pump and one protruding breast that is letting you down by refusing to let down. At this moment it seems it would be easier to open a Coke bottle with your teeth than to express your breastmilk for your baby. Yet two hours ago, the same breast which now refuses to cooperate leaked all over your good shirt and jacket when your boss asked: "So how's the baby?"

What do you do? Relax! Relaxing will help trigger the let-down reflex to make the milk flow. This may seem difficult at first as you may feel awkward and uptight.

Most mothers feel like that when they are learning to express, but with practice and support, you will soon find that you will be able to trigger your let-down like magic and expressing and storing your breastmilk will be second nature.

This reflex enables your baby to get the milk that your breasts have made. The cells around the alveoli contract and squeeze out the milk, forcing it down the ducts towards the nipple.

Making sure your milk lets down will increase the amount of milk you can express and help maintain and increase your supply. You may feel a tingling sensation when this occurs, or a feeling of sudden fullness.

Milk may drip from your other breast or milk may flow or even squirt freely as you express. You may also feel your uterus contracting in the early days when your milk lets down, especially if this is not your first baby.

Let-downs can occur several times during a feed or while expressing, but most mothers only notice the first. These secondary let-downs can be encouraged by swapping breasts when your flow eases while expressing.

The let-down reflex is a conditioned response to your baby's sucking. It can be encouraged by the sight or sound of your baby. It can occur if you hear your baby cry, or even think about him. It can also be encouraged by stimulating the breast and nipple area, as many couples discover during love-making.

However, anxiety or pain can cause the let-down to be slow or inhibited. That's why it is so important to relax.

ENCOURAGE THE LET-DOWN
- Try to relax. Try to express in a quiet, warm relaxing area, away from distractions. Breathe slowly and deeply. Drop your shoulders so that your chest also relaxes. You may like a warm drink or some soft music. A warm shower or a warm washer on your breast may also help.
- Gently massage your breasts by stroking down towards the nipple and gently rolling the nipples between your fingers. Massage cannot actually push the milk out, but it can help trigger the let-down.
- Think about your baby and how your breastmilk is helping him. If he is premature or sick in hospital, you will find it easier to express if you stay near his crib or just after you leave him.

If you are separated, gazing at a photo of him may help your milk let down.
- Have someone to support you. Many mothers find it easier to express if they have an encouraging partner or friend. Your NMAA Breastfeeding Counsellor will also give you information, suggestions and encouragement as you learn how to express your breastmilk.

CLEANLINESS

Great care is needed with cleanliness when you are expressing and storing milk for your baby. This is especially important if your baby is sick or premature.

FOR THE SAFETY OF YOUR BABY:
- **Clean and disinfect all containers before and after use.**
- **Before starting, wash your hands thoroughly with soap and water and dry them on something clean such as a disposable towel or tissue. Reusable towels should be kept for your use alone.**

- **Express directly into a disinfected container.**
- **If you are storing your breastmilk in the same container, as soon as you have finished, cover with a lid, label with the date and put it in the refrigerator. Otherwise, pour the milk into another disinfected container immediately before covering with a lid, labelling and refrigerating or freezing.**

HOW TO HAND EXPRESS

This is one milking session where you will not need a three-legged stool, but you will need a bucket, or any other disinfected wide-mouthed container. Seriously though, you might like to use a specially designed milk-expression funnel, available through NMAA.

Before you begin, wash your hands and dry with a clean towel. It is a good idea to place another clean towel on your knees to catch any drips or to dry your hands if they become wet and slippery.

You may not get more than a few millilitres to start with. This is not a sign that you do not have much milk. It just means that you are not as effective at getting it as your baby.

If your supply really is low, frequent short expressing sessions will gradually build it up.

If the flow seems to slow or stop, try expressing the other breast in the same way. You can change hands and breasts as often as you like until the milk no longer flows well. Your hands and fingers will become stronger with practice. Massage your breasts towards the nipples from time to time to encourage the milk to flow.

If you are expressing for all your baby's feeds, try some longer and shorter expressing sessions. You may find you get two or more let-downs during the long sessions, and will therefore produce more milk.

Don't expect to get copious amounts to start with. Expressing by hand or pump takes patience, time and practice. Keep trying. A good place to experiment with hand expressing is in the shower. The warm water helps your milk let down and you don't have to worry about catching the jets of milk which may squirt anywhere.

Before long, hand expressing will be as easy as one, two, three, four, five...

BREASTFEEDING ... NATURALLY

1. Place your thumb and forefinger on either side of your areola. It may help to imagine a line between them running through your nipple. If you cannot easily see the lower part of your breast, a mirror may help.

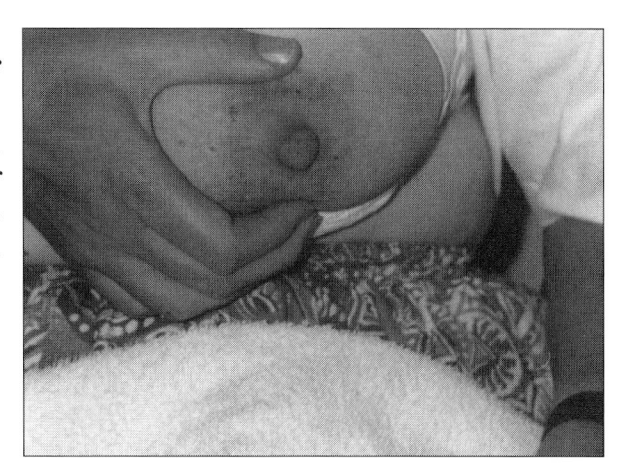

2. Gently press your thumb and fore-finger back into your breast tissue until you feel the bulk of the breasts. Your breasts may feel hard, lumpy and a bit sore if they are full. Go easy. This should not hurt. As you express, your breast tissue will soften and it will become easier, especially when the let-down occurs and the milk flows.

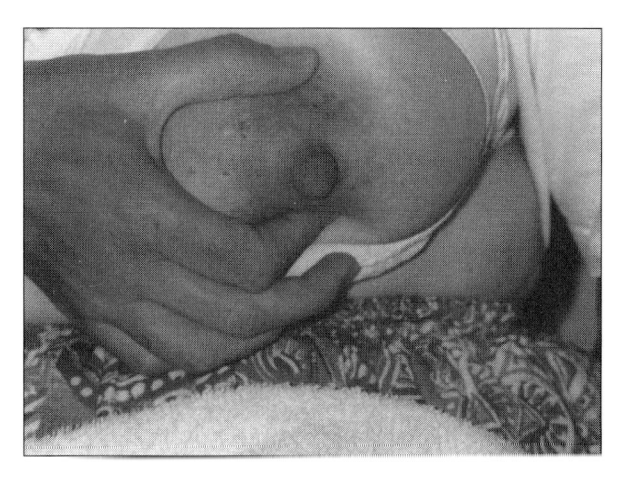

3. Press your thumb and fore-finger toward each other using a slight rolling action. This will compress the milk sinuses and cause the milk to flow out of the nipple. Until the let-down reflex occurs, the milk may drip from the nipple and you may need to hold your bowl close to catch it.

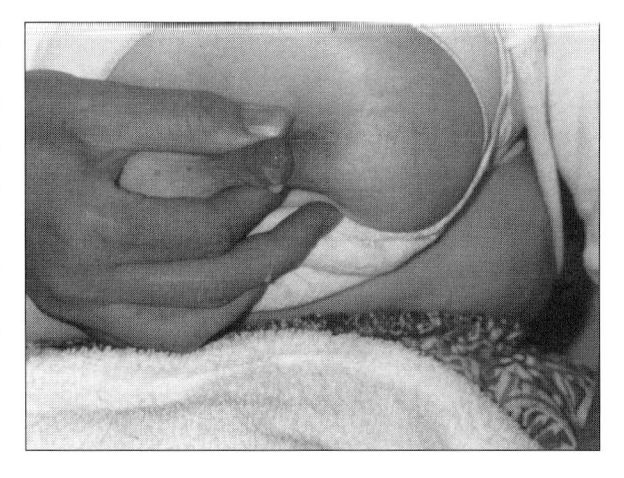

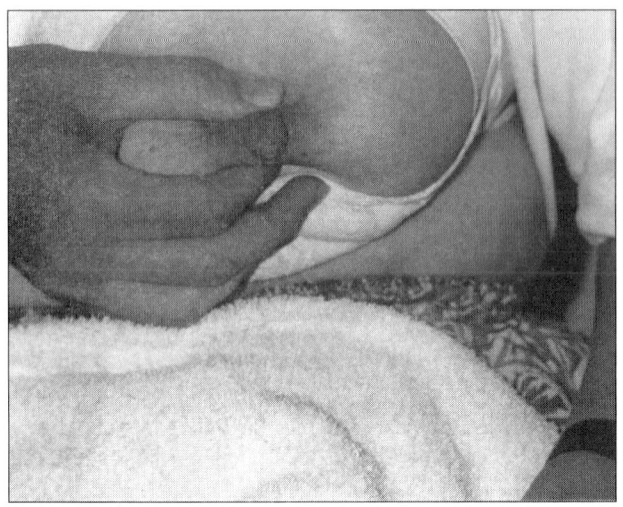

4. Continue this compressing motion in a rhythmical way until the let-down reflex is triggered. The milk may spray from the nipple. Several jets of milk can occur with each compression. It may take a few minutes for the let-down to occur. This is normal. The let-down is a conditioned response and will soon occur quickly each time you express.

5. When the flow eases, move to another section of breast, working your way around the areola. Remember to place your finger and thumb on either side of the nipple as before. If your hand tires, try the other hand.

• **A video, Hand Expressing and Cup Feeding, which shows the techniques described above is available from NMAA.**

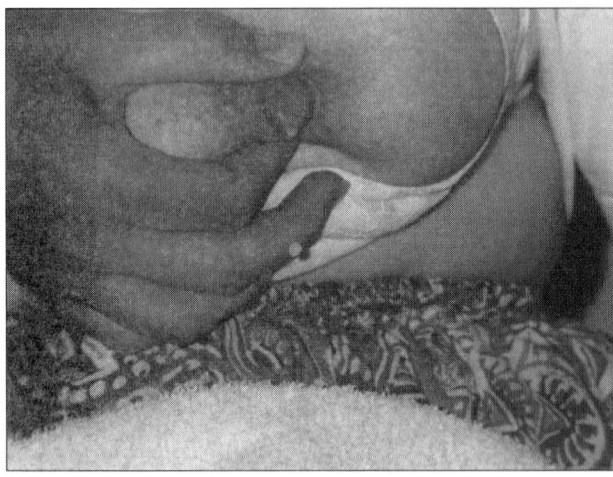

Photographs by Yvette O'Dowd.

BREAST PUMPS

Many mothers find that hand expressing is the quickest, most gentle and convenient method of expressing their breastmilk. However, there are times when a manual or electric breast pump is more practical.

A pump can make expressing easier, however it is still important to encourage the let-down reflex and the flow of milk.

Hand pumps are the most commonly used as they are compact, inexpensive and portable. They come apart for easy cleaning and most are well-designed.

They are available from NMAA and from many pharmacies. There are several different types of pump on the market now, and more are becoming available. However, before you rush out to buy one it may be wise to check with NMAA which one is likely to be best for you. Breastpumps which have successfully passed the NMAA testing process are available from NMAA's trading company, Merrily Merrily Enterprises.

HAND PUMPS

The **cylinder pump**, consisting of two cylinders, is easy and effective to use. A flanged breast cup is attached to one cylinder which is placed over the nipple. Both cylinders and the pumping action are in a direct line. You control the suction by drawing out the top cylinder. The cylinders are made of plastic with the milk collected in the lower cylinder which may also be used as feeding bottle. This type of pump is approved by NMAA as it allows for easy collection of breastmilk without damaging your nipples.

The **angled cylinder pump** is similar, but the cylinder is angled downward. A piston is pulled downward (on the first stroke) giving you good control of the suction and has an automatic suction release to avoid nipple damage. The milk is collected in a small plastic feeding bottle, fitted to the pump. Most standard feeding bottles are also useable. This style is also approved by NMAA.

The glass or plastic cone with rubber bulb is not recommended because it can be painful and cause nipple damage. The suction pressure is very difficult to gauge. These pumps are also difficult to clean and disinfect properly. There are also some with rubber bulbs attached by a tube to breast, cup and bottle. These are also not recommended because of lack of suction control.

ELECTRIC PUMPS

Several types of electric pumps are available and prices can vary widely. However, they can be hired from some NMAA Groups, pharmacies or hospitals. If you want to use an electric pump after the birth of a premature baby it is best to arrange this before you leave hospital, as sometimes there is a waiting list. If hiring from NMAA, contact your local Counsellor first. NMAA will show you how to use the pump and you will be offered ongoing support from a trained NMAA Counsellor.

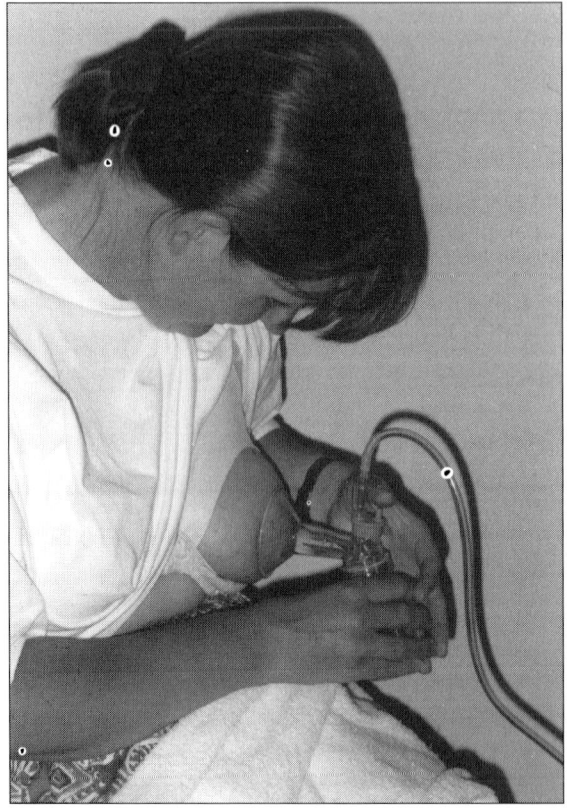

Photograph by Yvette O'Dowd.

SPECIAL BAGS DESIGNED FOR STORING EXPRESSED BREASTMILK.

These are available from NMAA and pharmacies. They are made from specially chosen materials to ensure that plastics do not leach into the milk, and expressed breastmilk (EBM) stored in them thaws more easily than in most other containers. However, boilable, freezable plastic cups with tight-fitting lids (not those which have been used for fatty substances or cream), or small glass baby foods jars which may be disinfected are also suitable.

HOW MUCH TO EXPRESS

How much you express depends on your reason for expressing. If you want to reduce engorgement when you have too much milk, you only need to express enough to feel comfortable. This can be done in the bath or shower, unless you want to store your milk.

Some mothers who are regularly expressing for a sick or premature baby can easily start a good flow of milk and quickly get 90-120 ml from both breasts every three or four hours. Others cannot get such amounts in one go, and find it easier to express small amounts more frequently, such as 30 ml every 1-2 hours.

The amount you can express is not an indication of the amount you are producing. Some mothers with thriving babies and an obviously good supply find it difficult to express. Sometimes, just after a birth, the amount of milk produced is judged on the amount that can be expressed. This is a false measure. Expressing is a knack. Your baby is born with the ability to milk your breasts. You will need to learn, and learning takes time.

SAY WHEN?

How much expressed breastmilk (EBM) you will need for your baby depends on his age and weight. It is best to ask your medical adviser or health nurse. If they are unavailable, a rough yardstick is 150 ml per kilogram of body weight over 24 hours. However, the needs of each baby vary widely.

For a single feed, a few small bottles should satisfy your baby. If you are planning to express milk for one feed to be given to your baby while you are away, you could express a small amount (say 20-30 ml) at each feed during the preceding 24 hours and keep this in the refrigerator, or express whenever it suits you sometime beforehand and freeze the milk.

It is a good idea to store the EBM in small quantities, eg 50 ml. If your baby wants more, then a second lot can be offered. However, if a large amount is offered and your baby is not hungry, the milk left will have to be thrown away, and no mother likes to waste this "liquid gold".

STORING YOUR EBM

You can store your expressed breastmilk in a variety of ways.

1. Small, sterile bags especially designed for storing breastmilk are available from NMAA and pharmacies. These are made from special plastics that do not leach into the milk. Milk stored in these containers thaws more quickly than that stored in other containers.

2. Baby feeding bottles. Breastmilk stored in glass bottles loses some anti-infective properties, which is undesirable if it is to be fed to a sick or a premature baby. Breastmilk stored in plastic bottles loses some of its fatty components. If you are expressing for an occasional feed, it doesn't really matter which you use.

3. Boilable, freezable, plastic cups with tight-fitting lids. Not containers that have been used for cream or fatty substances.

4. Small glass baby food jars (but some anti-infective activity loss will occur in the milk – as above).

5. Other suitable containers. Use small containers, just enough for one feed, or a couple per estimated feed, to avoid waste.

6. For a premature or sick baby check with the hospital about suitable containers – it may supply them.

PREPARING CONTAINERS

All containers – except pre-sterilised EBM bags – will need to be carefully prepared before each use. You may either boil, steam or use a chemical disinfecting solution. Whichever method you use, all items must be thoroughly cleaned first.

Cleaning is the most important step. Before boiling, steaming or using a chemical disinfectant always:

1. Wash your hands thoroughly with soap and water. Dry them on a clean towel (disposable or cloth) that is used for no other purpose.

2. Separate all parts of the containers. All removable parts of breast pump components need to be separated to ensure thorough cleaning. Rinse in cold water.

3. Completely remove all traces of grease, milk and dirt, etc, with a small amount of dishwashing liquid and warm water. Do not use soap. Use a brush kept specially for this purpose. Clean the flanges

and rubber components of your breast pump by rubbing salt on both sides and through any holes.

4. Rinse at least twice in cold water.

BOILING

1. Thoroughly clean all parts, as above.

2. Completely immerse all parts in water, bring to the boil and continue to boil gently (completely submerged) for 20 minutes uninterrupted.

3. Remove items without touching their inside surfaces. Long-handled plastic tongs which have been boiled with the containers are useful. Shake the containers to remove excess water, then

4. Place to dry on paper towels.

You may wish to place lids on containers while they are still warm, as they may shrink as they cool and not fit. Make sure your hands are clean first.

5. If you are not using the containers immediately, store in a new plastic or paper bag, plastic wrap or clean container. Seal well. These can be stored like this in the refrigerator for up to 24 hours.

CHEMICAL DISINFECTING

1. Thoroughly clean all parts.

2. Make up a fresh solution of sodium hypochlorite according to the manufacturer's instructions and completely immerse all items for at least an hour.

Check that none of the items contains air bubbles.

3. Remove the items without touching the inside surfaces. Long-handled tongs which have been immersed with the containers are useful. Shake the containers to remove excess solution, then;

4. Place on paper towels. If you use a commercial container to make up the solution, you can then drain the items on the rack provided. Make sure your hands are clean.

5. If you are not using the containers immediately, store in a new plastic or paper bag, plastic wrap or clean container. Seal well.

These can be stored in the refrigerator for up to 24 hours.

STEAMING

Electric steam units or those for the microwave can also be used to disinfect your expressing and feeding equipment. Follow the manufacturers directions.

METHODS OF STORAGE

As milk starts to deteriorate at room temperature after about six hours, it is important that it is properly chilled, frozen and thawed.

CHILLED MILK

Expressed breastmilk can be stored for up to 48 hours in the refrigerator at four degrees Celsius before use. It is normal for expressed breastmilk to separate into several layers. To reuse, just shake the container.

FROZEN MILK

Expressed breastmilk can be deep frozen for three months at minus 18-23 degrees Celsius or less in a separate freezer with its own temperature control.

Breastmilk should not be stored for long periods in a frost-free freezer that is part of a refrigerator because these freezers have a defrost cycle which could mean that the milk is subject to cycles of slight thawing and then refreezing which has an undesirable effect on milk protein and can increase the risk of bacterial growth.

Breastmilk stored in freezer compartments of refrigerators where the temperature is less stable should only be stored for two weeks.

FREEZING BREASTMILK

1. Label the container with the date
2. Place it, with the lid on, in the refrigerator to cool.
3. When cold, place it in the coldest part of the freezer (usually the back of a front-opening freezer, or the bottom of a chest freezer).
4. Chilled milk can be added to frozen milk as long as the container is immediately returned to the freezer.

FROZEN MILK WILL EXPAND IN THE CONTAINER, SO FILL ONLY TO THREE QUARTERS OR THE CONTAINER MAY BURST.

THAWING AND WARMING EXPRESSED BREASTMILK

1. Frozen milk must be warmed QUICKLY but not in boiling water, as it will curdle. DO NOT LEAVE IT TO THAW AT ROOM TEMPERATURE.

2. Place the container under cold running water, gradually allowing the water to get warmer until the milk becomes liquid.

3. Warm chilled or thawed breastmilk in a jug or saucepan of hot water or in an electric drink heater until the milk reaches body temperature.

Test by dropping a little on your wrist.

You do not have to warm the milk if your baby prefers it cold, although it probably shouldn't be used chilled. Somewhere between room temperature and body temperature is usually fine.

4. Do not use a microwave oven as it heats unevenly and the hot spots in the milk may burn your baby's mouth. Research also suggests that microwaving changes the immunological and nutrient quality of breastmilk.

5. Don't boil your expressed breastmilk for your baby.

Apart from being unnecessary, it destroys many valuable components in the milk.

USE YOUR THAWED MILK WITHIN 12 HOURS. UNUSED THAWED MILK MUST BE DISCARDED, NOT REFROZEN.

TRANSPORTING EBM

You may need to transport your expressed breastmilk between home and hospital, work and home, or home and a caregiver's.

Recently expressed breastmilk should be stored in a container which has been thoroughly cleaned within the past 24 hours, and if the milk is later to be frozen, then the storage container should have been disinfected as well.

Ideally, recently expressed breastmilk should be stored in refrigerated conditions, but can be safely kept at temperatures up to 27-32 degrees Celsius for up to six hours.

Do not leave frozen EBM at temperatures of 26 degrees Celsius for more than two hours.

If thawing occurs, the milk must not be refrozen.

FEEDING YOUR EBM TO YOUR BABY

How you feed your milk to your baby will depend on his age and preferences. You can use either a small cup or a standard baby bottle. A breastfed baby may accept a cup more readily than a teat, and this will help avoid confusion between teat and nipple. However, if your baby is having regular feeds of EBM, perhaps while you are at work, he will probably enjoy the extra comfort of sucking at the bottle. Caregivers are often more used to giving bottles and may prefer these.

Do not introduce a bottle until your baby has learnt to suck correctly at the breast and is gaining weight well. Some older babies refuse to accept a bottle from their breastfeeding mothers, but will happily accept it from another caregiver. An older baby who refuses a bottle, may take the milk more readily from a cup.

In some special circumstances, such as very low supply, you may like to try NMAA's breastmilk supplementer Supply Line, which delivers the milk to your baby through a fine tube as the baby sucks at the breast.

Any left-over milk must be discarded as bacteria from your baby's mouth will have contaminated it.

IN AN EMERGENCY

It is a good idea to build up a small cache of frozen milk in case the milk you have expressed is spilled or spoiled, or you do not have enough expressed milk to satisfy your baby.

It is best not to give artificial milk such as infant formula if your baby is under six months of age, especially if you or your partner has any history of allergy. However, if you need to or decide to use infant formula, ask your doctor or child heath nurse which is most suitable for you. The child health services have emergency telephone numbers in State capital cities.

CHAPTER ELEVEN

As your baby grows

- **Up to three months**
- **Changes to feeding patterns**
- **Biting, teething, breastfeeding and dental health**
- **Introducing solids**
- **Feeding an older baby or toddler**
- **Weaning.**

THE FIRST THREE MONTHS

The changes that occur to your baby (and your lifestyle) in the first three months of his life are the most dramatic that will occur over his whole life span. By three months, he will prob-

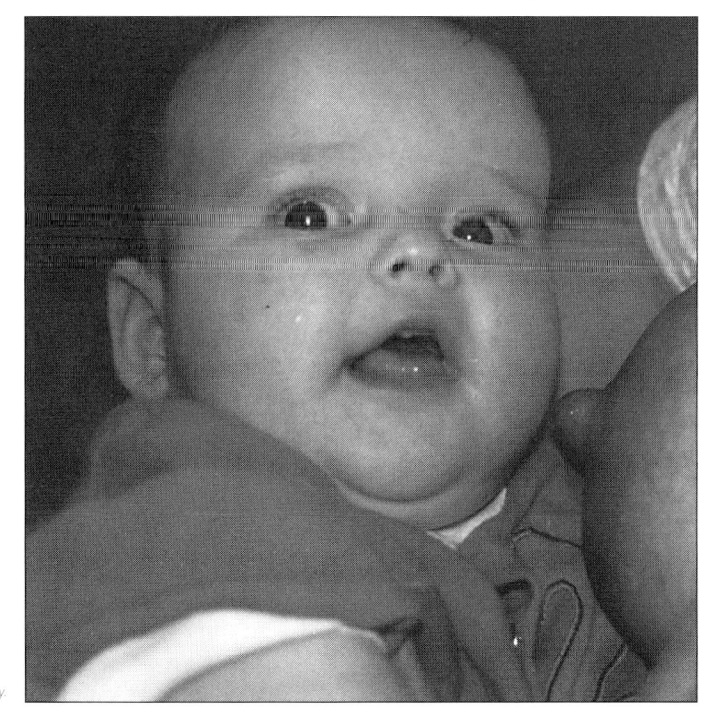

Photograph by Lesley McBurney.

ably be anywhere between four and eight kilos in weight, his face and limbs will have padded out, giving him a much rounder look, he will probably have rewarded you with his first smile, and will be making different sounds. He may even manage a chuckle if you coax and tickle him, or a squeal or two.

His eyes will have developed so that he can follow objects more easily and when you put him on his tummy he will probably be able to lift his head. He may also be able to roll one way, grasp objects, reach for things.

He will know the sound of your voice and may even turn his head when you speak. He will be able to support his head and may even be trying to move if he is placed on his tummy on the floor.

He will also be much more aware of you and your role in his life. In short, the really "helpless" stage will have passed and you will be enjoying a much more interactive stage as your baby grows stronger and more aware of his new world.

By now, breastfeeding is usually well-established. However, as your baby grows and changes so will his need for breastmilk and you will need to be prepared to be flexible.

For a start, at around the age of three months you may notice that your baby seems hungrier than usual. He may be fussier after a feed and unsettled. This is not an indication that your milk has "dried up". It is simply his way of saying that he needs more. You can provide this by feeding more often for a few days to build up your supply. You may have already had to do this when your baby was about six weeks old, another period when babies are growing rapidly and often need more food.

To increase your supply you will probably need to decrease some of your other activities, spending extra time instead with your baby at your breast. This may seem inconvenient at first, but in the long run a few days of intense feeding will be far less inconvenient than months of disinfecting, washing and mixing formula to give complementary feeds of cow's milk formula. (*See Chapter Six for suggestions on how to increase your supply.*)

Alternatively, you may notice that your baby's weight gain has slowed. It is common for a baby's weight gain to plateau at around three months. Do not be too perturbed by charts in clinics which indicate how big your baby should or should not be at this age. These averages are calculated from a mixture of bottle-fed and breastfed babies and do not accurately represent the patterns of fully-breastfed babies.

If your baby appears alert, with good skin tone and is reasonably content, and continues to have six to eight pale wet cloth nappies (or two to three well-soaked disposable nappies) a day, then there should be no cause for alarm.

It is more accurate to look at your baby's weight gain over a period of a month. Weekly gains can vary from 50 grams to 250 grams. However, overall, a gain of 500 grams a month indicates that your baby is growing well.

However, if you are still concerned you may like to talk to your NMAA Counsellor, your doctor or child health nurse.

Every child is different and you may notice that your baby seems to need extra feeds at other times too. Frequent feeding can boost your supply at any time that you feel your baby needs more.

At this age, you and others may expect your baby to have an established routine. But what you, your mother and your neighbour may expect is likely to be quite different from what your baby expects.

Some babies do fall into a fairly predictable pattern of feeding, waking and playing by the age of three months. Others don't.

You will probably find that it is better to go with the flow and follow your baby's lead about when he prefers to sleep and feed rather than create unnecessary stress and anxiety for yourself and your family by trying to fit the baby into a routine.

This doesn't mean that you have to be tied to the house. A young baby is usually happy to sleep almost anywhere, at your breast, in a backpack or Meh Tai sling, in your arms, in a pusher or on a rug under a shady tree.

He is also equally happy having his breastfeeds at the shops, a meeting, your workplace, your friend's house or at home. Eventually you will learn to predict his needs and he will learn that these can be met by you and others in a variety of ways and in a variety of places. Besides, babies are growing and changing all the time, so routines are subject to change too.

However, it is fair to say that by the age of three months most breastfed babies are more settled and you will start to reap the rewards of establishing a good breastfeeding relationship, including intimacy, convenience and optimum nutrition for your baby.

BITING, TEETHING AND DENTAL CARE

You may be advised by some well-meaning people that the eruption of baby's first tooth is the signal to wean – or it will be a case of fangs for the mammaries.

While your baby may sometimes accidentally or playfully nip you before or after a feed, it is impossible for a properly attached baby to bite as his tongue is placed over his bottom teeth.

Babies are generally adept at keeping their top teeth from clamping down, so there is no reason why you cannot continue to breastfeed your toothy baby. In fact, if his gums are sore or inflamed or itchy due to erupting teeth he will probably be seeking the comfort of your breast more often.

Babies commonly get their first teeth between six and nine months of age – about the same time that they begin showing an interest in sampling other foods. However, breastmilk is still a vital part of a baby's diet even when other foods are introduced.

Your milk will also continue to provide valuable nutrients for the development of strong teeth and bones and will further protect your baby from illness during this sometimes difficult time.

This is important as some babies seem to be more vulnerable to colds and general ill health during teething. While some do not indicate they are teething until the tooth itself appears, others seem to develop a variety of symptoms, such as fever, a runny nose or cough before the tooth erupts, others drool constantly which can sometimes cause a chin or face rash. Some teething babies have inflamed cheeks or bottoms, some are in pain and are understandably irritable as a result, and some will refuse to breastfeed as the suction increases discomfort.

If your baby does try to give you a nip, after your first yelp, firmly and calmly tell him 'No' and remove him from the breast. He will soon learn not to bite the breast that feeds him. Biting usually only occurs when the baby is bored, distressed by teething, has discovered a new game, or to get your attention if your concentration is elsewhere. A teething baby will usually try to bite anything handy to help relieve the pressure on his gums.

To avoid further bites, encourage him to bite on something else hard for a few minutes before each feed or rub his gums with a special gel or something cool. These can be obtained after discussions with your pharmacist or medical adviser. Don't encourage him to play with the nipple after the feed.

DENTAL CARE

You may have heard of "nursing caries" or seen posters of young babies and toddlers with rotten teeth. This is quite a misleading label. Your breastmilk will not damage your baby's teeth. In fact, it is an important aid in developing strong and healthy teeth and bones as the casein in your milk coats and protects new teeth from decay.

Nursing caries refers to a pattern of tooth decay caused by milk or sweetened fluids such as juice or cordial collecting behind the front teeth of a sleeping baby over a period of time.

This occurs when the baby is regularly put to bed with a bottle of milk, cordial or juice. The baby stops sucking, but the liquid still drips from the bottle, creating a pool above the tongue until enough collects to force the baby to swallow.

Over time, acid produced by the sugar in the mouth erodes the enamel covering the teeth, gradually eating the teeth away. In mild cases, the front teeth are pitted.

This decay is caused by the baby being left with the bottle at bedtime. Reports of any similar tooth decay in babies breastfed to sleep over a long period are difficult to prove, according to Virginia Phillips author of *Feeding Baby and Child – A Guide for Australian Parents*.

As Phillips says, although breastmilk is a sweet fluid, differences in the breastfeeding process should protect most breastfed children from nursing caries.

Firstly, a mother cannot leave her breast with the baby to drip milk into the baby's mouth. Secondly, the way the baby's mouth and tongue are used during breastfeeding is different. The mother's nipple is drawn well into the mouth to spray milk at the throat, rather than pooling it over the tongue.

Thirdly, there is no space for the milk to pool as all the space has been taken up by the baby's tongue, (which is well forward), the mother's stretched nipple and the baby's cheek pads. Also, to receive any breastmilk, the mother's let-down reflex has to work, or the baby has to suck. If a breastfed baby is fed to sleep, the milk flow stops when the let-down reflex has finished and the baby stops sucking.

However, if your baby is drinking fluids from a bottle at any age, be sure to remove the bottle before he settles down to sleep.

As soon as your baby's teeth appear, buy a small soft toothbrush and make a habit of brushing his teeth. This can be treated like a game at first. Use only water until your baby is old enough to understand that toothpaste must not be swallowed. Later, use a junior toothpaste that is low in fluoride, as the stronger toothpastes, combined with fluoridated drinking water, can sometimes cause an overload, resulting in greying or browning or white flecks known as dental fluorosis.

Encourage a preference for water rather than juice to quench thirst. This is cheaper for you and better for your baby, who is much better off getting his juice from whole fruit, which also provides fibre.

If you are still breastfeeding, do not be too perturbed by suggestions that your baby will not receive adequate amounts of Vitamin C if you do not give juice. To ensure you and therefore your breastfed baby gets plenty of Vitamin C, treat yourself regularly to an orange, some blackcurrant juice or some broccoli.

WEANING

For some people, the most difficult thing about breastfeeding is giving up. The sucking reflex is perhaps one of the strongest in the human species. You only have to walk down any street to see how even in adults, this need must still be gratified.

Despite health warnings, there are those who still smoke, others chew gum, and most of us use (and sometimes abuse) food for oral gratification as well as hunger. Children well past what is normally considered weaning age, continue to suck dummies or thumbs and it is common to see a child of three or four still sucking a bottle. Is it any wonder, then, that many breastfed children cling to the comfort, warmth and reassurance of their mother's breast for as long as possible? Yet the approval you gained from breastfeeding your infant may not be as forthcoming if you continue to breastfeed your toddler.

Be reassured that the time to wean is when you and your baby want to – not when others tell you to.

If your baby is being breastfed according to need, your breastmilk will provide all his nourishment and fluids he requires for the first six months of life.

You do not need to introduce cereals or fruit juices or any other food before this. In fact, if you do, your baby's appetite for breastmilk will be diminished, your supply will be affected and you may inadvertently begin the weaning process.

You may hear that babies should start other foods at four months. This is a recommendation to the wider community, most of whom are not still fully breastfeeding their babies. Formula-fed babies are more likely to need other foods sooner as they are not receiving the ideal food, ie breastmilk.

Weaning is said to begin as soon as you introduce any food or fluid other than breastmilk. However, most people regard weaning as the time when your baby has fewer and fewer breastfeeds until he is being completely nourished by other foods.

Ideally, you should follow your baby's lead. As children grow, so does their interest in the world beyond their mother's breast. Your baby's growing interest in his new world, with new people and new foods and tastes will encourage him to wean when he is ready.

At first he will only be interested in breastmilk, but gradually he will take an interest in what you are eating. After the age of six months, he may even try to grab the food from your hand or your plate. This is part of the development process – he is doing what he does best at this age. The second or third time he grabs your food is probably because it was a pleasurable experience the first time.

Breastmilk is still his most important source of nutrition, so you should always offer a breastfeed first. In the first stages, he will still seek your breast for food and comfort, but gradually this will lessen. As a result, your milk supply will gradually lessen and there will be days when he will not want to breastfeed at all until one day you will realise that the breastfeeding relationship is over.

> 'In most non-industrial cultures, children are allowed to be babies until another baby is conceived or born...The Ibo people of Nigeria call the newly-weaned child "the child who brought the child", and reward it for having separated itself from the mother, making the next baby possible.'
> — from 'Mamatoto – A Celebration of Birth' produced by The Body Shop and published by Virago Press.

In our society, where mothers have an "adult" life separate from their mothering responsibilities, or when they need or want to return to paid work early, babies are encouraged to separate from their mothers much earlier. This can make it difficult if you and your baby wish to continue breastfeeding after the first year or even past your baby's second year.

Some women find that they are being pressured to wean their babies just when they are beginning to feel that breastfeeding is going well. If breastfeeding has taken a little longer to establish, and you are both just beginning to enjoy it, it can be extremely annoying and disconcerting to be told that you should now give up.

Some people also fear that continuing to breastfeed an older child will encourage overdependency. In fact the opposite is true. A child who is confident and secure in his mother's love is much more likely to be independent and relate well to the world around him than one who has been forced to wean before he is ready because of other people's expectations. Your toddler or older child will still receive many nutritional and immunological benefits from your breastmilk, as well as important emotional security.

There are several advantages of breastfeeding an older baby and weaning slowly. Your child will be able to outgrow his infancy at his own pace and if he is ill and refusing to eat you can be confident that breastmilk will provide valuable nutrients and fluids. Your older child can also be weaned straight from your breast to a cup, thus avoiding the inconvenience of a bottle. Many children who are weaned from the breast early develop a dependency on the bottle, from which they must be weaned later. Ideally, weaning should be spread over several weeks or months, dropping one breastfeed at a time.

Weaning is a process of letting go for both you and your baby so it is important for both you and your baby's physical and emotional welfare that it occurs gradually and when you are ready.

Sudden weaning can leave you with sore and engorged breasts and at risk of developing mastitis. It can also result in a flat chest as the fat deposits that give your breasts that rounded look take longer to return if weaning is sudden.

Weaning can also be an emotional time, especially if this is your last or only baby. While some mothers feel relieved to have their bodies back, others feel sad that a special relationship has ended. Others may feel a mixture of relief and regret. It may help to focus on the positive side. Your child is obviously growing and developing well. You can now be more flexible about your clothes and your time.

Whatever your feelings, you can be reassured that you have done the best for your baby and that this is the beginning of another exciting stage in his life and yours.

> 'I don't feel like I want to wean him because it's the only time in the day that the world stops, once he starts feeding and I know that I'm going to sit or lie there till he's finished. It's just time when you're really alone together.
>
> 'If I gave him a bottle and said here's a bottle, go and sit and drink it, it's not the same. The other really good thing is that when I'm feeding him I'm touching him and he's touching me. He goes from the tummy button to the nipple, backwards and forwards and I just stroke him and cuddle him at the same time.'
> - Julie, mother of Bradley, aged two.

BABY-LED WEANING

You may be surprised to find that one day your baby makes it clear that he does not want to continue breastfeeding. He may fidget, refuse to feed or simply say that he has had enough. If this happens before the end of the first year or he is unwell, there may be other causes. However, if your toddler is healthy and has not shown interest in breastfeeding for a few days, he is probably ready to wean. This can come as quite a shock – especially if you planned a long and leisurely breastfeeding relationship.

You may feel rejected, even angry, and a general sense of loss. In this case, you may need help to accept your baby's decision. Your baby will still need your cuddles and love and will have had an excellent nutritional start to life.

MOTHER-LED WEANING

There are several reasons why you may want to wean your baby before he has indicated that he is ready. You may be planning another pregnancy, or may already be pregnant. Some mothers like to continue to feed an older child throughout the pregnancy and this is quite safe, but others prefer to wean. You may be returning to paid work, you may be feeling pressured by friends or family to wean or you may simply have had enough.

If you are no longer enjoying it and are feeling frustrated by your child's demands and he is healthy and happily eating other foods, this may the be the time for some active discouragement.

If your older child likes to breastfeed at bedtime, you may like to try a new routine where his father puts him to bed. New activities and contacts with other people, distractions such as books and toys at normal feed times, having an alternative breakfast temptingly laid out when he wakes, wearing clothes that make feeding difficult, limiting the number of feeds and not getting undressed in front of your baby are all ways that will help him to wean.

This is a difficult balancing act as you must be firm and consistent but still loving. If you are harsh and rejecting, your plan may backfire and your child may become more insecure and turn to the breast more. If your child becomes ill or distressed for any reason during the weaning process it is best to back off for a while.

Weaning a reluctant toddler is sometimes a process of two steps forward and one step back, with several false stops along the way. However, as far as we know, most children start school fully weaned and toilet-trained despite their mothers' fears and frustrations.

HOW TO WEAN

The process of weaning your baby can be as personal as deciding when to wean. Much will depend on your baby's personality, his need to suck and your circumstances. Here are some general guidelines, but overall it is best to play it by ear.

Whether you wean your baby on to a cup or a bottle will depend on his age. If your baby is less than 12 months old, you will need to discuss an appropriate infant formula with your child health nurse. Offer an alternative such as formula, cow's milk or unsweetened juice (this will also depend on his age) at the breastfeed that he is least interested in. Continue this substitution one feed at a time, every few days to a week until he is no longer having breastfeeds. When dropping the number of feeds per day, it is best to avoid going from one per day straight to none. Try to go from one each day to one every couple of days. In this way, you are less likely to become engorged.

Your baby may need some extra cuddling time to help him through this, and some babies and toddlers especially need skin-to-skin contact at this time.

If your breasts are becoming lumpy and uncomfortable, you can express a little or offer your breast to your baby briefly. Do not empty the breast as this will only encourage more milk to be made, and you will be back where you started.

Other ideas that may help are:

- Offering a dummy for extra sucking
- Giving a substitute feed or meal before a breastfeed
- Offering only one breast at each feed and making sure baby has plenty of other fluids
- Feeding to a definite routine
- Reducing opportunities for breastfeeding
- Changing daily routines to break the habit of feeding at particular times
- Encouraging the father to give substitute feeds at usual breastfeeding times
- Encouraging the father to meet your baby's needs at night

RAPID WEANING

If you need to wean quickly, over several days, drop the alternate feeds in the first day, expressing just enough for comfort. You can cut out the rest of the feeds in the next few days, making sure that you still give your baby plenty of cuddles and attention.

In the rare situation that you may need to wean immediately, you may experience a few days of painful engorgement.

This will gradually subside, but initially you may need painkillers.

Cold packs or chilled cabbage leaves applied to the breast will also help reduce discomfort and swelling.

Do not use heat as this will stimulate milk production. Watch out for blocked ducts and breast infections. If you experience severe pain, your breast looks red and inflamed and you are feeling shivery and achey, you may have mastitis.

This occurs when there is a blockage in a duct and some of the milk banked up behind it is forced into the surrounding breast tissue, which then becomes inflamed.

A breast infection is usually the result of untreated mastitis, although some mothers feel no early signs.

The symptoms of an infection are similar but more severe than those of mastitis. The breast is usually red and swollen, hot and painful. The skin may be shiny and there my be red streaks. You will feel ill.

It is important to seek treatment immediately you suspect a breast problem. Antibiotics are often prescribed.

If mastitis or a breast infection occurs you should postpone weaning, as it is vital that your breasts be emptied as much as possible and your baby's sucking is the most effective method of achieving this. Don't worry about the milk harming your baby. The milk will not harm your baby. (See Chapter 8 on Problems and Breast and Nipple Care.)

LET YOUR BABY SET THE PACE

Food is one of the delights of life, but being forced to eat when we are not hungry can turn delight into disaster. No matter how long it has taken you to prepare it, no matter how frustrated you may feel, never try to force or coax your child to eat. First of all it seldom works. Sleeping and eating are the two things that you cannot force a child to do. Secondly, it makes for future battles and future fatties.

Let your baby set the pace. Always stop when he doesn't want any more.

Initially it is best to breastfeed your baby before offering other foods so that he is not too hungry and cranky to try the other foods you are offering.

If he is still have lots of breastfeeds (say six or seven) try just one meal of solid food a day, gradually building up to three. If you rush things, your milk supply will suffer and your baby will miss out on breastmilk, which is still the most vital food for his growth and development in the first year.

FINDING NEW WAYS TO BE CLOSE

Even if it was your decision to wean your baby, you may find that you are sad, weepy and even depressed after the last feed. This is natural. Your hormones will take a while to get back to normal. If they have not already done so, some women menstruate almost immediately while others take a few months.

You may also feel a sense of loss or grief now that this special time has ended, and worry about how you may now comfort your baby and find ways to be close.

It may help to talk to other mothers who have breastfed or your NMAA Counsellor.

Your baby may also take a while to settle, perhaps waxing and waning between wanting to be a baby again and wanting his independence. One way of maintaining some special close time while fulfilling your baby's need for new stimulation and experiences is to replace breastfeeding time with reading time.

With an arm around your toddler and a special book, you can give him your undivided attention while you both explore new and exciting worlds.

Listening to recorded books or music while having a cuddle together is another way of maintaining closeness and encouraging listening skills.

UNWEANING

Sometimes, circumstances such as illness or wrong advice can lead mothers to wean their babies and regret it. You may have been separated from your baby through illness, or your baby may have developed an allergy or illness after weaning and you may like to try to start breastfeeding again.

If you have adopted a baby, you may like to try to form a special bond with him by attempting to establish breastfeeding.

Whatever your circumstances, relactation or stimulating lactation if there has been no pregnancy requires patience, determination, time and above all support. Contact NMAA in your state; there are Counsellors whose experience and knowledge in these areas will be of invaluable assistance.

CHAPTER TWELVE

The importance of sharing

- **Where to get the support you need**
- **All about the Nursing Mothers' and what we offer**
- **Directory of other services**
- **Helpful reading list**

TAKE PART IN A REWARDING EXPERIENCE

Breastfeeding your baby is an exciting and rewarding experience for you both. However, as in all things that are worthwhile, there are usually both joys and difficulties. At both times, it helps if you are able to share your thoughts and feelings with like-minded people.

These may be your family, your friends, other mothers you met while your were pregnant or in hospital or through your child health nurse, at playgroup, the pool, the library, the playground, or by attending your local NMAA Group.

WHERE TO GET THE SUPPORT YOU NEED

When you first become pregnant, you will suddenly notice all the other pregnant women around you – and all the information targeted to them. You may be sitting in your doctor's waiting room, flicking through a magazine on parenting, and see an ad for NMAA, or a poster on the wall, or a health department pamphlet about the importance of breastfeeding with a NMAA contact number. Your doctor is one place to find out how to get support you need. Your local council is another as most have lists of organisations that may assist young parents. Your local child health nurse, playgroup, librarian, social worker, midwife, or even the shop where you buy your baby goods can be sources of information as well as friends and family.

ALL ABOUT NMAA – HOW SIX WOMEN BEGAN A REVOLUTION

Mary Paton was a young mother in 1964 when she and five others began the Nursing Mothers' Association of Australia. Mary had trouble breastfeeding her first child, and was browsing in a bookshop when she met another mother, Pauline Pick, who was also seeking breastfeeding information. They, along with friends, Jan Barry, Susie Woods, Glenise Francis and Pat Paterson, decided to form a self-help group for breastfeeding mothers.

Mary's home in Balwyn became the first unofficial headquarters for the Association, with the large space under the Paton marital bed the unofficial first filing cabinet.

Today, NMAA with headquarters at Nunawading, Victoria, has 13,000 members, local Groups in every state and is recognised both in Australia and overseas as the country's foremost authority on breastfeeding. Breastfeeding is considered by the government and health professionals the undisputed best and complete and only food required for all babies in the first six months of life. NMAA is supported by a panel of distinguished advisers.

However, when Mary Paton and friends first met to form the Nursing Mothers' Association of Australia, breastfeeding was not considered hip. The 1960s were in full swing. Rock 'n' roll had revolutionised the music industry and social mores were changing. Freedom was the catchcry of the era. Beehive hairstyles, miniskirts and stiletto heels were symbols of womanhood and the baby feeding bottle was a symbol of motherhood.

The more gentle revolution started by Mary Paton and friends is not as well documented, but its effects have been just as far-reaching, if not more so.

It wasn't that breastfeeding was actively discouraged at the time. It just wasn't encouraged. Mothers were given the choice of breastfeeding or bottle-feeding, but if complications arose, it was assumed that the bottle-feeding was an equal substitute. In fact, as long as there was a bottle and a scientific infant formula around, persevering with breastfeeding was considered fanatical and risky.

Bridget Sutherland, now an Honorary Member of NMAA, left hospital with her first child 25 years ago with the words of the nursing sister ringing in her ears. "Of course, you'll be murdering your baby."

Mrs Sutherland was not suffering from postnatal depression, nor had she rejected her child. Her baby was considered at risk because Bridget was determined to breastfeed.

Now, the mother of three grown children (all breastfed) Bridget Sutherland proudly reports that they not only survived, but thrived.

Doctors and nurses at the time were not trained to handle breastfeeding problems, and within the modern nuclear family there were few older women to turn to for advice.

The six founding NMAA Members soon found the "fledgling" Association had outgrown the nest. When the space under the Paton marital bed could no longer hold all the NMAA documents, it was decided that a proper office should be set up. This was achieved through selling memberships and designing, making and selling breastfeeding and mothering aids.

In 1972, Australia became the first country to reverse the decline in breastfeeding, and Dr Elizabeth Wilmot, then the director of Maternal, Infant and Pre-school Welfare, credited NMAA in her annual report.

In 1983, an Australia-wide survey, conducted by Nancy Palmer, a nutritionist with the Commonwealth Department of Health, found that the number of babies who had ever been breastfed was 85 per cent. Fifty-four per cent were still being breastfed at three months 40 per cent were still breastfed at six months, and 10 per cent were still breastfed at 12 months.

An Australian Bureau of Statistics survey conducted between 1985-90 found that the number of babies who had ever been breastfed was 77 per cent.

In Victoria in 1993-94, at three months 53.5 per cent of babies were fully breastfed, and at six months 39.3 per cent of babies were fully breastfed. This is the only state where records are known to be kept.

Even the Pope recommends breastfeeding, for its excellent nutritive qualities, as well as its birth-spacing effect.

However, the battle for the best nutrition for Australian babies is far from over. A report in the Melbourne 'Age' on August 8, 1995, said that according to a Federal Government report, Australia would not meet World Health Organisation breastfeeding targets unless it imposed stricter guidelines on infant formula promotion. In Victoria, statistics show that only 44 per cent of babies are fully or partly breastfed at six months, which is far lower than the year 2000 target of 75 per cent, 'The Age' report said.

Today, the challenge for NMAA, its Members, and those committed to providing the best nutrition for Australian babies is to continue the trend towards breastfeeding. The needs of all mothers and their babies is of vital importance.

That's why NMAA and its work is so important – as a lobby group, to ensure that government policies reflect the needs of families, as an educator, and a great support network to breastfeeding mothers and their families. NMAA informs them and supports them in their decision to feed their babies naturally and gives them the knowledge and confidence to do so successfully.

In our society it is difficult for mothers to be recognised for their work. NMAA provides this, as well as opportunities for friendship and understanding and pride in our job as mothers and our commitment to providing the best start in life for our babies through breastfeeding.

Involvement with NMAA has also given many women not only the confidence to breastfeed, but the confidence to achieve in other areas too.

This book contains the combined wisdom of thousands of women – those who had the courage and conviction to have founded NMAA, its members and those health professionals who support its goals.

We hope that you will take this wisdom for yourself, make good use of it, enjoy it, and pass it on to your friends, your daughters, and their daughters. You may even have your own pearls to add to it as you learn what it is to be a mother in this changing world.

NURSING MOTHERS' ASSOCIATION OF AUSTRALIA
NATIONAL HEADQUARTERS
5 GLENDALE STREET,
NUNAWADING, VICTORIA.
INQUIRIES: (03) 9877 5011

SERVICES
■ Group meetings in hundreds of neighbourhoods all over Australia, for pregnant, brand new and experienced mothers.
■ Counselling on breastfeeding problems by telephone, by letter and in person is available to both Members and non-Members.
■ Literature on many aspects of breastfeeding and child-care is published and distributed by NMAA.
■ Mothering Aids – an increasing range of mothering aids is available from the local NMAA groups or by mail from NMAA's trading company, Merrily Merrily Enterprises.
■ Library books on breastfeeding and child-care may be borrowed from local Groups.
■ Magazine – Members receive the entertaining and informative Nursing Mothers' Newsletter.
■ Lactation Resource Centre collects and files the latest information on breastfeeding from worldwide sources. Phone (03) 9877 5011.

TELEPHONE COUNSELLING SERVICES

ACT and SOUTH NEW SOUTH WALES
Canberra (06) 258 8928

NEW SOUTH WALES
(02) 639 8686

QUEENSLAND
(07) 3844 8977/3844 8166

SOUTH AUSTRALIA
(08) 339 6783

TASMANIA
Southern (002) 23 2609
Northern (003) 31 2799

VICTORIA
(03) 9878 3304

WESTERN AUSTRALIA
(09) 309 5393

For more information about **NMAA**, write to us at **PO Box 231** Nunawading, 3131 or check your local telephone book.

INDEX

Abscess (see Breast abscess)
Adoptive breastfeeding, 220
Advice, dealing with, 94
Alcohol, and breastfeeding mother, 134
Allergies, 161
Alveoli, 22
Appetite increases, 101
Areola, 22, 23
Baby Care Rooms, 124
Baby-Friendly Hospitals, 33
Baby sling, 47
Bilirubin, 62-64
Birth Centre, 37
Biting, 210
Bottle-feeding, 7
Bowel motions, of breastfed babies, 10, 16
Bra, maternity 44
Breast,
    abscess, 154
    anatomy of, 21
    changes during pregnancy, 40, 41
    engorgement, 60, 150
    expressing from, Chapter 10
    medical problems, 148-154
    pads, 46
    pain, 17
    refusal of, 162, 168
    structure of, 21
    size of, 22, 42
    surgery, 157
Breastfeeding,
    ability to, 22, 42
    advantages of, 6, 8
    and working, Chapter 9
    benefits of, 6
    after Caesarean birth, 91
    getting started, Chapter 4
    how it works, Chapter 2
    in hospital, 54-56
    a premature baby, Chapter 5
    preparing for, 32
    twins, 83-89
Breastmilk, composition of, 97-100
    jaundice, 63
    leaking, 112
    low supply of, 104-108
    mature, 30
    oversupply, 110
    thawing of frozen EBM, 207

Breast pumps, 198-200
    Disinfecting of, 223
Cabbage leaves, 60
Calcium, 5
Cancer, breast, 8
Caesarean birth, 90
Choosing a caregiver, 186, 187
Choosing a hospital, 33-36
Child-care, 183-187
Colic, 154-158
Colostrum, 5, 29, 50, 99
Complementary feeds, 35, 61, 70, 107
Contraception, 107
Counselling, telephone, 225-226
Crying, baby, 119
    and sleeplessness, 120
Dental care, 211
Diarrhoea, 10
Diet, 17, 129
Drugs, 134
Ducts, 22
    blocked, 151
Engorgement, 60, 150
Environment, 9
Excercise, 130
Expressing, and storing breastmilk, Chapter 10
    at work, 181
    by hand, 196-198
    workplace requirements, 175
Fatigue, 76
Foremilk, 28, 99
Freezing EBM, 204
Frequency of feeds, 101
Gastric reflux, 159-160
Hand expressing, 196-198
Hindmilk, 28, 99
Home birth, 33
Hormones, 77, 127
Hospitals, 33-36
Hot weather, 99
Immunoglobins, 98
Increasing milk supply, 108
Infant formula 5
Inverted nipples, 43
Iron, 5
Jaundice, 62
Lactoferrin, 29, 98
Lactose intolerance, 161
Let-down reflex, 25, 182, 194
Looking after yourself, 127

Low supply, 104, 108
Mastitis, 152
Meconium, 29
Medical problems, 148-154
Meh Tai baby sling, 47, 69
Menstruation, 137
Montgomery's tubercles, 22
Nappies, 16
Night feeds, 70
Nipples, 23
    cracked, 149
    inverted, 43
    sore, 58, 144-148
Nurturing, 18
Nursing Mothers' Association, 95, 221-226
Oestrogen, 136
Outings, 123
Ovulation, 136
Oxytocin, 24, 26
Partner, 13, 38
Pesticides, 125
Positioning, baby, Chapter 4
Postnatal depression, 77, 139
Postpartum amenorrhea, 137
Premature baby, 79
Prolactin, 24
Protein, 26
Refusal, of breast, 162-168
Relactation, 220
Settling baby, 68, 69
Sex, and the breastfeeding woman, 134-141
Sleepy baby, 115-119
Sleeping, 71-73
Smoking
    during pregnancy, 133
    during breastfeeding, 133
Soap, 59
Sodium, 29
Sore nipples, 58
Storing expressed breastmilk, Chapter 10
Sucking, 55, 169
Supply Line, 110
Supply, of milk, 31, 103, 131
    reducing, 111
Teething, 210
Thrush, 64, 149
Too much, 110
Travelling with a breastfed baby, 123
Twins, 83
Uterus, 17, 25

Wakefulness, 72-74, 117, 118
Weaning, 212-216
    Baby-led, 215
    How to, 217
    Mother-led, 216
    Rapid, 218
Weight gain, 113-115, 209
Weight loss, 59
Wet nappies, 16, 209
WHO Code, 9
Working and breastfeeding, Chapter 9

FURTHER READING

Feeding Baby and Child   Virginia Phillips
Food for Under 5s   Rosemary Stanton
Politics of Breastfeeding   Gabrielle Palmer

A series of booklets on specific breastfeeding topics is available from the **Nursing Mothers' Association of Australia**. Please contact your local **NMAA** Group in your telephone directory.

Breastfeeding
... naturally